March 22, 2013

Dent[illegible] [illegible]d

[illegible] mother

from Kimberly [illegible]

Occasion of my 66th

Birthday -

Requiem a

word she could not

have known was

serendipitously profound

REQUIEM *for the* WEST

REQUIEM *for the* WEST

A collection of stories, essays, and photographs from forty years of living in the Rocky Mountains

Roger C. Brown

Preface by

FORMER GOVERNOR RICHARD LAMM

SUMMIT FILMS PRESS
Gypsum, Colorado
2004

Dedicated to—
my wife Anne Helene Garberg Brown,
my sons Gordon, Michael, Nicolas, Christian, and Tor Erik,
and my friend Barry Corbet

All photos are by Nick and Roger Brown, unless otherwise credited.

Distributed to the trade by
SUMMIT FILMS PRESS
P.O. Box 420
Gypsum, CO 81637
summitfilms.com

ISBN (cloth): 0-9763761-0-5
ISBN (paperback): 0-9763761-1-3

A CIP record of this book is available from the Library of Congress.

10 9 8 7 6 5 4 3 2 1

Printed by Johnson Printing, Boulder, Colorado, United States of America.

The paper used in this publication meets the minimum requirements of the American National Standard for Information Sciences—Permanence of Paper for Printed Library Materials, ANSI Z39.48-1992.

Contents

Preface
Goodbye To My West . . . and All Those Things We Took for Granted

Richard D. Lamm

Colorado has changed dramatically in the past forty years. Perhaps there has been more change in this short period than at any other time since the gold rush of 1859. We see a decade's worth of change every year, as one Colorado dies and a new one is born. Life is change—no civilization is ever static—yet there is a great nostalgia in my heart for Roger Brown's Rocky Mountain West. We are the same age, have the same values, and love the same things.

Every generation defines "the good old days" in personal terms. I am no different. There was something very special to me about Colorado in the 1950s and 1960s. It was a unique, wondrous place for those who loved the outdoors. It is worth pausing to remember.

The air in Colorado—including Denver—had an unbelievable quality. It literally sparkled. One could get up in the morning and see the mountains with crystalline clarity. The sun shone with a special brilliance, offering a sharp counter-point to the cool mountain air.

In the good old days you could enjoy more scenery during a drive to Boulder than most eastern families could see on a two-week vacation. Colorado had the most beautiful interurban roads in America—they were flanked by green fields where horses and cows grazed against a backdrop of snow-covered mountains.

Civilization always creeps up on human consciousness. Few Coloradoans fully understand, even now, that land use decisions have already been made that will fill up all the remaining open space between our major cities We will soon see fenced back yards in place of green fields, and we will have lost another great Colorado amenity. We will have citified the Front Range, and as Roger points out, are at work on the rest.

But it was the outdoor life that many of us came for—the skiing, the mountain climbing, the whitewater trips, the hunting and fishing. We headed for the mountains every Friday after work, throwing down our sleeping bags wherever sleep overtook us. In the old days you could still catch a native trout, gallop a horse for miles without encountering a fence, track a mountain lion, and float down a lonesome river. You could escape the regimentation of the civilized world. You could be free.

We thought it would last forever. We took it for granted. We took for granted being able to camp where we wanted, safely and in privacy. We took for granted drinking from a running brook, leaning down and looking at the mosaic of pebbles, moss, and ferns while we held the cold water in our mouths to warm it a few degrees before swallowing.

There were so few people in the mountains in those days—it was like having our own magnificent kingdom. We seldom met other people, and when we did, the camaraderie of shared purpose made instant friendships. The mountains were a refuge from the noise and congestion of the city. Few airplanes, no litter, few jeep trails, few signs of civilization. Although it was not possible to live your life in a totally pastoral setting as one might have fifty years before, you could spend a weekend in the backcountry with little likelihood of seeing anyone else.

The mountains in winter were even more special: dangerous, but with a captivating beauty, a magnificent stillness. We skied all day, filled with incredible well-being; watched storms swirl around the mountains, plumes of snow streaming from the peaks. Then one day, as my wife Dottie and I were just reaching the top of Jones Pass, a snowmobile careened over the lip of the ridge and almost hit Dottie. She protested reflexively and we last saw the snowmobiler going down the pass brandishing his middle finger. The mountains were changing.

Baruch Spinoza wrote of hiding sugar cookies in his papers for the unexpected joy of coming across them late at night. Such was the joy of discovering whole deserted towns in the backcountry that looked as if people had, a half-century before, just closed the doors to their cabins and left. It was a dividend, a link with a generation of determined but departed pioneers. Stoves, tables, chairs, bedsprings sat mute in the cramped, dark interiors. The stove doors began to go first to collectors with an itch, and within three years it was difficult to find a stove with a door. Then the stoves themselves went. Then the next generation of "collectors" took the weathered wood off the walls for their game rooms and bars. The 1960s saw more destruction to the ghost towns than all the winter storms and summer heat of seventy years. Now few are left.

Thomas Jefferson believed that a density of ten persons per square mile was about the limit of human tolerance "Whenever we reach that the inhabitants become uneasy as too much compressed and so off in great numbers to search for vacant country," he wrote. So also did another generation selfishly seek out space and solitude. On more than one occasion in the late 1950s we would put on knapsacks and walk for three or four days down the beach south of San Francisco. I never saw a sign of people along the miles of empty white beach washed by a blue ocean We would scuba dive and find ten-pound lobsters and a myriad of other fish and plants. Seals were in abundance and all but tame. We cooked shellfish over the coals of our campfire and slept under the stars.

Dottie and I went back to the scene of those walks recently with our children. Now quarter-million dollar houses march row upon row without so much as a vacant lot for respite. In half a generation the landscape has gone from the sublime to the ridiculous. I tried to explain to my thirty-five-year-old scuba diving son what it used to be like—but I soon gave up. It is hard to appreciate heaven unless you've been there.

But my metaphor is wrong. It was not the heavenly quality that we worshipped. The West in those days was like a magnificent cathedral that magnified all the bittersweet aspects of earthly existence—the West's expanses recalled the feeling one often gets in a great church where all one's aesthetic religious historical and personal feelings come rushing to the surface. The West was life painted in primary colors.

It was never a simple existence. One did not escape to the West as people escaped to Majorca or Tahiti or Paris. One lived in the West on its terms not one's own. The pioneers confronted the joys and sorrows of living close to the land—life and death, harvest and drought, sunset and storm. It was a vigorous total life that immersed one in existence not that immunized one to it.

Although we did not pretend to be pioneers most people who came to the West in the 1950s and '60s came to live life more fully. People would take incredible pay cuts so they could worship in the cathedral we called the Rocky Mountains. We came not to make a good living but to have a good life. Tragically, we are now witnessing the reverse: a flood of people who see the West as a good living rather than a good life. It is big bucks, not Big Sky, that motivate them. They are anesthetized to the grandeur of the West.

We saw the West change before our very eyes. I remember San Jose surrounded by orange groves, San Francisco without skyscrapers, Denver when the D&F Tower was our largest man-made structure. I was in the last party that ran Glen Canyon after the gates of Glen Canyon Dam were closed. We spent three days wading the Virgin River in Zion National Park. I took my kayak down the Rio Grande one last time as Cochiti Lake was forming, and I remember well kayaking the Dolores and the Yampa and not seeing a single party other than our own.

I have seen a new Manifest Destiny overtake America. I have seen the economic imperative change forever that spiritual refuge that was the West. I have made a truce with change—but many of the friends with whom I climbed the mountains or kayaked the rivers refused to accept it. They are the "new Indians," and many of them have refused to be herded onto the "new reservations." We get a post card occasionally from Montana or British Columbia or Australia asking us whether it is human need or human greed that makes us stay. They have escaped a world where, in Walt Whitman's words, men "in the name of Christ and Trade deflowered the world's last sylvan glade."

I know I am being selfish. Yet I see the energy crisis and the economics of growth. The story of the West has always been the creative tension between the furies of plunder and the forces of preservation. But now one dominates.

There is no hyperbole that can describe how fast the West is now changing. An avalanche of change is sweeping it. Coal, oil and gas, light industry, information technology, brewery's and growth rates triple the national average—any one of these we could possibly absorb, but taken together they spell chaos for our fragile environment. Our change, like our growth, is geometric.

I also know that Roger Brown's and my West will never be the same. I mourn our West as the painter Frederic Remington mourned another West. I mourn as John Audubon did when he met a man who had killed as many as 6,000 passenger pigeons in one day. I understand the pressure of people and regional offices, of new ski areas, and of tourism and highways. I understand, but I weep with the West for the past we've left behind.

No man can be certain that he has indeed become a wise man
so far as it is possible for any of us to be wise—
unless he has passed through all the fatuous or unwholesome incarnations
by which the ultimate stage must be preceded. . . .

We are not provided with wisdom,
we must discover it for ourselves after a journey through the wilderness,
which no one else can take for us,
an effort which no one can spare us,
for our wisdom is the point of view
from which we come at last to regard the world.

—Marcel Proust

Introduction

THIS IS A PICTURE BOOK AND A PERSONAL BOOK about a place I call home, a place where I have lived for forty years. It is the place where I have raised three sons and started them on what have become successful filmmaking careers. Two younger sons are starting out their lives here as well. So the book is autobiographical, to some degree, and it is about family and friends.

Evolution, God, or whoever or whatever it was that shaped this part of the world, did a fine job. Our mountains, lakes, rivers, forests, grasslands, and deserts are as beautiful as any on earth. Culturally, until recently, we have been rural: cowboys, foresters, farmers, small towns, tourism businesses, hunting, fishing, skiing, etc. But this is all changing.

I care deeply about this land and many of the people who live on it, so I do not take lightly the task of being critical. I would rather just close my eyes and ignore some of the things that have gone wrong, but some of us have to speak out. Unless steps are taken to protect what remains of the relatively pristine environment of the Rocky Mountains future generations will not have the opportunities my family and I have had growing up in this wonderful place. Paradise is being sold out.

People accuse me of being part of the problem, and they are right. The state of Colorado, numerous resorts, and several airlines have paid me well to sell their services over the years. I have probably made more tourism promotional films about Rocky Mountain destinations than anyone. I have also produced several popular ski films and commercials that have promoted mountain sports. So I have had a lot to do with bringing people here. I have tried to rationalize that I have been encouraging tourism, not residency, but that's a thin excuse. Why wouldn't people want to move to paradise if they could? No, I am guilty.

Although I came to the Vail Valley in 1961 as a ski filmmaker it wasn't long before I got involved in other projects: water issues, shale oil mining, the Outward Bound Schools, East African tourism, even a search for Noah's ark on Mt. Ararat in Turkey.

I moved from Vail to the Gypsum Creek Valley in 1978 to escape the busting-at-the-seams money-based expansion of that town. I built a solar heated house on twenty acres with a plan to live a rural life and become self-sufficient. Gordon, Mike, and Nick, (my three older sons) joined me in the film business in the 1980s. We began traveling all over the world doing sports adventure documentaries for television. Many of the photos in this book are from those travels.

In the early 1990s Nick and I took up the cause of the ranchers who were being forced off the land by a misguided urban based environmental movement. We worked with ranchers in several Western states and discovered the real soul of the West in the process.

In 1999 I married Anne Helene Garberg. We have two sons: Christian, age eleven and Tor Erik, age four. I write about experiences with all of the boys in the book. This creates some confusion until you realize the age differences. Gordon is thirty-seven years older than Tor Erik.

If I were asked to describe the West's biggest problem in four words I would say "out of control growth." Growth means jobs, work, money, and the good life on the one hand, but causes the loss of our rural countryside on the other. Subdivisions, trailer parks, strip mines, and gas wells are messing up our open spaces. Water diversions and reservoirs are drying up our streams. Gravel pits are punctuating our river valleys. Roads for gas wells and tire tracks from SUVs, ATVs and dirt bikes are ripping through the fragile semi-arid soils of our federal lands. Main streets are disappearing as small towns merge together into strip cities. "Big boxes," such as Wal-Mart and Home Depot, are pushing out many small entrepreneurs. The big ski resorts have been taken over by MBAs whose primary concern is the bottom line. As a result small ski town intimacy has given way to industrial strength playpen recreational complexes where the people who work there can't afford to live there. The use of cheap immigrant labor has brought the average working man's wages down to subsistence level.

The physical loss of our wild lands and free flowing rivers has also resulted in a less apparent but equally significant loss of the spiritually uplifting opportunities that can only be found in unspoiled Nature. Contemplative exercises such as hiking and camping in remote solitude have been largely replaced by athletic endeavors where bravado, competition, and fitness are the focus. Nature is now something to be conquered, not savored.

Still, the beauty and the majesty and the excitement of the West is far from gone, so the word "requiem" may be premature. Perhaps the book should be seen more as an invocation, an invitation to live more responsibly, and to try to save some of the natural qualities with which the Rocky Mountain West is blessed.

Acknowledgments

I am indebted to many writers and thinkers who have addressed problems and issues similar to those we have in the Rocky Mountains and to those responsible forward thinking people who live here. I refer to them and quote them in many cases. They are as follows:

- former Governor Richard D. Lamm
- community architect, State of the World Conference producer, and pilot John McBride
- mountain philosophers Barry Corbet, Maurice Herzog, Lucien Devies, Willi Unsoeld, Gary Templin, Murry Durst, Kurt Hahn, and Charles Froelicher
- wilderness advocates David Brower, Howard Zahniser, and Roderick Nash for his thorough book on the subject, *Wilderness and the American Mind*
- grazing and desertification experts Allan Savory and Dr. Wayne Burkehart
- energy expert Randy Udall and economist E. F. Schumacher
- agrarian philosophers Wendell Berry and Marty Strange
- pilot Phil Freedman
- the Dalai Lama
- editor Jennifer Engle Rix
- designer Polly Christensen

Map One: The Southwest

The Colorado River, Interstate 70, and some of the cities that depend on the Colorado River water.

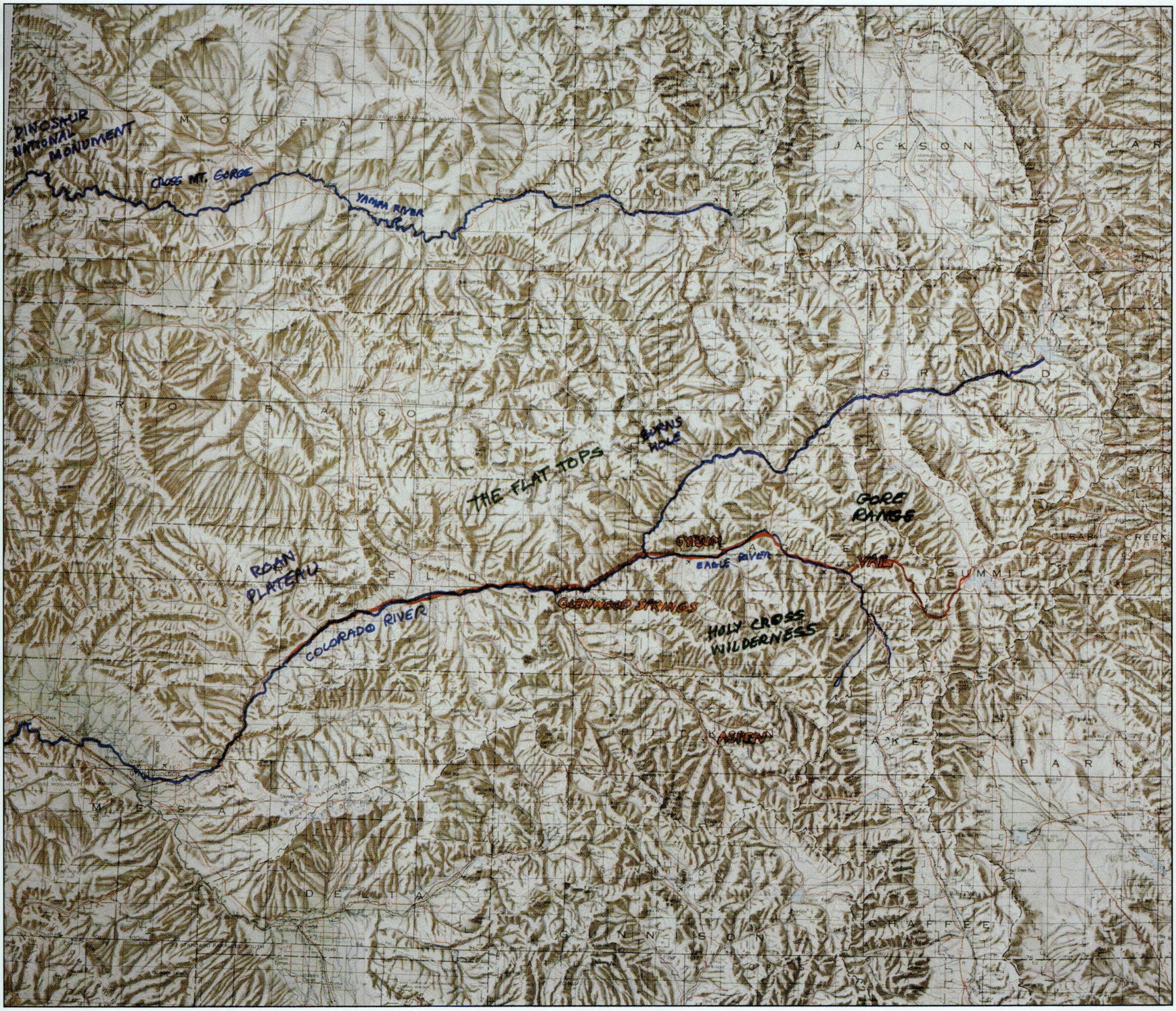

Map Two: Location Notes on the Northern and Central Colorado Rockies

The Yampa, Colorado, and Eagle rivers. Vail, Gypsum, Glenwood Springs, and Aspen. Dinosaur National Monument, Cross Mountain Gorge, The Roan Plateau, The Flat Tops, The Burns Hole, the Gore Range and the Holy Cross Wilderness.

"Father Sky created the sun, moon, stars, and Earth. Mother Earth provides what is needed by those who show reverence and respect. For Utes, there was a vast and varied land—sometimes gentle and sometimes severe—where they survived by living respectfully in harmony with their environment, whatever that might be."

—Virginia McDonnell Simmons, *The Ute Indians,*

Chapter 1

Dinosaurs and Other Early Stuff

Previous spread: The Yampa River in Dinosaur National Monument.

OK. OK. I KNOW, I AM A DINOSAUR in some people's minds, a misanthropic romantic, a Luddite, an obstacle in the path of progress. So be it. I admit to some of the above, although I don't hate people. I just think it's possible for them to behave better. Also I don't think extraordinary wealth and excessive material consumption are necessarily the best measures of success. So, there's the confession and a hint at the mission.

Most of this book is about people and places in Colorado, but similar experiences and problems can be found throughout the Rocky Mountain West and in many other mountain regions of the world.

The Continental Divide

Colorado contains a big piece of the roof of the nation called the Continental Divide. It is the high point that sheds the rain and water from the snow, east and west. Thousands of little trickles join into streams that become mighty rivers. The Arkansas, the Platte, the Rio Grande, and other rivers flow east while the Colorado flows west. The water in these rivers is the lifeblood of millions of people living between the Mississippi River and California. All the land west of the Continental Divide, over to Colorado's border with Utah, is considered the West Slope, western Colorado.

The Continental Divide was created about seven million years ago when upheavals pushed the Rocky Mountains upward. They reached a high point about five million years ago. Ice, snow, rain, and wind all chewed on these peaks, reshaping them, while ice age glaciers carved out the valleys. The cirques and moraines of the glaciers are still here for all to see, as are the depositions of fertile soils that grow hay, and condos, in the flat lower valleys.

Volcanic rock can be seen here and there, and hot springs also give evidence of natural pipelines that go deep down into the hot center of the earth. This great messy jumble of sliding tectonic plates has also exposed quantities of precious metals, like gold and silver. These metals set the the stage for the "get rich quick" mentality that is now finally overwhelming the beautiful (if sometimes hostile) always vulnerable land.

I have personal experience in some form or other with most of the geography. I have walked or skied over it, kayaked, fished, or bathed in it, flown over it, and now I guess I'm crying over it. For the sake of space, time, and clarity I will develop just a few examples. Everything, however, is under threat or already beyond repair.

The Beginning—Rocks, Bones, and Petroglyphs

There is no better place in the nation for me to start this story than in the far northwestern corner of Colorado for two reasons. One, a defining early environmental battle took place here in the 1950s; and, two, the geology, paleontology, and archaeology are right on the surface of the ground for all to see.

Eastern Utah, parts of Wyoming, and western Colorado were once covered by a large body of water called the Curtis Sea. As the sea withdrew plains formed, with lakes and streams, and deltas. The climate was subtropical which provided perfect habitat for dinosaurs, both vegetarians and meat eaters. They were the dominant life form for about 140 million years. It was a violent eat-and-be-eaten world, but an honest place where each creature understood the other's intentions. No public relations firm was around to make the other dino look good or put a positive spin on greedy mistakes.

Occasional floods would carry the dinosaurs' dead bodies down the rivers and into eddies and on sandbars where they were buried and became fossilized. Then there was a big uplift about seventy million years ago that brought the bones to the surface.

Around the turn of the last century a fellow by the name of Earl Douglass from the Carnegie Museum started finding fossils in eastern Utah. Then in August, 1909 he discovered dinosaur remains where the famous Quarry is now located. This was a dinosaur bone bonanza, so rich that a visitor center was built over the deposit to protect it from the elements and offer the public an amazing insight into the world of paleontology. In 1915 the Dinosaur National Monument was created. It includes several miles of magnificent canyons on the Yampa and Green rivers. Today the federal government might be less inclined to protect this area. Bones on top can sometimes be an indication of oil below, and oil rules.

In the 1950s the Dinosaur National Monument became a battleground for those interested in saving wilderness and those who wanted dams for irrigation. The Bureau of Land Management (BLM) proposed a dam at Echo Park on the Green River and another at Split Mountain Gorge not far from the Quarry. David Brower and Howard Zahniser of the Sierra Club lead the way in a battle that eventually stopped the BLM. The fight received national publicity and did much to introduce the value of "wilderness" to the American public. These efforts set the stage for the eventual passage of the Wilderness Act in 1964.

A dam was built at Flaming Gorge on the Green River upstream from the Park, and some folks still have their eye on Cross Mountain Gorge, a sweet little class 4-5 rafting and kayaking run a few miles east of the of the Monument boundary on the Yampa River. I shot a kayaking film there for *ABC American Sportsman* in 1979. It is a beautiful little canyon with far more difficult whitewater than exists anywhere in Dinosaur National Monument.

Many think that once a Wilderness Area designation battle has been won, it's been won forever, but this is not the case. There are always some folks around that think everything has to be "used" or it's being wasted. Wilderness, for them, is seen as a non use. An ongoing, neverending struggle exists between use and non-use, and use and over use. The problem is that once pristine natural lands have been used there is almost no chance of getting them back. As Clinton and Gore said about old growth forest at a conference we filmed, "Once it's gone, it's gone forever."

Archaeology

The first Indians apparently came from Asia to North America about 18,000 years ago. They crossed a land bridge that connected Siberia with Alaska, where the Bering Straight is now, and migrated from there throughout most of North America.

There is evidence of a continuous Indian presence in the Rocky Mountains dating back between 12,000 and 13,000 years. There are thousands of archaeological sites around the West revealing a fascinating history of Indian life prior to the arrival of Europeans. Some Indian cultures had complex mythologies and rituals that were suppressed by the early Europeans, but they have been experiencing a revival in recent decades.

The first Indians were nomadic hunter gatherers, but around the time of Christ some of them started building permanent villages and practicing sedentary agriculture. The most well known of these settlements in the Rocky Mountains is Mesa Verde near Cortez, Colorado. Other tribes, like the Utes, continued their nomadic existence.

Ancient petroglyphs.

Opposite page: south San Juan Mountains, Colorado.

Rock Art

The Indians of the Fremont and Virgin Kayenta cultures were prolific artists, leaving hundreds of paintings and petroglyphs on walls throughout western Colorado, Utah, New Mexico, and Arizona. As near as archaeologists can determine most of the work was done between A.D. 1000 and A.D. 1200. I have found examples in hidden places deep in the Dolores River Canyon and along the Yampa and San Juan rivers where we were kayaking. I've encountered them on rock ridges and in caves, as well.

Many of the anthropomorphic figures look like creatures we can imagine coming from outer space. Their bodies are trapezoidal, topped by square heads with elaborate headdresses. Some carry shields, and animals are usually present. Some have been painted or sculpted with exaggerated sexual organs.

The drawings are intriguing, but other than expressing hunting and reproductive prowess it is difficult to determine what they mean.

Father Sky, Mother Earth

The Europeans encountered Ute Indian tribes when they entered the Colorado mountains. Virginia McDonnell Simmons in her book, *The Ute Indians*, describes Ute cosmology:

> "In the Ute Indians' traditional view of the natural world, Father Sky created the sun, moon, stars, and Earth. Mother Earth provides what is needed by those who show reverence and respect. For Utes, there was a vast and varied land—sometimes gentle and sometimes severe—where they survived by living respectfully in harmony with their environment, whatever that might be."

If we—and by "we" I mean European settlers past and present—had embraced this philosophy 200 years ago, much of this book would be very different. The Ute view is so simple it seems trite in this day and age, but that is our cynicism, not theirs. We have been told the Indian message from the beginning, over and over and from every tribe, but we still are not listening.

The Flat Tops, looking into Deep Creek.

Connecting with the Past

Archaeology is a science, practiced by professionals, and I am not one of them. So the following observations should be taken with a grain of salt. I am trying to capture the spirit contained in a natural curiosity about the past that I share with many old timers who spent a lot of time looking at the ground, but there is no attempt to say that these observations are backed up by any verifiable science. What follows is subjective and personal.

Looking for arrowheads is my way to time travel into the past, to connect to the universe, to meditate, to purge stress, and to regain sanity. I find stone artifacts almost everywhere I visit. I've found hundreds of points on several continents, but I never tire of looking. It's something I always dream of doing more of.

Cottonwood Pass, southwest of my house, must have been a migratory route for several tribes. It was an easy way around the Glenwood Canyon which was certainly too rugged to pass through during high water. There is a cave in this area where there are a few faded pictographs. It is clearly an old trail that the Indians used for hundreds, perhaps even thousands of years. The Indians would have come down off the Flat Tops, or along the Colorado River, to a point a little west of where Dotsero is now, and crossed the river to Cottonwood Creek on the south side of the Colorado River, and up over Cottonwood Pass and down into Glenwood Springs. Some Indians probably came all the way from the Eastern Plains on this route.

They healed their wounds and sore joints in the hot springs at what is now Glenwood. From there they could travel out into the desert southwest to maraud or trade with the Pueblo tribes. I have found a few pieces of pottery near my house, but these people were primarily hunter-gatherers so the pottery is scarce. I doubt if they spent the winter in the Gypsum Creek Valley. The country was too cold.

Magical Moments

It is fall. I am jogging a few miles behind the house in an isolated canyon on the side of Red Mountain. It is a hidden place I visit infrequently, a place where the Indians used to find the milky white flint they used for their arrow points. This is a gray afternoon, and while there are different shades of green and brown and dull red, the landscape seems monochromatic and silent. Other than a few pinyon jays nothing moves. There are probably rabbits and deer and coyotes around but they do not make themselves apparent to me or my dog, John Henry.

When I get near the bottom of the canyon I begin to see the white chips of flint on the ground. In some places the broken rock is so dense I can't avoid stepping on it. I have never found a point here; too many old timers have been here before me. Arrowhead collecting was a popular pastime in the 1940s and 1950s before the ski resort got started. I move up a ridge through the oak brush to what's left of an old cabin. The roof is gone. In back is an outhouse and a corral with a shed for horses. The flint chips are thick all around the cabin. Two years ago I thought the rock doorstep to the cabin looked suspicious. I turned it over to see the flat smooth surface of a large, old grinding stone *(metate)*.

A few Aspen trees and larger pines in the gully next to the cabin indicate there was surface water here once, but it's gone now. Lower down in the gully there is a washed out dam and below that pipes running further down toward a meadow. The pipes have been half buried by several years of spring run-off floods. Who ever lived here had enough water to irrigate a small field. There are

Below left: Old timer's arrowhead collection.

Below right: 4 1/4-inch notched knife found near Minturn in the early 1960s.

stories about outlaws that hide out in places like this, but who knows. The memory has been lost.

I can feel a presence, the ghost of the cowboy or outlaw, or perhaps the Indians that preceded him, or a cougar watching me. I have never seen a cougar in this canyon but I know they are here. Hunters with dogs treed three cougars one day last winter not far away. The hunters tell me it is a good place to hunt the big cats. They have killed several toms here over the years. Deer winter below, there are a few elk up higher, and there are rabbits everywhere—plenty of food for cougars.

The silence is spooky, but I don't want to leave this lost canyon. If ever I have been in a place where I think the ghosts might come to life it's here. If I could just stretch my imagination a little further something or somebody might appear. It is when I let go of the present that the ancient points appear on the ground before me.

When I look for arrowheads in a place like this I try to put myself in the Indian's shoes, or moccasins, I should say. They liked flat areas with trees, but sometimes they worked out in the open. Being able to see the enemy approaching was critical. I'm sure it was the flint that brought them here more than the pinyon nuts and the game.

The largest point I have ever found was almost within the city limits of Minturn near Vail in the early 1960s. I was coming home from a discouraging day of bird hunting up Grouse Creek, looking at the ground on the trail before me. About a half-inch of white flint was showing in the mud. I reached down and got my fingers under an almost perfect 4 1/4-inch, beautifully notched knife.

Another wonderful "find" occurs on August 6, 2003—the day I decide to write this book. It's hot and sunny in the Gypsum Creek Valley, a good day to take my nine-year-old son Christian up onto the Flat Tops above Deep Creek. My purpose is to locate grouse before the hunting season and it's also a good opportunity for Christian to get used to his new BB gun.

The road up is steep and rough. The unloaded truck bounces around on the washboard, threatening to leave the road if I don't adjust my speed. Thousands of big Mormon crickets are crawling on the dirt, impossible to miss. Finally we get to the top. This east side of the Flat Tops is magnificent with its grand flat meadows stopping abruptly at the edge of the Deep Creek Canyon. Sheer cliffs drop away, down to scree slopes where scattered pines and spruce hang on tenuously. There are holes in the cliff walls, some of which are large caves. Way below is Deep Creek, a glistening little ribbon of clear water winding through a pine forest. I'm sure there are lots of small trout in the creek. I want to climb down and explore but it's a two-day trip so it will have to wait.

We hike up above the grassy open meadows to the edge of the pine and spruce forest. The blue grouse is primarily a forest bird that sometimes feeds in the adjacent meadows. It's fun to catch them out in the open but more often than not I find them in the forest. Of course the hawks like to catch them out in the open as well, which is why they don't spend too much time there.

As Christian and I cross a steep opening between the trees I look down and see a white stone with the unmistakable shape of an arrowhead. The tip is broken off, but still it is one of the most beautifully made pieces I have ever seen, thin with lateral fluting and finely shaped edges, two-inches long. I marvel at the skill of the maker. It looks like a archaic piece, probably 2,000 to 3,000 years old.

Clement Frost, a Ute tribal chairman, once observed, "The land doesn't belong to us, we belong to the land." At this moment I feel like Christian and I belong.

My ears hear only silence. The persistent snap, snap, snap of breaking flint is long gone. No piece of sharp stone will ever again cut through to the heart of a running deer. Age old tall tales will never be repeated by the children of these hunters over the embers of a warm evening campfire. The ancient knowledge floated away long ago, into a dark silence, lost to an indifferent world.

And so the arrowheads we find in the dirt are both beautiful and sad.

Arrowhead collecting is pretty much a thing of the past in Eagle County. Most of them have been picked up. But then, once in a while, I still spot one. It glints in the dirt, a little rock tool, beautifully sculpted, made from a carefully selected shiny stone. My heart skips a beat. It is clear to me that the ancient people imparted mystical powers to these hunting implements, and that they killed with great respect for their prey.

These days I also find the tire tracks of dirt bikes running through many of the Indian camp sites. I'm sure the riders are oblivious to the destruction they are causing.

Larry Schultz, the man who built the road and water system for my home on the side of Red Mountain, told me stories of cutting open Indian tree burials nearby when he was a kid. Apparently the Indians wrapped their dead in skins and hung them in big old juniper trees in the winter when the ground was frozen. When he opened the skins stone tools and other artifacts fell out which he picked up and gave away to friends. Larry has had more than his share of bad luck in his life, maybe because he messed with those graves.

It is illegal to pick up arrowheads and other prehistoric artifacts on American Public Lands. The artifacts pictured in this book were either found prior to the passage of various state and federal Antiquities Acts, or they have been found on private land. The laws backfire in a way, because most old timers are reluctant to show their collections to professional archeologists who might be able to fit the artifacts into a bigger picture; pinning down where they were found, determining their age, the source of the rock, and so on. Show me a ten-year-old kid who says he saw an arrowhead on the ground and didn't pick it up, and I'll show you a liar.

Ankatosh
Warets
Ouray
Shavano
Guerro

Chapter Two

The Arrival of the Europeans

"We do not want to sell a foot of our land—that is the opinion of our people. The whites can go and take the land and come out again. We do not want them to build houses here."

—CHIEF OURAY of the Tabeguache Utes, circa 1860 as the Colorado Gold Rush began

"None but the Indians have ever lived in this country, and they exist only as a part of it. They have never attempted to assert themselves but have grown up like the trees. It is their food, their drink, their religion and their life."
—Donald John Hall

The Utes, and earlier tribes, lived in Colorado for several thousand years without substantially changing the natural design of the land. The first Europeans to explore the continent trapped and did some farming and grazing, but they didn't disturb the landscape all that much. They did, however, change the lives of the Indians dramatically.

It was the miners that had the first serious physical impact on the Colorado mountains. That started in 1858 when gold was discovered in Cherry Creek near where Denver is now, and a gold rush began, but I'm getting ahead of myself.

One of the first Europeans to arrive in the Rocky Mountain West was a Spaniard, Captain General Juan de Onate. He traveled north as far the Chama River in New Mexico in 1598. He and his men were on horseback. The Indians saw these animals and managed to run off with a few. By 1640, the life of the Utes had become very much more mobile. They had evolved into skilled riders who could hunt, fight, and move relatively quickly through the rugged mountainous terrain.

Previous spread—Chief Ouray and other tribal leaders (left) Courtesy of the Denver Public Library *and Antelope herd (right).*

Below: Elk herd.

There is a record of Ewing Young's exploration traveling west along the Colorado River in 1827. He passed close to where I live. My guess is he went over Cottonwood Pass, behind my house, to avoid the Glenwood Canyon. He was exploring, covering long distances, so it's doubtful he took the time to wander up the Eagle River to where Vail is now. After that there were most certainly many unrecorded explorations by trappers and prospectors. As these white men made more and more demands on Indian territory fighting broke out, and eventually the Indians were subdued and forced onto reservations. It was a process that took several years.

Each time Indians killed white men, no matter what the reason, the incident was used as justification for taking more land away from them. This is what many settlers, miners, military men, and assorted opportunists and thieves wanted—a chance to squat on the fertile valleys that the Indians had been forced to relinquish.

One of the most devastating incidents for the Indians was the Meeker Massacre. Nathan Meeker was in his sixties when he came on hard times and took a job as Indian agent at the White River Reservation in what is now Meeker, Colorado. Meeker wanted to civilize the Indians and turn them into self-sufficient farmers, but the Indians were more interested in hunting and horse racing. Conflicts developed and the White River Utes complained to Chief Ouray who lived near what is now Montrose. He asked the Los Piños agent, Abbott, to write letters to Washington about the problem but Abbott never did. Meanwhile, the Indians were purchasing whiskey and firearms from outside the White River Reservation. Tensions continued to grow until finally Meeker requested troops for protection. For the Utes this amounted to a declaration of war, so they ambushed the troops as they entered the Reservation. The battle lasted six days, until more troops arrived and the Utes surrendered. Meanwhile Meeker and nine employees had been killed and mutilated. Josie and Arvilla Meeker, Flora Ellen Price, and her two children were taken captive by the Indians but eventually released. The entire state of Colorado panicked at this point. No Ute was safe anywhere. Over the next few years the Utes lost most of their reservation lands in Colorado. Their exodus along Evacuation Creek in Utah has been compared to the Cherokee's Trail of Tears. There was much heartbreak, death and suffering. Today there is a Ute Reservation in Southwestern Colorado and another in northeastern Utah.

There is very little in the way of written history on the Utes in Eagle County, but some old cowboys can remember a few stories. Orris Albertson told me of a time when the U.S. Calvary was chasing a large bunch of Indians along the east side of the Flat Tops. It was a small group of soldiers, and judging from the fact that the Indians were eating a cow a day, the soldiers were not sure they wanted to engage them in battle. They trailed the Indians to the eastern end of Glenwood Canyon and then gave up. Apparently the Indians went up into the Cottonwood Pass country and over to where Montrose is now.

It's not hard to imagine what it was like for an early trapper or explorer in Colorado. Life was not that difficult if he was experienced and careful. His rifle had a large advantage over the Indians' short range bows. There was always plenty of game available if he had a good supply of powder and shot. And the rivers had lots of fish. The Indians were probably not as likely to bother him if he kept moving. The Indians tolerated the trappers because they traded with them

For the Utes, the yucca plant had many uses, including medicine.

Above: Georgetown Loop, 1989.

Top right: Minturn Roundhouse crash of Rio Grande engine, 1913. Courtesy of the Eagle Public Library.

Bottom right: Theodore Roosevelt on a political tour in Colorado. Courtesy of the Denver Public Library.

and respected their skills. It was the settlers whom the Indians resented because they laid claim to the land.

From the first of May until the end of September the weather is mostly pleasant, particularly below 8,000 feet. I'm sure the tough mountain men knew how to wait out the winter storms which usually only lasted a few days. Of course they were careful not to get caught up high when the snow started to accumulate.

Between 1860 and 1910, after the miners arrived in great numbers and the Indians were still hunting, there were no hunting seasons and the big game all but disappeared.

Nature could be a hard taskmaster as well. There were occasional bad winters when many of the animals starved to death because they couldn't dig down through the frozen crusted snow to feed. An old timer friend from Baggs, Wyoming, Sid Webber, tells of growing up without seeing a deer or an antelope for a two- or three-year stretch when he was a boy. A big snow had wiped them out.

Moose Hunter. Courtesy Brown family album.

The Railroads

In 1887 the railroad was completed from Leadville to Eagle and on to Glenwood Springs, and the country was opened up to even more settlers. The homesteaders came in on the train and wandered into the high valleys, hoping to be able make it with a few cows and sheep and a lot of hard work. Most of them failed. Parts of the deserted homesteads are still standing. I have rhubarb growing in my garden from stock that I found in a hidden, beautiful wide spot in the Piney River Valley on the west side of the Gore Range. Trout from the Eagle River, potatoes from the Brush and Gypsum Creek valleys, deer, elk, mountain sheep, cattle and domestic sheep from the whole county—all helped to feed the Leadville miners.

After the turn of the century another railroad line was built under the Continental Divide through the Moffatt Tunnel near Winter Park and down the Colorado River Valley to eventually join up with the railroad coming from Leadville. Glenwood Springs became a popular tourist destination because of the hot springs. Teddy Roosevelt came out to Glenwood Springs, using it as a base for hunting expeditions into the Flat Tops. Glenwood boasted polo fields, a popular pastime for the wealthy Denverites of those times. Polo ponies were raised and trained in the Gypsum Creek Valley. When I first moved to Gypsum in the mid-1970s you could still see the outline of a horse racing track in the meadows on the Gypsum Creek Ranch.

The headwater lands of the White River have always been some of the most productive hunting and fishing areas in the western United States. The Indians spent the summer months hunting in the high, grassy meadows of the Flat Topsand then followed the game down into the sagebrush country in the fall. They killed only what they could eat and wasted almost nothing, tanning the hides with the brains of the animals and eating the liver and other organs.

When the mines started up in Leadville, Aspen, and the other mineral rich towns, the population in the Colorado mountains grew to well over 50,000 people. Market hunters slaughtered huge quantities of game to feed these fortune hunters. Jack Burns, from the Burns Hole country, bragged about shooting forty-seven elk in one day. He only took the hindquarters of the animals, leaving the rest to rot. Others hunted deer and bear just for the skins, and there was a big trade in elk ivories, the two small remnant tusks found in the animal's upper jaws. Wagonloads of deer, elk, and mountain sheep carcasses moved from hunting country into the mining towns every day, finally depleting the seemingly inexhaustible supply. The situation became so bad that elk actually had to reintroduced into some areas. Elk hunting was stopped in four counties in 1903 and not opened again until 1929.

In 1891 President Benjamin Harrison established the White River Plateau Timberland Reserve, but there were no provisions to protect the game and loggers paid little attention to restrictions aimed at them. It wasn't until then Vice President elect Teddy Roosevelt came to Meeker to hunt lion in 1901, and he saw what was going on firsthand, that effective laws were enacted. Roosevelt took the power to manage the federal lands out of local hands and gave it to Congress. A federal grazing fee was established to control the cattleman. They resisted until the matter finally was settled in court, and Fred Light, a cattleman from the Snowmass area and a big offender, paid up.

Above: J. M. "Doc" Holliday as he appeared in the early 1880s. Courtesy of the Denver Public Library.

Below: Diamond Jack Alteri. Courtesy of the Colorasdo Historical Society.

Not everyone that visited western Colorado had the quality of character that Teddy Roosevelt exhibited. Gunslingers came through the country as well. Perhaps the most infamous was Doc Holliday. Doc sold himself as a dentist but his tubercular cough didn't help the dental business, so he spent most of his time pursuing another profession, gambling. He carried a sawed-off shotgun under his coat and wasn't afraid to use it if the game was going badly for him. At least eight dead men attest to the fact that Doc was a poor loser.

Doc Holliday spent most of his adult years in Arizona. He came to Glenwood Springs hoping the mineral water would help his tuberculosis, but he was beyond repair and died in 1887 at age thirty-five. He has been immortalized in numerous Hollywood western films.

Another colorful character hung out in Eagle County. "Diamond Jack" Alteri, a Chicago gangster, purchased a dude ranch at Sweetwater Lake in 1927 and used it as a hideout from those in the Chicago mobs that wanted to see him dead. He lost the ranch in 1935 because of unpaid taxes and was forced to return to Chicago where he was gunned down while leaving his hotel to visit the barber shop. Cowboy Orris Albertson remembers meeting Diamond Jack when he visited the Burns Hole country. Orris says he was a gentleman, friendly, and not at all threatening.

In my view, gangsters in the today's West are not so easy to identify and not seen as criminals, but the damage they inflict is highly visible. Their crime is exploitation. Their victim is the land.

These real estate developers mine the scenery as surely as the power companies strip the coal out of the ground near Craig, and the hard rock miners once took gold and silver from Central City and Leadville, leaving piles of tailings behind. The trophy homes these developers build—and the CEOs, stock market barons, assorted speculators, and other extremely wealthy types buy—sometimes exceed 10,000-square feet in size. Security gates warn passers-by to stay away. The beautiful mountain views once sitting above ranch meadows and easy to enjoy from back country roads are now plugged with these ostentatious displays of conspicuous expenditure. Acres and acres of prime agricultural land are ruined in the process, but there are no laws against it.

After Pete Dodo, a rancher in the Upper Eagle Valley, sold his property to the Arrowhead developers, he watched in shocked disbelief as they built the golf course. "My family spent years leveling that ground and taking out the rocks so we could grow hay there, and now they are putting all those little hills and sand traps in. Crazy, if you ask me."

Mining and Ranching

Mining, more than any other industry, has shaped Colorado's past. It is difficult to walk anywhere on federal lands for very long without stumbling on a hole where someone has tried to dig something up out of the ground. Even the Indians had places where they picked up special rocks for making tools. Mining is a major industry in Colorado today, not as much for precious metals, but for coal and natural gas. At one time people thought we were going to have the largest mining operation in the world, to extract oil from the shale in the Piceance Basin. But that didn't work out.

Mining is an exploitative industry by definition. No one has ever successfully tried to justify it as anything else. The only kind thing that can be said about mining's impact on the natural environment is that it is relatively small. There are far more square miles of paved roads and parking lots in this country than there are square miles of mines. Still, some of the big open pit mines in the state are not comfortable to look at. Our nation operates on fossil fuels, we are almost totally dependent on energy from oil, coal, and gas, however, so it seems hypocritical to complain. Many say the question isn't whether to mine or not, it is how to mine with minimum impact. On the other hand there are excellent renewable sources of energy like the sun and wind which are both abundant in Colorado. Efforts are being made to harness these sources, but at the moment I would have to say it's too little, too late.

Mining and the railroads brought settlers to Colorado in large numbers. Farming and ranching were natural outgrowths of the need the miners had for food. Those people who got into the business of supplying the miners often fared better than the miners did. But the ranchers had their share of problems to solve as well.

First, the semi-arid ranch lands in the mountain valleys needed water to grow enough hay for winter feeding. Hundreds of miles of irrigation ditches were built for this purpose. The cowboys move their cattle off the irrigated meadows in the spring and up into the high country, letting the hay grow undisturbed. After the second hay or alfalfa crop is cut and bailed, the cattle are herded back to the home ranch and sold or kept in the hay meadows over the winter. Some ranchers move the cows and sheep to lower warmer elevations near Rifle and Grand Junction to avoid the cold.

Another group of cattlemen complicated matters by coming to Colorado from places as far away as Texas to fatten their cows on the tall mountain grass. These free-range cattlemen would move in for the summer and then drive their cows to Denver in the fall and then to bigger markets in the East like Kansas City and Chicago. There were no restrictions on where they could graze. The grass

Above: Moving mining equipment, late 1800s. Courtesy of the Eagle Public Library.

Right: Nick Brown at an abandoned mine near the top of New York Mountain, Holy Cross Wilderness.

Cattle roundup in Burns, Colorado.

belonged to the first cowboy who could get his herd to it after the snows melted. Over-grazing became a serious problem as a result.

Ranchers who had their home operations in Colorado, like Frank Benton from the Burns Hole, complained bitterly and pushed Congress to remedy the situation. Eventually the Taylor Grazing Act was passed. This Act tied the use of the federal lands to the ranches that were located next to them. The grazing allotments were managed by the federal government and are still in use today.

Some men brought large herds of sheep into the Colorado mountains. The cattlemen decided that sheep were damaging the range and tried to drive the sheep herders out. Shootings occurred, but eventually they settled their differences as some ranchers began running both sheep and cattle. In fact, some land is brushy, drier, and more suitable for sheep, which are browsers like deer. Cattle are grazers and prefer grass that grows in the meadows and irrigated pastures of the valley flat land.

The Flat Tops and the Glenwood Canyon

One hunk of geography stands out in my mind, both for its spectacular beauty and the way it has been treated since the first Europeans encountered its forbidding walls.

"Getting to know you, getting to love you, getting to learn all about you." I forget the song but not the message. Love—real love—grows over time. Ecologist Wes Jackson has written a book with the wonderful title, *Becoming Native to this Place*. That's what has happened to me. Being a native isn't about where you are born, it's about putting in the time in one place, learning to care, and sending down roots. It's about exploring; touching, feeling, smelling, and digging up the

Dome Peak, Flat Tops Wilderness Area.

past which enriches the present. The Flat Tops and the Glenwood Canyon are in my back yard. They have fascinated me from the day I first saw them and they are part of what I consider home. So I'll introduce them now and revisit them later.

The Deep Creek Road, which is the southeast entrance to the Flat Tops Wilderness Area and Flat Tops National Forest, is about a fifteen minute drive from where I live. Red Hill blocks my view to the north and west so I can't actually see the great Flat Tops monolith from my home but it's not very far away. As soon I drive onto I-70 north of Gypsum I can look down the Eagle River Valley to a big hill with a little tiny road winding up over the top. Mountain range isn't quite the right description for this chunk of country but the name Flat Tops hits the mark. It is a fifty-mile by fifty-mile-wide plateau, a big block of rock, steep walled all around with rolling hills on top and occasional sharp canyons like Deep Creek, and the Glenwood Canyon for that matter, cutting through it.

The Colorado River swings south near McCoy and goes for about forty miles along the east side of the Flat Tops. The geology is spectacular. Basaltic volcanism from the Miocene epoch of the Tertiary period walls in the river in parts of this area. Eventually the Colorado River joins the Eagle River and heads west toward Glenwood Springs. At this point it cuts deep down into two-million-year-old Precambrian granite. Above the granite is stacked Sagauche sandstone, then Dotsero, Manitou, Chaffee, and Leadville sedimentary formations. The giant walls rise straight up from the river in many places. Occasional black holes mark cave entrances. Trees cling to little flat places here and there. The canyon invites exploration but the scale and size are formidable. There is so much of it.

Fifteen miles west of the confluence with the Eagle, the Colorado River exits the main canyon at the city of Glenwood Springs. Here a huge hot springs flows from deep in the bowels of the earth at the rate of 2,000 gallons a minute. The Indians used the warm comforting sulfur smelling water to heal their wounds long before white men arrived. Probably the first white man to bathe in the Glenwood hot springs was Richard Sopris, a gold prospector, who arrived there in July 1860. It's been getting more and more popular ever since. I try to do a few laps at least twice a week to keep arthritis and worn out disks from crippling me.

The rugged Rocky Mountain terrain didn't hold back westward expansion. The Denver & Rio Grand Western Railroad was completed through the Glenwood Canyon in 1887. Two years later funding was provided for a wagon road, and that road was continuously improved until it is now a four-lane interstate, one of four crossing the United States.

When I was interviewing Stewart Udall about oil shale in the early 1970s, the then about-to-be-built superhighway through Glenwood Canyon came up in the conversation. Stewart said, "It's such a beautiful canyon, why change the road? Let people slow down and enjoy the scenery." It was a nice sentiment for a nation where the automobile is the most significant icon after God, and "thou shall go as fast as possible" is the Eleventh Commandment. No one paid much attention to Stewart's suggestion.

Interstate-70 in Glenwood Canyon is now the crown jewel of the American Interstate system, a four-lane raised steel and asphalt testament to our irrepressible ingenuity, and conclusive proof that the question is no longer "can we do it, but should we do it?" The old two lane highway in the canyon would have backed up traffic for hundreds of miles in both directions if left unchanged. The I-70 speed limit in the canyon is fifty miles an hour, but most folks go faster. Very few slow down for the scenery. Speed rules.

The Colorado River keeps on moving west into Utah and down to Arizona, on through many more big cuts in the earth like the Grand Canyon, until it reaches Mexico and the Sea of Cortez. But no water reaches the sea these days. It is used up by cities and agricultural projects all along the way. Las Vegas, Phoenix, and Los Angeles depend on Colorado River water.

There have been several big fires on the Flat Tops. Years ago beetles attacked the forests leaving an almost impenetrable tangle of dead trees, trees that burn hot and fast when they catch fire. Some logging has been going on continuously since the early 1900s, but it's not highly visible. The dominant features, other than the big stretches of burned forests, are the vast open grasslands punctuated by patches

East entrance to Glenwood Canyon.

Colorado River and I-70. in Glenwood Canyon.

of Aspen trees here and there. The tops of the hills are rimmed by jagged lines of black timber. Dead snags mix with sharp-pointed spruce and pine. If you're a hunter you see immediately where the big animals graze and where they hide. The trick is to catch them out in the grass where you can get a clean shot.

The Flat Tops harbors the largest herd of elk in the state as well as thousands of mule deer and a few herds of bighorn sheep. Numerous lakes, some very remote, have trout in them. The biggest trout I have ever caught in Colorado was in Keener Lake at the top of the Derby Creek drainage . I have seen grouse almost every time I have visited the Flat Tops, but I have only hunted them recently.

Armies of elk and deer hunters, myself included, move onto the Flat Tops every fall, bringing all their toys with them: trailers, four-wheelers, whatever makes the hunting easier. Somehow the Flat Tops survive, and in the spring the deer, elk, and cattle move back up the slopes to feed on the high country grass.

*"Woe unto them that lay field upon field
and house upon house that there be no place to be left
alone in the world."*

—Isaiah

Vail 1962

Chapter 3

Vail: Birth and Maturation of a Ski Town

Above: Vail Olympic training, 1963.

Previous spread—
Vail Valley, 1962 (left) and Vail Valley, 1990 (right).

If Colorado is a reflection of the nation in some way, then Vail is an aberration of the good and bad of both. Tons of money have built opulent modern chateaus for the rich and powerful and excellent facilities: performing arts centers, indoor ice rinks, alpine gardens, ski lifts, etc., for anyone who can afford them. But it is a place of extremes. No one is starving in Vail, and it's too cold for the homeless to survive, but a dozen immigrant laborers might be sleeping in a small trailer on the one hand, while a solitary caretaker is living in a 10,000- or 20,000-square-foot home on the other hand, except for a few weeks a year when the owners show up. The town makes no moral judgment about its new residents, everything is based entirely on their ability to pay. Vail has become a modern feudal society in many ways, a place that is dedicated to the care and feeding of the very rich. Dennis Kozlowski, the "Creed of Greed" Tyco entrepreneur, had a place in Bachelor Gulch until he was arrested recently. Aspen is the same—a town where Enron's Ken Lay had two multimillion dollar homes, and others like him still do.

Having lived through the entire development of Vail from the beginning I think I can offer some perspective. Please bear with me while I relate some personal stories. The stories are scattered through many chapters and may not always seem relevant, but each adds another dimension to the whole, painting a picture of the past and present that is hard to see in any other way. The history is important because I think what happened in Vail reflects what has happened in most of the big American resorts. Vail is victim of its own success.

The Beginning

Vail was born a beautiful baby, and we all loved her.
We loved the mountains that gave her to us,
we loved skiing on her graceful slopes and trails.
We delighted in the friendships we made
on the lifts and in the homes we built, and
in the children we raised there.

Money was one of those things it was embarrassing to get too focused on. Some had it and some didn't, and so what? We all struggled in different ways to create the resort. We were pioneers with common goals, and we were incredibly happy.

Skiing in the early days of Vail.

My story is not unique. Several people who arrive in Vail in the beginning with no money in their pockets do very well: Rod Slifer in real estate; Pepi and Sheika Gramshammer in the hotel business; Dave and Renie Gorsuch with ski equipment and clothing stores; Joe and Ann Staufer with the Vail Village Inn; and dozens more. With determination and a little imagination it is hard to miss.

My love affair with Colorado begins in Vail in 1962. I lived in Boulder for a year before this, but I don't get hooked until I move up into the mountains and start building a home. I am twenty-seven, married, with a son on the way. Living in the mountains is a dream I had developed long ago growing up in the suburbs of Boston, and now it is coming true.

Colorado seems an innocent place in the 1960s, but it is probably me who is innocent, naïve, and idealistic. I don't know it at the time, or at least I don't think about it, but Colorado has had a history of exploitation since the miners arrived in the 1850s. Making money has almost always been the dominant goal.

My early twenties are turbulent years. I am pursuing an interesting but lonely career in photo journalism. I need time by myself to write, but I want to have a girl to share my ideas with and be in love with. I don't submit anything I write to any magazines: it is too personal and private. So I have no positive feedback or any indications that I might be getting somewhere. I keep falling in love and getting hurt or hurting someone. The confusion between desire and some deeper need for a companion is tearing me apart. I am divided between the contradictory goals of having an exciting career and the deeper instinctive need to find a mate, settle down, and have a family. I am living hand-to-mouth and almost always broke, but I know inside that I am learning, accumulating experience, and finding my way. My career is evolving slowly, but at least it is evolving.

It seems, looking back, that those years were a high point in the development of the nation. American idealism was ascending. The conservatism that followed World War II was giving way to a more liberal sense of social responsibility. But there were some terrible reality checks. Martin Luther King Jr. ended the lie that America had been living with since the Civil War by putting some teeth into the idea of equality, and he was assassinated for his efforts. Jack Kennedy brought the illusion of hope to the world with his charm, good looks, and intelligence, and he was gunned down in Dallas, Texas. I am working on my house in Vail when I hear the news about Kennedy. I cry, and I find out later, while traveling in countries like Turkey, that the whole world cried for Jack.

It is pivotal moment in my life when Bob Parker, then editor for *Skiing Magazine*, sees *Out to Ski*, a ski lecture film I have made and asks me if I am interested in making a film for a new ski area that is just getting started called Vail. The hitch is that the Vail partners don't have much money. They can pay for the cost of the film stock and processing, but they will have to pay for my labor with a

Blue grouse on Flat Tops.

residential building lot. The Head Ski Company job pays me enough to live on so the deal sounds good. I do the shooting on weekends and put a lot of VIPs on Head Skis, so Howard Head forgives my moonlighting.

A Vail partnership costs $10,000 at the time. This includes a building lot and lifetime ski passes for the whole family. Since I am donating labor on the film they give me a lot but not the ski pass. The lot has a value of $2,500, so with the lot I secure a bank loan and build a house. I invest about $75,000. I sell the house for $310,000 in the mid 1970s. Two years later it sells for over a $1,000,000. Real estate is obviously the business to be in. No one sees this as a problem until the local working people have been bought out of town and the big new mansions stand vacant much of the year,

My first wife and I are broke much of the time in those early years. I hunt and fish, first for fun, but then in tight times the venison helps our grocery bill and I become a meat hunter. A good-sized herd of deer live on the ski mountain behind the house. I drive up Mill Creek in the dark after a fresh snow and hike up the old logging roads looking for tracks. We have either-sex licenses. I don't always look at the head of deer before I shoot, and this is how I kill one of the biggest deer in the area. I shoot, the animal goes down, and I walk up to see a huge set of antlers on the head of this gray-nosed old buck. I am very excited for the first half-hour or so, but the deer is heavy and very difficult to drag through the forest to my car. By the time I get the animal home and butchered I consider myself a professional. Hunting is hard work. We eat the liver and heart and I have the skins tanned. Living off the land feels good.

I have a partner in the film business at that time, Ken Miller, who grew up in Minnesota fishing with his Dad. Ken and I go over to the Piney River and catch great quantities of brook trout. Over the years the Piney just keeps getting better and better as we cut back the brook trout population and the cutthroats, Yellowstones, and browns have a chance to grow bigger and bigger. The river seems inexhaustible. I teach my sons Gordon, Mike, and Nick how to fish there. It is guaranteed. We always come home with a nice mess of trout.

In the early spring and fall, hundreds of sheep plug up Highway 6 when they are being moved to and from the mountain pastures. The sheep herders run their herds right through the middle of Vail. If a dog chases their animals they shoot it. If you have a garden it is a fair meal for the sheep. Hard feelings develop so the sheep herders soon find a way to go around the town. The sheep business keeps shrinking over the years, first near Vail, but then in the rest of Eagle County. Herding is a lonely business. The sheep ranchers hire Basques from Spain, South Americans from the Andean altiplano, and Navajos from Arizona. We run into these herders in the back country. They are always happy to share a cup of coffee and talk even though our Spanish is no better than their English.

My marriage can't stand the pressures of being broke a lot of the time and traveling out of town when I do get a job. We divorce, in spite of having two children. Later I marry again, this marriage lasts for eighteen years and one more son, Nicolas, is added to the family.

Fishing on the Eagle River.

Luck plays a roll in almost everyone's life at some point. I am clearly in the right place at the right time in Vail in the early 1960s. Don Fowler, the United Airlines Denver manager, sees the film I made for Vail and decides United Airlines also needs a film promoting Colorado skiing. The logic is simple. United has good summer traffic into Denver but winter business is slow. Most eastern skiers that can afford it take their winter vacations in Europe, but with new resorts like Vail and Breckenridge popping up, and older resorts like Aspen and Winter Park in the picture, Colorado is in a position to give the European Alps a run for its money.

Don Fowler corners the president of United Airlines in a restroom at their executive offices in Chicago and sells him on the idea. I start making the film on Don's word. I actually don't get paid until the show is complete. When we are searching for a name for the show Bob Parker suggests "Ski Country, U.S.A." That name sticks and is still the name of Colorado's winter sports promotional organization today. The film is well received. Other big companies like Hertz get involved in subsequent promotions and then other airlines like TWA, Western, and Frontier join the effort. These promotional films become my bread and butter for ten years. The *Ski Country, U.S.A.* program is obviously a huge success. We have unleashed a monster.

Bob Parker becomes Vail's publicity director as soon as the resort opens. He is a genius at stretching his marketing budget or to put it another way, at getting free publicity. If I need untracked powder skiing shots I can call him early in the morning on a clear day after a snowfall and ask him to keep the back bowls closed until I have time to shoot a few runs. If I need good skiers from the ski school he arranges it. Bob opens up off limits areas if I need to get onto some cliffs for jumps or powder in the trees. If it is potentially dangerous situation he makes sure we have a patrolman with us who can clear the area of avalanche danger.

It is a symbiotic relationship. He hires me to do the Vail promotional films, and I bring my film projects for airlines and ski companies to Vail. In this way

Roger Staub.

Vail receives a great deal of free promotion and I have the prefect studio, pretty much under my control, right in my back yard.

When Vail hires the Olympic Gold Medal winner Roger Staub as the Director of Skiing they don't think of him as a manager. He is a figurehead which means he is readily available almost whenever I need him in front of my cameras. Roger is a poetic skier with a dry sense of humor that shows up in some of the funniest sequences we ever put on film. He seems to relish the absurdity of letting his body go, carving smooth turns into terrain at speeds that would mean certain disaster for someone of lesser skill. The word "graceful" takes on a whole new meaning with Roger.

Roger is always good company, easy to laugh, and as elegant in his manners as he is on skis. It is a painful loss when he falls out of the sky while hang gliding near his home town of Arosa, Switzerland. For me, Roger is the personification of the fun and style that characterizes Vail in the early years.

I occasionally shoot film of the founder of Vail, Pete Seibert, skiing powder, climbing in the Gore Range with Dick Pownall and some of the other 1963 American Everest Expedition members. I interview him for the Vail history show, but Pete and I have a somewhat uneasy relationship because of my strong stands on environmental issues. I become a participant in the East Meadow Creek lawsuit (*Parker vs. the Forest Service*) in which we stop the Forest Service from logging next to the proposed Eagles Nest Wilderness. This is the first time anyone has successfully sued the Forest Service. Pete is upset with Bob Parker and me on this issue since Vail depends on the Forest Service for its permits. Later Pete convinces me to go to Mexico City with him and show *The Edge,* an adventure sports feature documentary I have just finished, to some Mexican politicos. They really like the film, although they are more into big game hunting than kayaking or climbing. Pete's efforts pay off, however. The Mexicans invest heavily in Vail.

I am shooting on so many different ski films in some years that I have to take advantage of every sunny powder day. I cannot afford to miss one of them. Even now when a Colorado bluebird day breaks I get a twinge in my stomach that says, "Why aren't you shooting?"

Vail is a great place to live during these early years. Everyone knows everyone else. There is little separation between rich and poor. You are measured by the way you ski, not by your bank accounts. But it doesn't matter if you are a lousy skier as long as you are a good sport and come up smiling. There is a strong sense of camaraderie. We know we have a special community and we work to keep it that way. Enjoying the mountains and each other is more important than making a fortune, at least for awhile.

As Vail grows it changes. There is a kind of seesaw development going on. The mountain becomes more and more crowded as more hotels and condos are built. In turn, Vail Associates builds more lifts and opens more terrain to satisfy the demands of the new skiers. Subdivisions spread westward out of the Gore Creek Valley and along the Eagle River.

Then Beaver Creek is built. It seems empty in the first years, no lift lines and almost empty trails, but the gated village idea is popular and big homes and condo complexes start going up. The real estate developers sell the idea of ski in and ski out second homes. Time sharing ("interval ownership") brings these expensive accommodations within reach of even more people. It becomes quite fashionable to own a place in the Vail area.

Growing pains during these years bring Vail Associates to the brink of bankruptcy on more than one occasion. This forces the Board of Directors to get more seriously corporate. They decide founders don't necessarily make good managers. Pete Siebert goes off to Utah to try to create another Vail called Snow Basin and goes broke in the process.

Big money folks with big egos have entered the picture by now. Millionaire Harry Bass, an early investor from Texas, decides he wants to own Vail and secures a controlling interest. Things don't work out for Harry, so he sells out to junk bond magnate George Gillette. George has a grand vision for Vail which he quickly implements. More lifts and more ski terrain are opened. The airport in Gypsum is expanded to accommodate larger planes. This allows some guests to avoid the Denver International Airport and the long and sometimes snowy drive over two passes to Vail. But alas, George goes broke and sells out to Apollo Partners. They install Adam Aron, a thick-skinned MBA, to run the company. Meanwhile Breckenridge and Keystone are acquired, and Vail Associates becomes Vail Resorts.

Adam Aron relies more on real estate sales than lift ticket revenues to create a profit picture so when the real estate market slumps after the September 11 World Trade Center bombings and the accounting scandals that shake the corporate world, Vail finds itself once again in financial trouble. This is exacerbated by Vail's accounting practices, which also have to be adjusted.

Vail is now a very different place from what it was in the early years.

Roger Brown skiing powder, 1962.

The First Problem

I don't think a physical place can be destroyed easily without first destroying the spirit and beliefs of the people who live there. As long as we were young and strong, and confident in what we were doing, the mountains somehow seemed safe. If a super highway in the wrong canyon, or an inappropriate logging operation next to a wilderness area, or transmountain water diversion threatened us, we simply stopped it.

What has really changed us over time is an in-migration of large numbers of people with different values. It's like Tibet: the Chinese have moved hundreds of thousands of lowlanders onto the plateau, overwhelming the native Tibetans. In Colorado, large numbers of basically urban people have moved into the mountains. Instead of adopting a mountain lifestyle, however, most have brought their urban ways with them and have demanded urban amenities. Those of us who want to live as mountain people have become a small minority.

Howard Head, the inventor of Head metal skis, said to me once, for what reason I am not sure, "That was in another time and in another country. And besides, the wench is dead." Or close to it. So much for crying over spilt milk. Colorado is a mess.

Above: Roger Brown, 1967.

Above right: Barry Corbet, 1967.

Summit Films

Summit Films, like Vail, was born out of a dream. What could be more satisfying than making movies about the things we love to do?

In the late 1960s and early 1970s we evolved into filmmakers with reputations for knowing what we wanted to say and how to say it. Our success gave us the confidence to buck established thinking, not only in mountain sports but on other subjects; the environment, paraplegia, and anything else that seemed important to us. We set our own standards.

Much of life is about successful partnerships, symbiotic relationships that are "greater than the sum of their members." The results can take many shapes: the children of a family, the founding of a town, or, in the case of Barry Corbet and me, our films.

I first met Barry in Jackson Hole, Wyoming, in 1963. He was a well known mountain climber at the time, in search of another way to make a living. Being a climbing guide and a motel owner wasn't enough—he wanted to express himself creatively. Filmmaking was one possibility.

Barry had been at Dartmouth when I was there, but we never met. He left before graduating. It had nothing to do with his academic skills, climbing in the Tetons was a more attractive option than hanging around to pick up a degree.

A big new ski area was about to be built in Jackson and I was there to talk with the owners about making a promotional film. I was already established in the film business, having done shows for Vail and United Airlines. Barry and Muffy owned a motel near the old ski area in Jackson. I stopped by for a slide show he was giving in order to raise money for the 1963 American Everest Expedition. He went to Nepal and most of the way up the West Ridge of Everest a few months later. I made more films and came back to talk to the Jackson Hole Ski Area people again. They agreed to hire me if I would hire Barry because Barry lived in Jackson and could capture those fleeting moments after a snowfall when everything is so beautiful and there is fresh powder to track, That put us in the film business together. Barry turned out to be very good—not only at shooting but at writing and particularly at editing to music.

Roger filming Hart Ski Team, 1968.

We made films for Head Skis, Scott Ski Poles, Hart Skis, Waterville Valley, and another for United Airlines. The films were successful, particularly a series of shows we did for the Hart Ski Company. We were called the Antonionis of ski filmmaking, the artists who were giving ski films a new dimension. It was a wonderful and exciting time. Unfortunately it came at a terrible price.

The Time

Barry Corbet and I are products of 1950s and 1960s. We both come from conservative families. We were both assaulted by liberal attitudes that were emerging at that time. We were both young, we had confidence in ourselves, and doubts about the establishment.

In the early 1950s everyone was still trying to understand how Adolf Hitler, a man of such absolute evil, could have gained so much power. At the same time we were being debilitated by a fear of our own invention: the atomic bomb and possible nuclear annihilation. Instead of peace there was the Cold War. Many of us began to seriously question the traditional moral values we had been raised with.

A philosophy had emerged in France: Existentialism. Its most influential proponent, Jean-Paul Sartre, claimed that God does not exist, that man defines what he is—his essence—by his own actions. "Man is free," he wrote. "The coward makes himself cowardly. The hero makes himself heroic." We are all responsible for choosing one course of action over another. It is the choice that gives value to the act. Nothing that is not acted upon has value.

Powder skiing in Vail.

This was a philosophy that we could live with. We would have no one to blame for our actions but ourselves.

Many of our contemporaries missed the point. They only embraced Sartre's negative views, that life can only be horrible and absurd. They rejected moral laws; the religious commandments, the restrictive obligations to family and community, and they acted—by dropping out. It was the birth of a new permissive amorality.

For the rest of us, Existential thought simply presented an opportunity to create a meaningful existence outside the established system.

The Films

The films we made were personal expressions more than promotional vehicles for our sponsor's products. We explored the "why of skiing;" not the "what to use," the "how to do it," or the "where to go" aspects of the sport. As a result without consciously trying, I think we connected to aspirations in our audiences that were similar to our own. This is why the films are still popular with these people thirty-five years later. They gave form and shape to undefined good feelings, and they wake up the past.

Of course the innocent enthusiasm of one generation can be seen as melodrama by the next. As we said in *Ski the Outer Limits*, today's outer limits will be tomorrow's commonplace, and this is exactly what happened. From a sensational action point of view the films we made in the late 1960s and early 1970s are tame by today's standards. We may have conceived the idea of "extreme," but it soon took on a life of its own, and we could only stand back and watch the baby grow. (More about this in chapter 9.)

Skiing may be a frivolous activity, but it's where we started our filmmaking careers and we experienced a wonderful freedom in the process. I don't know if being skiers made our films better, or if our films made our skiing better—probably both. I think when you search for the essence of something as intensely as we did, it's possible to cross a threshold that gives the object of exploration a new dimension. The skiing, in this case, became a distillation of perfectly harnessed gravity used to float on a medium that is neither air nor a solid surface. The experience becomes more than physical, it moves into an almost spiritual realm. We are stoked. As Barry wrote in the script for *Ski the Outer Limits*:

Air and snow.
Powder snow is a game in two elements.
A wave of exuberance.
To the master, powder calls for economy of motion—beautiful expression.
It is not often given to man to create poetry, let alone recognize
the act at the time of creation.
Float . . . against a delicious pressure,
Or plow through.
Ravage the purity of the slope.
Powder is the ultimate in sensuous experience.

One major piece of equipment allows us to introduce a whole new dimension to ski films, the D. B. Milliken super slow-motion camera. We film the action, particularly the aerial acrobatics, at 200 or even 300 frames per second. This amounts to eight to twelve seconds of screen action for every one second of real time. We get wild shots of acrobatic skiers Tom LeRoy and Herman Gollner flipping into Corbet's Couloir (named for Barry) in Jackson Hole. Audiences can see what is really going on for the first time and they love it. The skiers look like birds soaring on air currents, and the powder snow floats as if gravity has ceased to exist. We also do extensive travel shots, skiing with our subjects, shooting forward and back and sometimes skiing backwards to get an interesting angle. This gives the audience a feeling of being in the film and doing the skiing

The unique photography was important but the stories and themes are what sustained the audience's interest. They appealed to everyone, not just skiers.

The Incredible Skis

The Incredible Skis is about two pairs of skis that had minds of their own and took their riders on wonderful trips. It is a "once upon a time" children's fairy tale.

Ski Magazine calls *The Incredible Skis,* "A Film to Dance By." The sequence the magazine seems to like best is a slow-motion scene of my English setter, Jo Jo, running through a field of daisies superimposed under Swiss skiers Art Furrer and Roger Staub "weaving a wedel in the same rhythm." Barry and I don't see it as a big deal, we are just exercising the tools of our trade. I explain in an interview, "There is no other way you can put these elements together (except in a film). That's what film does, rearranges time and space and creates new relationships through juxtapositions."

Some say our next film for Hart, *Ski the Outer Limits*, is the most popular ski film that has ever been made, but it is a bittersweet effort because of Barry's accident. John Fry, then editor of *Ski Magazine*, says, "What co-producers Brown and Corbet have successfully accomplished in *Ski the Outer Limits* is to integrate all of the obvious spectacular skiing—and it is spectacular indeed—into a theme that is meaningful."

"Out of this," says Barry Corbet, "emerged our conclusion: namely, that a point arrives where skill and personal flair take on a character of their own beyond the conventional limits of the sport as we normally think of them. We call these the "outer limits."

We are drunk with success. Nothing seems impossible. Films are expensive, but I have learned to hate budgets and regularly neglect them. The attitude spills over into other areas. I am willing to fight for my beliefs on all fronts, particularly on environmental issues. This results in a battle with the all-powerful Denver Water Board.

Corbet's Accident

May 2, 1968. I am sitting in my office catching up on paperwork, pleased that the sun is out because Barry Corbet and Norman Dyhrenfruth are in Aspen trying to shoot the rest ofthe *Coors 8th Interski* film. They only need one more day of sun to finish up.

About 10:00 A.M. an uneasy feeling comes over me. I can't concentrate and I have an urge to get into the car and drive over to Aspen. Silly, I think, but I still can't work, so I sit there. The phone rings about 2:00 P.M. It is Barry's girlfriend Mary Hutz. There has been an accident. Barry has been hurt. It is serious. It is his back or his legs—she isn't sure. The helicopter has crashed and now another helicopter is coming from Denver to get Barry out.

I immediately leave for Aspen. I don't know anything about paraplegia at the time, so that idea doesn't enter my thoughts. And I really don't think Barry can die. He is too tough for that although he has been having a lot of bad luck in the last few years: a broken tendon in his knee followed by a blood clot that collapsed a lung and signs of more blood clots. In spite of this, he had managed to climb six of the seven highest peaks in Antarctica, and he has just finished filming the Winter Olympics in Grenoble, France, for another film we are doing. Bob Redford carries Barry's tripod at Grenoble in exchange for a pass to get on the race courses. Redford is preparing himself to make a film called *The Downhill Racer*.

I try to reconstruct the events of this fateful day. Apparently the little CJ helicopter was flying higher than it was supposed to. It moved slowly, making several trips to carry the skiers and film crew up into the mountains in back of Aspen. No one knew it at the time, but they were working illegally inside the Snowmass Wilderness Area. We probably never would have known if it hadn't been for the accident.

Barry and Norman are shooting skiers Bill Duddy, Scooter Lacuta, Carolyn Teeple, and Betsy Glenn. Norman places himself off to the side for a long pan shot. Barry gets into the helicopter. He doesn't have a camera stabilizing mount, he hand holds the small Arri S camera out the window of the door. He has a seatbelt on but no shoulder strap, and the seatbelt is loose because it's designed to hold two people. He shoots several rolls of film this way. Norman continues to film from the ground while Barry follows in the air close behind the skiers, almost level with them at times. And finally the pilot flies too low. He hits a knoll, and loses control and goes into a series of bounces. From Norman's film (he has the presence to keep the camera running) and other recollections, it appears that Barry gets thrown out of the helicopter on the third bounce. He flies through the air and lands hard, breaking his leg and his back. Later examinations indicate he has also ruptured his intestines in two places, probably from beating against the seatbelt before it snaps.

The helicopter finally stops rolling in an upside down position. The pilot's seatbelt has held. Two ribs are broken and he is in shock but otherwise not critically injured.

Bob Craig, a mountaineering friend, and Barry's girlfriend, Mary Hutz, are at the hospital in Aspen when I arrive. All they know is that a rescue helicopter is on its way. So we all wait, anxious and uncomfortable, hoping for good luck, yet knowing something very serious has happened.

The rescue helicopter with Barry lands at the hospital about 5:00 P.M. We speak to him but he is in shock, and although his eyes are open he does not recognize any of us. He has a big gash in his face that is no longer bleeding. It is terribly clear to me that he is very badly injured and probably close to death. I feel guilty. It should have been me up there. Maybe I wouldn't have asked the pilot to fly so low. The doctors rush Barry to the emergency room and go to work. Meanwhile the helicopter flies back for the pilot and Norman. As soon as it lands Barry is loaded aboard and taken to Denver.

Struggling with the problems of a broken back, ruptured intestines, a history of thrombosis, and a broken leg, the doctors have to carry on a delicate juggling act just to keep Barry alive.

On July 2, Barry moves out of the hospital and into an apartment nearby where he edits *Ski the Outer Limits*. He has mastered the use of a wheelchair and has learned to drive a car with hand controls. He is a phenomenon to the rehabilitation people; no one has ever adjusted so quickly.

Condoriri, Bolivian Andes.

All this time Barry keeps one goal in mind, to regain the use of his legs. Because the spinal cord has not actually been severed he feels there is a chance. A few small muscles near his knee show some signs of life, and some of the sensory nerves work, giving him a great deal of pain, but that is all.

James Salter, the screenwriter who wrote *Downhill Racer*, interviews Barry for a possible theatrical feature script that will incorporate real episodes of Barry's life. The film is never made, but some events are fictionalized in Salter's book, *Solo Faces*.

What happened in reality is not very different from the book. Gary Hemming, an old climbing partner, shows up at Barry's place. Gary is convinced that because Barry's spinal cord is not actually severed, he can walk—that his paralysis is mental, not physical. Gary tells Barry to get up out of his wheelchair, and, of course, he can't.

As the days go by, Gary becomes more convinced that Barry can and should be able to walk.

"Get up!" Gary demands one evening.

"I can't!" The commands and denials are repeated. Reality begins to fade. Or perhaps reality is finally being addressed; it's hard to say. Gary brings out a loaded revolver, points it at Barry, and pulls the trigger. Click. Then Gary points the gun at himself and pulls the trigger again. Click. Barry doesn't know it, but the firing pin in the revolver is broken off. He slides to the floor and tries to stand up, but can't.

Gary has failed to make Barry walk, but he has not failed to express the profound love and pain he feels for his friend. He only wants Barry to walk, a desire I have also felt everyday of my life since the accident occurred. I have never known anyone who got more pleasure out of climbing and skiing than Barry.

Gary Hemming leaves Denver for Jackson Hole, Wyoming, where he meets up with Pete Sinclair, Pete's wife Connie, and Barry's ex-wife Muffy. And one evening Gary goes out and shoots himself in the head.

Perhaps the best expression of the philosophy that Barry Corbet, Pete Sinclair, Gary Hemming, and the other climbers of that era lived by is found in Maurice Herzog's book, *Annapurna*:

> "In overstepping our limitations, in touching the extreme boundaries of man's world, we have come to know something of its true splendor. In my worst moments of anguish, I seemed to discover the deep significance of existence of which till then I had been unaware."

Lucien Devies, another expedition member, lays down the final justification:

> "It takes courage to draw the veil from those moments when the individual approaches the universal. That wonderful world of high mountains, dazzling in their rock and ice, acts as a catalyst."
>
> Man overcomes himself, affirms himself, and realizes himself in the struggle towards the summit, toward the absolute."

Mountain experiences like these allow us to cross a threshold into a place that holds different values and meanings. The civilized world, with all its comforts, suddenly seems dull, even empty, something to escape. Once this unspoiled mountain world is planted in our souls it does not let go. A permanent longing makes our hearts ache, we have to return. It is the last refuge in difficult times. The destination does not have to be the barren summit of some great mountain, but it must be pure, a place that feels like we are the first humans to be there.

This reminds me of a taxi driver in the Virgin Islands who said, after seeing all the heavy sharp-cornered camera cases I would have to put in his cab, "You can mess with my wife, but don't mess with my car or you will mess with your life." Try to mess with those last pieces of pure Nature in the mountains and some of us are ready to fight to the death to protect them.

Pete Sinclair is at Barry's apartment in Denver when we write the script for *Ski the Outer Limits*. It is only five months after the accident, but it is a heartening few days. Pete offers ideas and words that we like and use in the script. I can see little moments when Barry gets so caught up in the editing and writing that he forgets what has happened to him. He smiles and jokes and lights up when the words and pictures come together in the right way. In those brief happy moments the terrible hopelessness that I feel and hide leaves me, too.

My son Nicolas is being born in a nearby General Rose Hospital at the same time as we are doing the edit. Two births are going on a few buildings apart: a baby boy and one of the best films we have ever made.

We have weathered the storm, but we are irrevocably changed. There is no backing up the clock and doing things differently. The years have passed but the

Ama Dablam, Nepal.

pain for me hasn't. It will never go away. Barry, on the other hand, has created a different life for himself and seems quite content.

Ski the Outer Limits wins grand prizes in several film festivals, both nationally and internationally. Suddenly we have enough work to start hiring others. We assemble an all-star team. There are the old timers like Dick Durrance, a famous early Olympic ski racer; Norman Dyhrenfruth, the organizer and leader of the American Everest Expedition; and Joern Gerdts, a *Life Magazine* still photographer who wants to get into filmmaking. Cutting edge experimental filmmaker Bob

Fulton and Paul Ryan, a *cinema verité aficionado*, also come on board. Summit Films becomes highly charged creatively— and perpetually on the brink of bankruptcy.

We continue to explore ideas that are important to us, and find sponsors willing to put up with the experimental nature of our work, but our "golden days" eventually come to an end. We can't sustain a payroll that supports our indulgence. Gerdts, Ryan, Fulton, and the others leave the fold.

Being a paraplegic is never easy. Barry has numerous physical problems; a bladder infection, or another broken leg, or tendonitus—always something. He goes down the Grand Canyon when we shoot *The Edge* and subsequently takes up kayaking. He uses his arms like legs and they become super powerful, but the ligaments and tendons and joints aren't up to the strain, so he has to eventually give up boating .

We stay partners for seven years after the accident, through the production of *The Edge*, but editing sports films is a painful experience for Barry and finally we split up. Barry gets a job editing a definitive magazine about paraplegia and is still pursuing that career today.

". . . to know the wilderness is to know profound humility, to recognize one's littleness, to sense dependence and independence, indebtedness and responsibility."

—Howard Zahniser

Chapter 4
Wilderness

Above: Dick Pownall above Main Gore Lake, 1963.

Previous spread: Reflections on New York Lake.

"Without any . . . wilderness we are commited . . . to a headlong drive into our technological termite-life, the Brave New World of a completely man-controlled environment . . . We simply need that wild country available to us, even if we never do more than drive to its edge and look in."

—Wallace Stegner, 1960

The Time

The 1970s. The success of our ski films gives clients the confidence to believe we can do work in other areas. Trans World Airlines contracts us to do a film in East Africa. Bill Coors of the beer brewing family and Olive Watson, wife of IBM's Tom Watson, helps raise money to do an Outward Bound Schools film. We land a contract to do a film on Martin Marietta's electronic capabilities and get to document the beginning of computer chips. Barry does a very emotional definitive film on paraplegia. We make an environmental show on transmountain water diversions, not for profit, but because it is the right thing to do.

Now, looking back, I see that for me these were the mean, terrible, successful years. The mid-thirties are very often the most productive years in a person's life, and I am no exception. I am filled with huge amounts of creative energy, but also unbridled ruthlessness and ambition. I have a sense of fair play, and I care deeply about many things: family, friends, work, and honor. But I have very little patience for what I see as weaknesses, and I don't know the meaning of the word "compassion." I accept no religion, and spirituality is an embarrassing word.

The late 1960s and early 1970s were very contradictory times in the world scene as well. *Apollo 11* lands on the moon. Neil Armstrong says the immortal words, "That's one small step for man—one giant leap for mankind." On the other side the Vietnam War is demoralizing the nation. Almost 60,000 Americans lose their lives and nobody knows for sure why or for what.

Audiences are responding to our films. They are captured by what they see as the healthy idealism of outdoor adventure. "Explore your limits on a mountain or in a desert or a jungle or on the sea. Find yourself in a wilderness."

The Wilderness Act

The Wilderness Act was approved by Congress on September 3, 1964. It says, in part:

> ". . . a wilderness system will be established to assure that an increasing population, accompanied by expanding settlement and growing mechanization, does not occupy and modify all areas within the United States and its possessions, leaving no lands designated for preservation and protection in their natural condition. . . . these lands will be administered for use in such manner as will leave them unimpaired for future use and enjoyment of the American people, . . . and preserved in their wilderness character."

The areas designated must be:

> ". . . undeveloped federal land retaining its primeval character and influence . . . The imprint of man's work must be substantially unnoticeable, There must be outstanding opportunities for solitude or a primitive and unconfined type of recreation . . . and the area must be at least 5,000 acres in size."

My home sits in the middle of several Wilderness Areas: the Flat Tops, the Eagles Nest, the Holy Cross, and the Snowmass to mention a few. Some are only minutes away, none more than an hour-and-a-half drive.

Wilderness justifies its own existence. One only has to go there and stay awhile to understand how important wilderness is to our well being. Wilderness experiences give us an opportunity to reconnect with Nature's original design.

Wilderness Experiences

I begin hiking in the Gore Range (later designated the Eagles Nest Wilderness) in the spring of 1962, right after I move to Vail. I think that because the snow is gone in the valley it will also be gone higher up. I soon sink into deep, wet snow up to my waist. I keep going back into the wilderness year after year, learning a little more on each trip. Early July is the best time to see carpets of brightly colored flowers. The trout in the high lakes are hungry in August and September. Mushrooms also show up in mid- to late August if it's been a wet summer. I learn where to find blue grouse and timberline bucks.

I introduce all my kids to the wilderness, not necessarily to teach them self-reliance, but just for the fun of camping, climbing, and trout fishing. These have been some of my most memorable experiences.

It is on a hike up Homestake Creek that I learn about water diversions. This inspires me to make *The Water Plan* film. We take on the Denver Water Board and keep them from building water diversions on the small streams in the Gore Range above Vail. It is David and Goliath, Vail vs. Denver.

Some folks don't see the value in saving something like wilderness. They say if it can't be used, it's useless. They want roads, interpretive centers, shelters, and toilets. Others wouldn't mind having a few dirt bike routes or meadows open to snowmobiling. To them I can only say: It *is* being used, by Nature, to follow its own course, without human intervention. We can learn a great deal by observing the process, fires included.

If more tangible justification for setting aside Wilderness Areas is necessary I point to Outward Bound and similar survival schools that teach self-reliance. Here the wilderness is being used to help adolescents mature into responsible adults. A lot of ghetto kids have had their lives straightened out in these programs. A few adults mature through these survival experiences as well. We've done two films for Outward Bound.

There has always been some pressure to open up the Wilderness Areas to other uses, but never as much as right now with the energy extraction obsessed Bush Administration.

Fire—Nature's Toothbrush

September 19, 2003. My old adventure buddy, Doctor Phil Freedman, flies me over the Flat Tops to do aerial photography. Our route takes us from Deep Creek on the east side of the great monolith to Trappers Lake in the northwest corner and then back.

Top left: Hot fire.

Top right: Gypsum Creek Valley fire. Even glass from a broken bottle can start a fire on a hot day.

Middle left: Trappers Lake, Flat Tops, fall 2003, almost completely burned.

Bottom left: A beetle-killed forest; the next fire on the Flat Tops.

Above: Recovery—Aspens grow back.

It's a perfectly clear day. the air is quiet and the aspens are solid yellow. The sliced-off mesas drop abruptly into rocky cirques and bumpy meadows where hundreds of small shallow ponds and occasional larger lakes beg to be fished. Old, partially dead spruce forests string out across some of the higher ridges. The aspen groves roll down the slopes in ribbons toward the Colorado River. Then red oak brush takes over and below that pinyon and juniper. We get into a layer of forest fire smoke at 13,500 feet, but it does not affect the clear view below. Unfortunately, last year's forest fire at Trappers has not begun to heal. The whole area is black and gray and sad. It's a wonderful adventure for both of us, another good memory to add to our adventures that started back to Nepal in the 1970s.

At one point I say to Phil, "I wonder why we go to Tibet with all this right here?" In fact, the American Wilderness is better protected and more pristine than most of the remotest parts of the rest of the world including the Himalayas. On the other hand, it is the little subsistence level villages and nomads in the other parts of the world that make those places so interesting. It would not break my heart to see some sheep herders up here on the Flat Tops, but we don't.

Most forests in the Rocky Mountains have burned at one time or other. Some burned so long ago that almost all the signs of fire have disappeared. Only an occasional black trunk gives the secret away. But once you've seen a forest fire you don't take anything for granted.

Fire is something that is always on your mind if you live in or next to a forest. I spend a lot of time clearing dead wood away from around my house. Fire is an incredible, horrible, frightening thing to behold, an example of Nature at work, but very hard for us humans to accept because what is being lost will not return again in our lifetimes. In a different time frame, Nature can be seen as simply brushing her teeth, cleaning out the debris in order to stay healthy.

William Henry Jackson photo of Mount of the Holy Cross, 1900. Courtesy of Denver Public Library.

Thousands of country homes in Colorado are vulnerable to forest fires, and a few burn almost every year. But if, in our desire to escape urban pressures, we build homes where we shouldn't, then we only have ourselves to blame.

Firefighters were lost on Storm King Mountain just west of Glenwood Springs, Colorado, in July 1994 when erratic winds whipped the flames of what was thought to be an easy to control situation. The fire raced uphill faster than the firefighters could run, killing fourteen of them before they could reach the top of the ridge and possible safety.

Two Sacred Peaks

The area of Holy Cross Mountain and the Bowl of Tears Lake keeps coming up as I reminisce and listen to other old-timers. It's a pilgrimage site and has been for some time. William Henry Jackson photographed the mountain in the late 1800s.

A big "cross" dominates the steep east face of the mountain. It is not as distinct now as it was a hundred years ago. One story is that the Tenth Mountain

Cross Creek below Patricia Lake, Mount of the Holy Cross in the background, 1982.

Division troops overshot their target and lobbed a mortar onto The Cross during training exercises at Camp Hale in the 1940s. Another more plausible story is that some of the rotten rock defining The Cross simply fell off naturally.

My first experience with the mountain, and the lake below it, occurs in 1963. I decide to go for a fishing trip on Memorial Day weekend. I drive up past the Tigawan Cabin to the Half Moon trailhead. I plan to visit the Tuhare Lakes on the other side of Notch Mountain but there are so many people on the trail I get frustrated and look at the map for another place to go. Bowl of Tears is the closest lake as the crow flies. All I have to do is climb over Notch Mountain. No

Nick's first trip to the Bowl of Tears, August 1982.

matter that it is 2,900 feet up and then another 1,200 feet straight down to the lake. I am young with lots of energy and strength and little judgment.

There are old stone structures on top of Notch Mountain where pilgrims can sit and gaze at The Cross. They are partially buried in the snow and look like they haven't been used for years. I can see Bowl of Tears way down below. It is mostly ice covered, but the north side has a little open water. The descent down the cliffs goes quickly. When I reach the lake and look into the water I can see several giant trout swimming methodically along the shore. This is a trout fisherman's dream. I shake with anticipation as I assemble my fly rod, attach the reel, and pull the line through the guides. The fish are down several few feet, so I put on a Gold Wrapped Hare's

Ear and sink it down into the water almost to the bottom. When fish come near I pull the fly up in front of them but they have no interest. During the next two hours I try every fly I have with me but I never get a strike. Finally I have to admit defeat and head for home. The map indicates I can circle around the north end of Notch Mountain and avoid climbing so high. I pick my way through some willows and cliffs and come out onto a boulder field that I scramble over until I reach the Half Moon trail that is used by climbers to reach the north flank of Holy Cross Mountain. I get back in the trailhead parking lot just as it is getting dark. Now I know where there are some very big trout and I know how to get there fairly quickly—quick enough for day trips.

I return to the Bowl of Tears many times, and once in a while I catch some of the big cutthroats. I only run into one other fisherman in those early years, a miner who lives in Gilman. I have had countless dreams over the years, seeing those big fish cruising around. Occasionally I take the family or one of the kids to the lake, and we sometimes camp overnight. Later, I bring an Outward Bound School troop in and film them climbing up beside The Cross. Over time the big fish either all get caught or die of old age, but they are replaced by smaller fish that are easy to catch. When we move to Gypsum in 1978 I stop going to the Bowl of Tears. I find other high lakes closer to home that are harder to get to and less frequented. I take one more trip to the summit of Mount of the Holy Cross with a friend, but that is more of a peak bagging event than a pilgrimage.

Pilgrims encircling Mt. Manasarovar in Tibet.

North side of Mt. Kailash in Tibet.

Then, in 2000, I go back into the Bowl of Tears to get some water for our baby son Tor Erik's baptism at the Gypsum Lutheran Church. I start early in the morning and take my shotgun along since it is grouse season. I wander off the trail but never out of sight of the Notch Mountain massive. Luck is with me; I bump up a few grouse. When I get to the open rock scree slope, I hide my gun and the birds so I won't have to lug them all the way to the lake and back. I'm glad to see the trail is faint, not many people have been using it. I drop off the ridge down to Patricia Lake and get slowed by some willows that I have to push through. From there the trail goes up over polished rock that was once under a glacier. Finally I reach the Bowl of Tears. The water is murky, and only one fish breaks out in the middle of the lake. I fish for a while but don't see any trout close to shore, and I don't get any strikes. Nothing lasts forever, I guess. I head back to the trail head and the car.

Preacher Jeff appreciates the holy water and rations it carefully so that it can be used for several baptisms.

Mount of the Holy Cross reminds me of another mountain I have visited in Tibet—Kailash. It also has a lake nearby: Manasarovar. I am kicking myself now that I didn't bring back holy water from my visit there in 1999. Kailash and Manasarovar are two of the most sacred sites in the world for Hindus and Buddhists. The Brahmaputra River (called the Tsang Po in Tibet), the Karnali River, which eventually runs into the Ganges, the Sutlij, and the Indus all start near Mount Kailash.

We run into Tibetan pilgrims circumambulating Mount Kailash and Lake Manasarovar. Most are on foot hiking around the mountain, but many use horses on the longer trip around the lake. Other than a few cheap tennis shoes their clothing is wool, no nylon encased down, no pile. They burn yak dung in small fires that are used to cook. They leave no garbage because they have no garbage.

A pilgrimage in Tibet is a search for transcendence. The pilgrims give up the comforts of everyday life in order to make themselves more receptive to a higher spiritual calling. I'm not sure we have any equivalent to a Himalayan pilgrimage in this country, but going to a place like Holy Cross Mountain and Bowl of Tears certainly brings one closer to God or whatever guiding force one chooses to believe in. Visiting almost any place in the Colorado high country wilderness is an uplifting experience. I feel fortunate to have spent so much time in these sacred places, both here and around the world.

Top: Cooking with yak dung in Tibet.

Bottom: Heating tea with solar energy in Tibet.

The High Lakes in the Flat Tops Wilderness

Ben Wurtsmith, a rancher friend, gives me the history on a piece of the eastern edge of the Flat Tops Wilderness. It is clear from his stories that early settlers tried to use most of the high country for one purpose or another, if not for irrigation, then for grazing or logging or mining. Wilderness is a relatively recent concept.

Most of the larger lakes at the headwaters of North Derby Creek are named after men who tried to harness them for irrigation of Derby Creek Mesa. You can still see some of the pipes and valve wheels at the outlet of Keener Lake. Mr. Edge also tried to harvest hay in the meadows between Keener and Edge lakes. It must have been a long haul down over the very rocky rough road to the lower lands. Keener was apparently a wealthy man who owned a yacht that he sailed when he wasn't visiting his ranch in the Burns Hole. Ben doesn't seem to know much about Hooper and Bailey, but they were all ranchers in the early days of the Burns Hole.

Ben tells me about the buffalo skulls they used to find in the high country, particularly in the Edge Meadows area. His theory is that they were killed by people hunting meat for the mines. There are shallow holes in some places that Ben says are buffalo wallows, places where the buffalo would roll on the ground, turning the grass to mud. It would be interesting to know how old the buffalo skulls are and if they where killed by white men or earlier by Indians. Ben and

Keener Lake.

most of the other ranchers in the area have the buffalo skulls hanging up on walls or kicking around in a corner somewhere.

Before the Flat Tops Wilderness area was established in 1975, there was a jeep road to Keener Lake and beyond. Ben said people completely trashed out Keener Lake which is one of the main reasons he supported the Wilderness designation. He worked with the Forest Service to move the trash out after the designation. He showed me where his mules got away from him at one point, scattering tin cans all over the countryside. At another point, he told me about his encounter with what might have been the last grizzly in the Flat Tops. He ran into the bear at fairly close quarters. When he raised his rifle, which was relatively light caliber, he could see that this was no ordinary black bear in front of him. He was much bigger and was gnashing his teeth as he stood his ground in front of Ben. Ben didn't shoot; he backed into the woods and left as quickly as possible. I asked Ben if he didn't shoot in order to spare the last grizzly. "No," he said, "I was scared. That gun I had wasn't heavy enough for an animal like that."

Ben said his folks and the other ranchers in the area let all the boys go up into the high mountains without supervision when they were quite young. They hiked everywhere and built rafts which they floated on the lakes even though they didn't' know how to swim. He said they could have gotten in a lot of trouble but didn't. They survived, and Ben thinks they are all much better people as a result of the experiences.

Climbing Mount Powell

I decide to take son Mike up Mt. Powell in the summer of 1981. He is fifteen years old. It turns out to be a real exploration for both of us. Little do I know the trail we start up on this day will eventually take him to the summit of Mt. Everest.

We decide to go light, no fishing rods, no ropes, no ice axes, just the Light Dimension tent, sleeping bags, pack frames to get us to base camp, and day packs for the summit.

I plan an early start but we don't arrive at Piney Lake until 10:00 A.M. We hike out the long, flat trail following the Piney River to the foot of the Gore Range instead of going left and following the river to its source. We pass through groves of big aspen trees and lodgepole pines. From here, the climb up is steep. We lose the trail for a while but find it again. We are alone; we haven't seen a soul since leaving the Piney River Valley. I start to feel a little tired but don't let on to Mike who is cruising along with energy to spare.

We finally reach timberline and set up the tent on a flat spot where others have camped before us. It is a small area next to some scrubby fur trees with dead branches we can use for firewood, There is a small perfectly clear stream about thirty yards away, and there are lots of mosquitoes so I'm glad we have the tent with us. Parry primrose are blooming along the stream's edge, and we find some miner's lettuce to nibble on.

Mike is fascinated by the high country, He climbs up through a rock slide to a snow patch, while I climb up to the cirque below Kneeknocker Pass to see how much snow is left there. Later we build a fire, cook dinner, and take another short hike before dark. I point out some tracks which I wrongly assume are elk. Mike can't quite believe how big the mountain looks that we will be going up in the morning.

I wake Mike at 5:45 A.M. We boil some water for instant coffee, eat some granola, and start hiking at about 6:30 A.M. This is my first excursion into the mountains since filming in Nepal and everything seems smaller and easier to me but I don't trust my reactions. I know this climb, like all others, will get difficult eventually.

Below left: Mountain goats.

Below right: Ptarmigan.

Above: Mike Brown with the Pangboche Lama, Nepal 1998.

It takes us an hour to reach Kneeknocker Saddle. There is a steep snow field on the other side. Mike steps out onto it but I caution him back. If he slips he could take a very fast ride to the rocks a few hundred feet below. I regret that I don't have a rope and an ice ax, but eventually we are able to pick our way down some rocks along the side of the snow to the bottom of the snow field. From here it is a 2,000-foot climb to the top, mostly on steep grass until it turns into a boulder field near the summit.

Marmots whistle and duck out of sight while pikas squeak at us incessantly from the rocks. We see large chunks of white hair that I am pretty sure come from goats. I had heard there are mountain goats in the Gore, but I have never seen any. I keep scanning the ridges for goats as we approach the summit. Finally, about 1,000 feet down on the northeast face, we see one.

We search for the cairn that marks the register on the summit but we find none. A note from disgruntled climber tells us that he didn't find the register either. Michael stands on the highest point which makes him higher than any point in the Gore Range. We can see down the east ridge to some lakes that look promising for trout. Michael picks up some rocks, then we snack, and start our descent.

"Let's go down over there, Dad." Michael has the adventure bug. Why back track when we can see new terrain? We walk down the long west flank of the mountain to where it drops off. I am skeptical about going into the cliffs, but Michael is insistent so I agree to go a little further to see what's there. It is difficult to see much from above, but we have lots of time and the weather is good, so we pick our way down through the top cliffs.

The columbine thrives in inhospitable places. Can we?

"Look Dad!" A herd of goats, thirteen in all, scramble off through the rock bands below us. There are two small kids and one yearling. Big chunks of white hair hang off their backs and rumps making them look diseased, but they are just shedding their winter coats. When they gain a ridge far to our right they stop and watch us. Our agility is no match for theirs, they have nothing to fear.

We arrive back at camp exactly at noon. In three-and-a-half hours we are at Piney Lake. We pass Austrian transplants and hotel owner friends Pepi and Sheika Gramshammer on the walk out. They say hello, but we have no easy way to tell them about the wonderful adventure we have just experienced. I can't remember very many trips where it was just Michael and me, usually one or both of the brothers is along. It is very special.

This is just the beginning of Mike's climbing adventures. He has been all over the world doing television shows on climbing expeditions, three on Mount Everest where he has managed to summit on each effort. It's gratifying to know that a two day wilderness trip at a young age could be the start of such an extraordinary career. And it's all the proof I need to fight for every inch of wilderness that can be saved.

Fishing the High Lakes with the Boys

August 1989. Son Nick and I go on several fishing trips into the Eagles Nest and the Holy Cross Wilderness areas. We invariably have good times, although on one occasion I have a scary accident. I want a shot of me climbing on a near vertical rock face with New York Lake in the back ground. So I give Nick the camera and start to climb. I am about thirty feet up the face when a rock comes loose

Clockwise: Nick approaching New York Lake, 1989; Nick and Roger camped at New York Lake, Holy Cross Wilderness; Tor Erik.

in my hand. As I fall backward the rock clips my head, cutting a hole in my scalp. Luckily, it isn't a direct hit or I might have been knocked out and possibly killed. It is a bloody cut. For a minute Nick thinks I am seriously hurt.

I decide to keep moving regardless, not knowing if I might go into shock at some point. Pretty soon I began feeling fine. As we cross the pass that separates the Lake Creek drainage from the Brush Creek drainage we stumble into a flock of ptarmigans and we started taking pictures again.

The boys and I visit the Piney River many times over the years and the lakes around Mount Powell where we hook into a tough old rainbow that I film for a *Colorado Tourism* film. Nick and I do a long, hard hike across the Gore Range from Piney Lake to Green Mountain Reservoir. The three boys and I do a big difficult hike in a circle from Mystic Island Lake to Lone Pine Lake and back.

We always catch trout, once in a while some big ones. We occasionally run into another hiker fisherman, but not very often. These memories fill my chest with longing, making me want to return again and again. The cliffs, the meadows, the dark water with its cruising lunker trout, the bright flowers, the lichen, the whistle pigs and the pikas, the passing storms, the little fires we build to cook

Top: Jim Ditts, attorney, Deep Creek, Flat Tops, Colorado, 1896.

Bottom: Nick at miner's cabin, NewYork Mountain, 1989.

and warm ourselves by, the stars that hang above us close enough to touch, and the excited yells. "Wow, Dad, I've got a big one!"

Fast forward twenty years. I find myself with a new family. The experiences repeat themselves. So little changes in the high wilderness. There are a few more jet contrails cutting up the blue sky but actually less trash because people pick up the old stuff and carry it out. This phenomenon proves that something is appreciated more when it is worked for. There are some good folks making trips into these remote places. They care.

Fish Story

Labor Day weekend 1996. My primary objective is Edge Lake in the Flat Tops Wilderness. Ben Wurtsmith has convinced me it will be good fishing, hopefully for big ones. It is easier to find than I anticipate, not very far from Keener Lake that Ben had taken me to the week before. People are camped at the end of Edge Lake when I arrive. They have a big tent, lawn chairs, etc. I don't know if these have been moved in by horses but I would guess so judging from the amount of gear.

I spot some fish breaking along the shore. I set up my fly rod, tie on a number 12 Orange Humpy fly, and catch several without much difficulty. They are cutthroats, between ten and fourteen inches long. Two guys with inner tube waders come down the middle of the lake spin casting, but they didn't seem to be having much luck. Some of the trout I catch are thin, indicating that perhaps there are too many fish for the size of the lake. I release those that unhook easily but still have five left for dinner and breakfast. Then I hike over to Keener. I want to catch a big one.

I get to Keener at about 5:00 P.M. It is windy. I fish where I caught the three pounder last week but I don't expect much luck. Experience has taught me that unless I can see the fish, particularly the large ones, I won't catch anything. The men with the inner tube boots show up and immediately launch. They fish until it gets dark. I set up my camp, built a fire, and go to bed. I have all day Sunday and I only want to catch one fish.

I wake with the light, get up about 6:30, and make a big breakfast. I feed my dog, John Henry, some of my bacon and eggs and a few fish bones for which he is very grateful. The men with the inner tubes go out at 7:00 and fish for about two hours. I start around the lake about 8:30. My experience with high lake fish is that they only surface feed after the sun has been up for a while and the insects have become active. The reflections are extraordinary, so I go back to camp for my camera. I move along the north shore fairly quickly, casting now and again but I am mainly just looking, hoping to see a big one. Two crows chase a golden eagle high above in the cliffs. The white eyes under the eagles wings seem to be looking at me. What a beautiful day it is.

The wind has shifted from earlier in the morning and started blowing from the East. This pushes all the floating objects including insects into the area where I am headed. This is fortuitous. I can see little bits of foam piling up near the shore, and then I see the swirl. I cast the fly onto the surface in front of me, and then I see him, the monster I have looking looking for. He is leisurely sucking in insects from the surface, heading straight for my fly. This is an incredible fish, thick and heavy with a slightly humped back and a wide mouth.

I have just put a new three-pound test leader on the line, and the fly is a 16 Orange Humpy, very light gear for a fish of this size. It is the first fly on the leader so every last inch of the thinnest part of the leader is still there. Last week I set the hook too hard on a somewhat smaller fish and broken a much thicker leader.

The rod is the flexible wand that the fish wears himself out on. If the rod is handled properly the fish will pull the line but it won't snap, because the rod will bend and the reel will release line and the water will give. It is this steady pressure that eventually wears the fish out.

A four pound trout.

The monster takes the fly, I gently set the hook and the fight is on. For a few seconds he doesn't pull very hard and then he panics. The line buzzes off the reel as he heads out into the lake. I think he is going to take all the line I have and then snap the leader, but he slows down about the time it is all out, and then he heads back. Now I have to reel in so that the line won't go slack, letting the fly drop out of his mouth. This goes on back and forth for twenty minutes. Each time I think he is tired enough to bring to the net he dives again, pulling the line off the reel. Cutthroat don't jump the way rainbows do, but they do come to the surface. Each time I see parts of his huge dorsal fin and tail I marveled at his size. This is truly a fish I have had hundreds of dreams about.

I do not release the big fish to fight another day. I'm from the old school of fishermen. We enjoy eating what we catch. And I don't want to let his rare experience become just another fish story. Who would believe me without a picture? But I stop fishing even though I can see other big fellows breaking. As you hear it expressed every once in a while out in this country, "I had all the fun I could stand for one day." I bring the monster on shore and take several pictures with the rod, reel, and net to give the shot perspective.

I'm pretty sure this isn't the biggest fish in the lake. The week before Ben said he saw one that he thought went over two feet. This one is only a little over twenty inches. He weighs four pounds even. It is the biggest fish I have caught in over twenty years. To get that large the fish has to be smart, either that or all the fishermen that have come to this lake for the last several years have to be stupid. I like to think he was smart—but I was smarter. I parade him past the inner tubers who are eating breakfast. They are politely complimentary but a little envious. I pack up my camp and put the rod away even though I will walk along a steam full of fish while hiking out. After a fish like the Monster the little ones don't hold much excitement.

I should mention that Friday night, the night before I left to go fishing, I went for a short walk behind the house. It was almost dark but I could still see a familiar white shape in the dirt. I reached down and picked up a 2 7/8-inch stone blade. I guess it was a sign of good things to come.

A Big Hike with Christian

How much cold can this fifty pound, seven-year-old boy handle before he gets hypothermic?

August 2001. It's been a busy-going-broke summer. When it gets like this, which has been often in my life, I put my head down and work, work, work. That's okay when you're a bachelor, but I have a family now and I shouldn't neglect them. So when my wife Anne Helene asks me to take our son Christian on a camping trip, I

Christian on the Yampa River.

agree. I have been wanting to hike into New York Lake and go trout fishing for the last couple of years. This looks like an opportunity to do both.

Christian is just about seven-years old. This is really too young to take him to New York Lake, which is only about a seven-mile hike but has major changes in altitude. We park the pickup at the old mining town of Fulford at 9,966 feet, climb to Nolan Lake at 11,200 feet where we camp for the night, climb to the top of a pass at 12,300 feet the next morning, then scramble down to New York Lake at 11,274 feet and back out to where the truck is in the same day.

In spite of being steep, the trail to Nolan Lake is not difficult. We get there a little after noon. The lake is in a spectacular cirque with cliffs to the southeast rising straight up several hundred feet. An open, ancient spruce forest covers the valley floor to the north and west.

I set up our rods, tie on dry flies, and we begin fishing. I explain the trout's ways; how to look for a break on the surface of the water or a fish feeding in the shallows. We sneak to the edge on the inlet and watch the fish dart away, leaving little clouds of muddy water behind them. Christian struggles with the rod, catching bushes behind him, then slaps the water, but occasionally he drops the fly lightly on the surface. The fish strike but Christian doesn't know how to set the hook, so the fish spit out the tasteless artificial flies and disappear. I manage to catch several brook trout as the day progresses, but Christian does not and is discouraged. We cook dinner and go back to the lake for evening fishing. After several strikes Christian yanks the line at just the right moment and lands his first trout. It's an exciting moment.

We crawl into our sleeping bags. I'm a little concerned about bears so I keep Christian close beside me. There have been a lot of starving bears reported this summer. It's been very dry and the bears have had trouble finding enough food.

The next morning we make a big breakfast of eggs, bacon, trout, and cereal. Christian is intrigued by the Whisperlite stove, which he learns to prime and light. Bold camp robbers steal our food if we give them the smallest opportunity. At about 10:00 A.M. we start out for New York Lake. There is no trail up through the steep, open, alpine meadows. The big spruce trees thin out and finally disappear as we reach timberline. I point out the Arctic gentian flowers, a sure sign of ending summer. We see a mother ptarmigan and her chicks that fascinate Christian, then we cross the pass and reach the edge of the deep basin that contains New York Lake. From here it's straight down a series of cliffs and benches until we reach the lake. The first bench down has the remains of an old mining camp. Christian finds a couple of rusty nails and puts them in his pack to bring home to his mother. We scramble 1,000 vertical feet down over cliffs to the lake. Trout are breaking everywhere, but by the time we have our rods set up they have stopped. We watch in frustration as they look at our flies but cruise by without striking. A few seem to be big—two pounds or more.

Black clouds are moving rapidly over us. My worst fear is being realized. Thunderstorms and rain have arrived. I know we will be exposed and vulnerable to lightning when we cross the high saddle on the way back. We start hiking out as fast as we can go. By the time we reach the second band of cliffs, the rain is coming down hard, soaking our clothing. How much cold can this little fifty-pound, seven-year-old boy handle before he gets hypothermic?

Christian climbs up fearlessly. It is a game for him. He is not afraid and I hide my fear for him. We stop behind some rocks to avoid the lightning that is now close to us. Thunder shakes the valley. We get soaked, but the rain eases off and we continue upward. Then it rains hard again and we find some protection under an overhanging cliff. We still have a long way to go. Christian's hands and feet are now wet and cold but he is still upbeat. The rain turns to hail and starts to accumulate on the ground like snow. Then it stops but the wind comes up. I wrap my pile jacket around Christian and we continue upward. If I can get him to the camp at Nolan Lake I can build a fire and warm him up and if he is hypothermic, I can put him in my four seasons North Face sleeping bag, which is super warm. He eats a few Hershey bars and seems oblivious to the foul weather. This is not the baby I have seen around his mother at home. Christian is "tough as nails."

We make it back to camp; I put a warm rain jacket, a wool hat, and mittens on Christian, and we head down the trail to Fulford. Pretty soon he starts peeling off clothes and pretends he is an automobile driving down the trail. He dances from rock to rock. Errrr, errr, go the sounds of his engine. I am amazed to see him so full of energy. He should be exhausted. We arrive at the car before dark. It has been an almost perfect adventure. We reached our objective, weathered a storm, camped, cooked, caught fish, and saw some wonderful remote country. It is the same kind of an experience I have had with Gordon, Mike, and Nick numerous times.

Will he be the next explorer in the family? Who knows, but he has caught the wilderness bug, of that I am sure.

Anne Helene and Christian at a cabin at Piney River, East Meadow Creek confluence.

Tor Erik, Anne Helene, Christian, and Llama Jackson.

Christian's Second Trout

July 2003. We are back at Nolan Lake for another fly fishing lesson. We get there about 2:00 P.M. and set up our rods.

Christian's casting is too fast and he swings the rod all the way from almost 8:00 o'clock to 4:00 o'clock. In the back cast the line hits the ground or rocks or a bush, weakens and breaks, and the fly is lost. In the forward cast the line only goes a short distance and then slashes the water scaring the trout. I instruct him to slow down and give the line a chance to stretch out behind him in the backcast and I tell him to keep the rod between 11:00 o'clock and 2:00 o'clock. When he does this the line floats high and then drops softly on the water. He still doesn't catch anything, so we make camp and prepare to cook dinner.

It turns out I have brought old matches that are soft and don't want to ignite. On top of this, the pressure valve on the Whisperlight stove breaks. For a while it looks like we are going to have cold cereal for dinner, but we keep trying and the Whisperlight finally gets going. I start a wood fire in case the Whisperlight fails again.

Christian tells me that when he went fishing at Sylvan Lake with his church group they watched a truck come in and dump fish into the lake. "Put and take" it's called and I suppose it's better than nothing, but it points out the value of Wilderness Area lakes where you have to walk in and there isn't enough fishing pressure to clean out the naturally reproducing populations. Someone put a few brookies in Nolan years ago and they have been doing fine ever since. In fact, the lake has too many fish. Many are long and skinny with big heads. Christian's story about the hatchery fish reminds me of the many disconnects I have seen in recent years. The Vail Resorts people had Disney characters, Goofy, Pluto, etc., skiing around on the trails as if to say, "Well, just skiing isn't enough. We have to add some fantasy to this."

It's the same fantasy exaggerated a thousand times in *Star Wars* flicks and *The Terminator* thrillers that have people thinking killing is an ordinary part of daily life. The media plays the war in Iraq like a football game to the American people. The Iraq people are numbers, not humans. So thousands of them die, soldiers and civilians, so what? We'll show them who is boss!

The next morning I tell Christian to go fishing by himself while I pack up the camp. I will catch up with him shortly. When I reach him on the other side of the lake he is back to his old habits so I repeat yesterday's instructions. We can see trout feeding close to shore so I tell him to try to drop the fly a few feet in front of where the trout is swimming. Wham! The trout strikes and is hooked. He plays it carefully until I can get the net under it. Christian has caught his first trout with no hands-on help from me. He is very excited. It's a big moment for him and for me too.

Grouse Hunting

September 13, 2003. Went grouse hunting with Christian. Lots of black powder hunters on the Flat Tops, some camped right on the edge of the grouse cover. After about forty-five minutes of hunting, John pushes a bird out of the current bushes. It's an easy shot, but I have to be quick. The bird comes down and Christian runs after it since it's wounded but not dead. My father was shooting birds in front of me when I was Christian's age, so it feels like I am passing down a tradition. We see a few more birds and I get one long shot that hits the bird but doesn't bring it down. We see blaze coated hunters around the camps now, getting ready for the evening hunt and I realize we should probably have worn some red. We are home before 3:00 P.M.

Grouse dinner.

September 14, 2003. There was a frost last night. Twenty-five degrees. Summer is over.

September 17, 2003. I pluck the grouse this morning. We have decided to prepare a dinner worthy of this wild bird. We dig three kinds of potatoes from our garden: red, white, and black. We pick red, yellow, and green apples from our trees. This is the first time in four years a spring frost hasn't killed the apple blossoms, and the trees are loaded. We add some local pine mushrooms and a few juniper branches to the display. Anne Helene takes some pictures. After this we stuff the bird with apples and red cabbage, wrap the breast with bacon, and put it in the oven.

A wine salesman at a local liquor store has recommended a sauvignon blanc that turns out to be just right. Anne Helene takes more pictures of the cooked grouse, vegetables, and wine on a table in front of the fireplace. We say a blessing and enjoy the white slightly gamey meat, fresh potatoes, and mushrooms. We have performed a ritual of sorts, grateful that the land has offered almost everything before us.

November 2003. We are in a full-on guerrilla war in Iraq, losing American soldiers almost every day, and the suicide bombing has spread from Iraq to Turkey.

Bald eagle. Photo by Anne Helene Garberg Brown.

Eagles

There is a golden eagle's nest in the red sandstone cliffs above my house. I assume the nest is old since the sticks are piled several feet thick. They are wise birds when it comes to hiding the nest location. They almost never fly directly out over the valley where they can be seen, but circle around low in the trees until they are far enough from the nest not to reveal its location. Then they gain altitude and hunt. The nest, like my home, is directly under the airport flight path so I assume the eagles have given up using it. But I see eagles cruising in the sky a few miles away when I'm mountain biking on Red Hill so I climb up to the nest one day to have a look. Sure enough there are two fledglings, all feathers with their heads hidden. What a nice surprise. I observe them from a distance for several more months after this until they grow up and fly off for the winter.

Eagles aren't common in the Rocky Mountains, but not all that rare either. Many of the rivers have bald eagles nesting in the cottonwood groves. The bald eagle is a fish-eater by choice but will eat carrion and small animals given the opportunity. Neither the bald nor the golden eagles are fussy eaters.

The easiest place I know to find eagles is on the road near a creek crossing just south of Baggs, Colorado. For some reason there is a lot of road-kill there, mostly rabbits, and the eagles, both golden and bald, pick the pieces off the pavement. Our majestic national bird, it turns out, is a not too fussy scavenger. There is a lesson in this.

September 2000. We are in Baggs, Wyoming, just across the Colorado border. A birder friend, Detlef Stremke, and his wife are visiting us from the former East German Republic. I first met Detlef in North Peary Land in Greenland, where he was observing birds that wintered in Germany and spent their summers in the Arctic. Now we are looking for the famous but rapidly disappearing sage grouse. It is their mating season, and they put on quite a show. Ray Weber, a rancher who helped us with *Western Ranching: Culture in Crisis*, tells us where to look. The sage grouse are fascinating, but watching two eagles and a coyote fight over a dead faun is truly amazing. The coyote tries to drag the carcass under a rock, but he is no match for the eagles who claim the meat.

Following is a collection of stories about exploring Wilderness Areas with my sons. I realize now these trips were some of the greatest gifts I could give to them and they to me.

Trout with Legs?

July 7, 2002. Christian is awake most of the night anticipating our planned excursion to Cherry Lake in the Red Table Mountains. What he really wants to do is catch his second trout. We figure that if there are no trout in Cherry Lake,

Cherry Lake, Red Table Mountains.

Top and bottom; Tiger salamaders.

there will be trout in the beaver ponds further down or in Erickson Lake in the next draw. We are optimistic about our chances for success.

The drive up to the top of the Red Tables takes less than an hour. There is a wonderful view of the Snowmass Wilderness Mountains as we get higher on the mountain. We park and scramble down steep talis slopes filled with wildflowers. Red paintbrush plants dominate, but yellow and white blossoms also pepper the green vegetation. Century plants send their spikes high into the air. Further down we run into columbines. Under all of this is the red sandstone rock, making the display of color seem unreal. Mosquitoes attack us but are bearable as long as we keep moving.

As we approach the lake we can see breaks on the surface. I think there must be trout after all. As we get closer the black fish become more visible. They have legs! I can't believe it. Then we see a couple dozen big salamanders crawling in the shallows, occasionally coming to the surface for air. Some are over six inches long, thick, with big heads and bulging eyes like a frog. They have the dull green markings of the tiger salamander I found in my pump house at home.

Christian spots more and more of the strange prehistoric looking creatures. Several swim out from under the log as we step onto it. Some have external gills that look like ferns growing out of their necks, others don't. The normal cycle for amphibians is to live for a time in the water as larvae and then transform into land animals. But some of these tiger salamanders don't metamorphose, they continue to stay in the water for years, never exchanging their gills for lungs. A few of these very adaptable creatures also develop broad U-shaped heads and long pointed teeth allowing them to catch and consume smaller salamanders. This cannibal adaptation is another one of Nature's amazing survival mechanisms. The cannibals will make it to another year and another breeding season.

We are witnessing a kind of reenactment of a transformation that occurred billions of years ago when oxygen started to build up in the atmosphere and some creatures found a way to metabolize it. With lungs instead of gills they were able to live out of the water. It was a slimey beginning and a slow process, but we are the end result—evolving from amoeba, to fish, to something like these salamanders, to primates, and finally to humans.

It's nice for Christian to see this—to know about his origins and to know that something similar may be in his DNA. We walk further along the shore of lake, seeing squirming masses of freshwater shrimp in the shallows. This would be a trout paradise if the lake was deeper and the water cooler. But luckily for the salamanders, there are no trout here.

Cherry Lake is in a proposed Red Tables Wilderness Area, but the designation is being questioned by the town of Gypsum. They want to develop water in the area. Jeepers and dirt bikers don't like the plan either, because it will close part of an old dirt road that goes up from Gypsum Creek Road, along Red Creek to the Red Table Cliffs, and finally to the top of the ridge.

The Ouzle and the Shrew

Almost every adventure sport has its counterpart in Nature. Certain creatures can do what we do, only better. In kayaking it's the dipper bird and the water shrew.

I met the ouzle during my first summer in Vail. It's a medium-sized, nondescript, gray character feeding primarily on aquatic insects. It has the ability to walk underwater and feed along the bottom of a stream. It can use its wings like fins. Currents don't bother it. In fact, it rides the currents to get from one good feeding spot to the next. I'm not sure how its eyes work, but they obviously see well when submerged. The name "dipper" may come from the bird's habit of bobbing up and down as it stands on a rock or log between dives into the water, or "dipper" may refer to its extraordinary amphibious performances.

The ouzle builds its nest in places where the swift current protects the chicks. I have filmed the yellow beaks of the young poking out of moss banks or clumps of debris and vegetation stuck in the middle of the stream. The parents deliver insects every minute or so, big bunches of creepy black things from the bottom of the creek.

The water shrew is less visible. I have only been able to observe these animals on two occasions. The first time was when I was fishing in Beaver Creek where the resort is located now. The second time was when I hiked into the top of Antoine's Cabin Creek in the Red Table Mountains south of Gypsum the night before the opening day of elk season. It was late in the afternoon and a light snow was falling. I found a flat spot in a meadow and quickly set up my tent and lit a fire. Then I picked up a pan to fill with water. As I approached the creek I saw what at first I thought was a strange gray fish moving along the bottom. I stood still and watched.

Suddenly the little gray fish seemed to expand and pop to the surface. It was then I noticed it had legs and was swimming. It came to a place where the water dropped down over some rocks, and it ran the white-water just like a miniature kayaker might. When it dove to the bottom its fur seemed to collapse against its sides giving it a sleek appearance. Then when it wanted to surface and float, the fur would fluff out making it buoyant. The little creature moved quickly and continuously, never stopping. I understand they eat several times their weight every day, and ounce for ounce they are the nastiest little monsters on earth. I'm glad they are not big enough to want to take a bite out of me. I know I would be no match for them if they were as big as my dog. I have looked into the mouth of shrews that my cat has killed. They have very sharp looking canine or "eye" teeth that must make short shift of anything they decide to eat. The water shrew is kind of a very mean Moses type character: It walks on water but it's not leading anyone to the Promised Land.

After a while the shrew disappeared behind some rocks, and I went back to camp to make dinner.

Why Outward Bound?

Because urban pressures appear to be debilitating the human spirit.

Because our society is exceedingly complex and it's dang confusing.

Because life abounds but most of us seldom see it.

Because we are killing that very environment which sustains us in life.

Because all of us are losing a sense of compassion for one another.

Because new and relevant values have to be found to replace the tired and no longer relevant ones.

Because it is easier to repress than it is to solve problems.

Because people need understandable stress.

Because you're here and you're worth whatever investment we can put in you.

Because most of life is not full of kicks, but there must be some kicks in life if it is worth living.

—Murray Durst's introduction to Outward Bound students

Chapter 5

Outward Bound

Above: Roger filming Outward Bound students near the summit of Mt. Holy Cross, 1971.

Previous page: Dick Pownall aid climbing near Main Gore Lake, 1963.

SOME FILM PROJECTS BECOME LIFE CHANGING EXPERIENCES for the filmmaker. *Outward Bound* has been one of these for me. The Outward Bound Schools (OBS) teach teenagers self-reliance through wilderness experiences. Similar adventures occur without the formal structure of wilderness schools all the time when young hikers, climbers, etc., take expeditions into remote wild areas, but there are two major differences between these excursions and Outward Bound. First, the Outward Bound School recruits a certain percentage of kids from low income families in cities who would never get to travel into a natural wild area any other way. These kids bring their own version of the law of the jungle with them. Second, the OBS founders and instructors have developed a philosophy and a method of teaching that can change attitudes and behavior in these impressionable young people, effectively helping them make the transition from adolescence to adulthood.

This kind of growth and maturing has been what we have looked for in almost all our adventure shoots. When a climber, kayaker, etc., takes on the challenge of a first ascent or descent they usually stick their neck out, and the experience often changes their lives. What's more important than the success or defeat, however, is the exploration of one's limits, both physically and mentally.

Beyond the personal challenges are other demands that, in the long run, may be even more significant; learning to work together and to watch out for one another in survival situations, for instance. It's a complicated process, but very important, particularly now, when so much of American leadership seems juvenile to the point of being dangerous. We need to develop mature responsible and compassionate people to lead the nation.

A closer look at Outward Bound as it operated in the early 1970s is revealing. Part of the OBS philosophy is to create "understandable stress" in a society where so much of the stress is incomprehensible—nuclear proliferation, AIDS, etc. The other side of the philosophy is that "life can't be all kicks, but there must be some kicks in life." There is a boot camp component and a fun component to the experience.

Outward Bound is one very good reason to protect remaining wild areas left around the world. Traveling in a wilderness environment for several days with minimum equipment brings you in direct contact with life's basic conditions: cold, heat, snow, rain, hunger, and exhaustion. You can see and feel the problems that threaten your comfort, and in some cases, even your survival. It's the same kayaking on a river, skiing in the back country, or climbing a big remote mountain. Time, energy, and food slip through the same hourglass and must be rationed carefully.

We make two films for the Outward Bound Schools. One is an overview of the whole program, the other is about the Coors Company's Third Chance program in which "two-time losers" (criminals who have been in jail twice) go through the rigors of an Outward Bound course. If they stick to the program and complete it, they are given a job at the Coors Brewery.

Barry Corbet produces these films from his wheelchair. He has several of us shooting: me, Bob Fulton, Norman Dyhrenfurth, Joern Gerdtz, and Dick Durrance on the first show, and Bill Trautvetter and Charles Groesbeek on the second show. To my mind, the *Outward Bound* show is one of Barry's best efforts. He incorporates all of our very different photographic styles into a single powerful statement, a statement that is as much his as that of the Outward Bound Schools.

The *Outward Bound* film takes me into several locations in the Eagles Nest and Holy Cross Wilderness areas near Vail. We climb up next to The Cross all the way to the summit one morning, which is probably foolish with so many beginners scrambling around on loose rock, but we encounter no problems. Bob Fulton and the other cinematographers visit the ocean oriented OBS school in Maine where they row Boston whalers on the open sea and the lakes region school in Minnesota where they participate in canoe trips. There are five schools in all, scattered across the nation, each one offering a different set of wilderness conditions to deal with.

My most significant contributions come in the form of super slow-motion photography. Scree slopes are made up of small rocks that have broken off cliffs over long periods of time, piling up at the base of the mountain. A steep, even surface is formed, almost like a sand dune, that you can run, even leap, down, landing softly as the little rocks give way to your weight. Some of the students discover what fun this is, and I ask them to demonstrate for me while I run the Milliken camera at 300 frames per second. The effect on film is amazing, gravity seems suspended as they float gracefully through the air, kicking their legs up, taking what seems like forever to land. It is another case where the visual filmed experience captures the exuberance of the action better than actually being there, unless of course you are the one jumping.

Experimental filmmaker Bob Fulton brings a whole different dimension to the experience with his single frame bursts and fast travel moves over glassy water surfaces, plants, and rocks. He creates a feeling which is simultaneously calm and exciting and very energizing.

"The Razor Edge of Imminent Dissolution"

Before the students are sent off on survival exercises they are taught basic outdoor skills. There is one amusing sequence in our film with the famous mountaineer Willi Unsoeld that gets at the "why" of these outdoor experiences.

Willi is teaching a group of students how to rock climb. He says:

> "I can still remember the early days of rock climbing. The thing we sought along with the skills, the spread holds and the jam holds and the fist holds, and the elbow holds, and all the various maneuvers, the thing we really sought was the razor edge of imminent dissolution, you know, where it is all right there in your fingertips, everything is in a living quiver of concentrated living."

At first you are tense and afraid because, as Willi says:

> "Like that *(snaps his fingers)*, it might all go." [He is referring to beginners who regularly peel off the rocks but are roped and protected with belays* from the instructors so they only fall a few feet.] More experienced climbers, on the other hand, sometimes get over-confident and go well above their last protection and end up falling long distances. There is a point where the muscles can't handle the load and you start to shake or quiver, just before you let go. . . ."
>
> "Gradually you get better, and you know what your fingers can do, and all the chill is gone, but sometimes you have to fake it a little bit when you get up there on very small holds and you're just hanging, and you think 'I better not let down my guard even a tiny bit,' and you watch your navel internally. It's internal navel contemplation, and when that quiver starts you think, 'OK *(click)*, shut it off,' because even though you're faking it, it might become the real thing. . . ." *(Visuals in the film: a series of falls.)*
>
> "It's not because it's any great thing to do, it's because of that nagging question—'Can I or can't I?' "

Willi's description reminds me of advice I once received from the great Olympic champion skier Stein Eriksen when I was training in Portillo, Chile. He looked at me in a heap on the middle of the slalom course one day after a fall and said, "That's good, Roger, you're not learning unless you're falling."

His remarks didn't make me feel better, but I understand at that moment that I should learn how to fall without getting hurt. If you are going to be a ski racer, particularly a downhill racer, you are going to take some rough spills. It hurts when you're going upwards of sixty miles an hour and something goes wrong and you slam down on the hard icy surface of the race course. You can feel your brain jarring in your skull. You learn to relax because if you tense up some-

* A *belay* is a safety rope that is attached to the climber and usually runs through *caribiners* (metal snap links) attached to the rock with *petons* (nails hammered into cracks in the rock) and into the hands of an anchored climbing partner. While one man climbs, the other holds the rope in what is called a belay position. The belayer can arrest a fall by holding the rope tightly, keeping it from sliding through the caribiners, or catching the weight of the climber from above, in some cases.

Rappelling. Courtesy of G. Regester.

thing is sure to break. Wilderness experiences are similar—you know there's going to be some sweat and pain involved, but it's worth it just to be immersed in unspoiled Nature. You may not be aware of the maturing process also taking place, but it is occurring nevertheless.

Another poignant moment in the film sticks in my mind. Two instructors are talking: one claims Outward Bound is a physical survival exercise, the other says it's more of a contemplative experience. As the film evolves we discover it is both. The students know they are going to be put into situations in which they will have to hike long distances and, in some cases, go without food. The situations are not life-threatening since an instructor is nearby to make sure no one gets in serious trouble, but he stays mostly out of sight. The students travel together in small groups. They become exhausted and get blisters but they know they have to keep going in order to reach their destination and return before all their supplies are gone.

Another part of the Outward Bound program is called the "solo." The students are given water and a few matches to light a fire and left by themselves for a few days. For many it is the first time they have been alone, without human contact, for an extended period of time. There are many different reactions: loneliness, fear, panic, and hopefully soul searching. When we did interviews with the boys on solos we got comments like, "For the first time I asked myself who am I, and why am I here?"

When Outward Bound Schools founder Kurt Hahn was asked, "What has led to the erosion of principle that man should give back to society as well as take from it?" He had this to say:

> ". . . (the problem) is largely connected to the unseeming haste with which modern life is conducted. It's the absence of aloneness. You cannot harvest the lessons in life except in aloneness, and I go to the length of saying that neither the love of man nor the love of God can take deep root except in aloneness."

Thus "the solo."

One of the greatest benefits Outward Bound and other programs such as the Peace Corps are creating is "outer direction" as opposed to egocentricity. Gary Templin wrote several years back, "In the frustrating search for identity young people rush madly into questionable activities (drugs, etc.) only to run into a complicated and inconsistent morality." Outward Bound tries to free them from this trap. The unforgiving nature of the wilderness forces the students to work together when they are in a patrol group and teaches them compassion for one another. Templin goes on:

> "A young person . . . should be totally sure of himself, capable of compassion, as well as possess mental and physical strength, be self-disciplined, and able to look outward in fulfillment of his responsibilities to the world."

That's the goal.

Prayer flags in the Himalayas.

Charles Froelicher, a dedicated Outward Bound supporter, explains the transformation further:

> "Without self-discovery a person may still have self-confidence, but it is a self-confidence built on ignorance and it melts in the face of heavy burdens. Self-discovery is the end product of a great challenge mastered, when the mind commands the body to do the seemingly impossible, when strength and courage are summoned to extraordinary limits for the sake of something outside the self a principle, an onerous task, another human life. This kind of self-discovery is the effective antidote for the indifference and insensitivity we have bred into modern youth."

While traveling in Tibet I am exposed to the story of the eleventh-century yogi, Milarepa. People tell me that he was at Mount Kailash and that the footprints we see in some rocks, blackened with finger grease, are his. The story sounds like an early extraordinarily successful Outward Bound adventure in some ways, an indication that the Outward Bound programs are built, inadvertently or knowingly, on ancient wisdom. Briefly the story is as follows:

> Milarepa's family came on bad times after his father died. Relatives, who promised to help, instead stole the family property for themselves. Milarepa's mother wanted revenge so she asked Milarepa to apprentice himself to a magician who could teach him how to cast evil spells. He did this and, as his mother demanded, brought great suffering not only to his relatives but to the entire village. Milarepa felt no joy from these actions, only remorse, and the magician also felt bad and sent him to the famous Dzogchen master Marpa. Marpa put Milarepa through incredibly difficult trials, forcing him to repeat useless tasks, demanding that he wander in the wilderness, eating not much more than nettles, living alone in a cave, not accepting help, coming close to death, until finally Milarepa became enlightened. Although he was eventually offered riches and comfort Milarepa continued to lead the life of a yogi, teaching the dharma and about the follies of greed and revenge and the benefits of compassion, until finally he reached full realization.

None of this discussion really explores the value of being immersed in the beautiful natural world that these wilderness experiences offer, yet this part of the experience is equally or more significant. Years later, a former Outward Bound student will tell you, if you ask, that he remembers more than anything the magnificence of place he was temporarily "trapped" in. But here I must kneel before the great Nature philosophers and writers like Henry David Thoreau, John Muir, and Aldo Leopold. More of that in other chapters.

I still carry the Outward Bound philosophy with me today. It's not easy to set aside selfish pursuits and become "other directed," but I try. As the years pass and I look back, it becomes clearer and clearer that compassion and kindness towards others is the greatest reward, not self-gratification.

"If there is magic on this planet,
it is contained in water."
— Loren Eisley

Chapter 6
Water

Above: Deer Lake, Flat Tops, one of many little gems full of trout.

Previous spread: An unnamed lake, Flat Tops Wilderness Area.

It is 1970. Courage or naïveté, call it what you will, but I get verupset with the Denver Water Board and its plans to dry up the Vail Valley in order to bring more water to growing East Slope cities. So I start a fight that eventually leads to the creation of the first minimum stream law in the West. This effort becomes one of the most difficult and rewarding adventures of my life.

February 26, 1995. Clear water, so clear that if it didn't collect reflections you wouldn't see it, in a high mountain stream, washing over gravel and rocks, dancing ever downward through a million little falls and pools, making its own music, inviting us to cast a fly, snap a picture, or take a drink, this is a experience that grips to my soul. I love this kind of water to the point of pain. I have always felt this way about these streams since I can remember.

I used to think clear free flowing streams were only in high mountain country, but then over the years, as I traveled, I found them in deserts and jungles. There is nothing wrong with turbid streams and rivers, they are part of the natural system as well, but they are not as beautiful in my view. Of course when I am in a kayak it is the movement, not the clarity of the water, that matters. Muddy opaque water gives off different reflections, more solid and mysterious, and less friendly, but the ride is the same in either case if you're in a boat. All streams and rivers give us visible currents to follow in a life full of mostly invisible currents.

In the early 1970s I encountered what I considered to be the ultimate rapist, the Denver Water Board. They had dried up several streams in other places in

Colorado, and now they wanted to divert the streams around Vail. For me this was the beginning of a passionate war.

Water is a given in our lives. We never really think much about it unless we don't have any. In the East, where I was raised, there was always plenty of water: the Atlantic Ocean where we caught flounder and mackerel, ponds where we chased turtles in the summer and played hockey on their ice in the winter. Water never failed to flow from the tap: for baths, squirt guns, watercolors, lawn sprinklers. The clear fluid was always there, like the food on the table and roof over our heads.

My college friends, Fred and Dick Shanaman, invited me to visit them in Tacoma, Washington during the summer of 1956. My father had died that spring, and they wanted to help me get over the loss. As I drove across the Great Plains I noticed that it kept getting drier and drier. Grasslands and sagebrush replaced trees in many places. Somewhere east of the Washington Cascades I realized I was in an actual desert. Then it got wetter again as I drove up a pass and dropped down into the giant coastal forests of the Northwest. I took it all for granted at the time. I had no idea how important water was in those arid areas. Hundreds of Easterners had tried to settle the dry lands of the American West at an earlier time and failed because of a lack of water, sometimes people even had gun fights over water rights.

The Pipes

It is ten years later. I'm now settled in a home in Vail, Colorado, and I'm out hiking along a mountain stream that suddenly ends abruptly in a big pipe. Below is a bed of rocks. I can't believe it.

I follow the pipeline to the Homestake Reservoir. From there I learn that the water is piped and pumped many miles through the mountains, under the Continental Divide, to where it eventually becomes the domestic water supply for the cities of Colorado Springs and Aurora.

Everyone knows how beautiful a mountain stream is. Beer and cigarette ads will show you if you haven't visited one personally. The clear mountain stream is second only to the eagle as a symbol of freedom and purity in the American psyche. Thank God for these images and for Madison Avenue, or our fight to save the streams would have been much more difficult.

I'm only aware of two situations. First, the Homestake Project (Colorado Springs' and Aurora's water supply), which is located in the Sagauche Mountains southwest of Vail, has minimized the water flow in Homestake Creek and has completely dried out three of its tributaries. Second, the Denver Water Board has similar plans for most of the streams coming out of the Gore Range (now the Eagles Nest Wilderness Area) that lies northeast of Vail. One of these, the Piney River, happens to be my favorite trout stream. Much of the Piney is fairly remote. I am often the only one fishing there, and over the years I begin to look at it as my private fishing stream. I teach my sons how to fly fish on the Piney.

Not knowing anything about water law I simply assume that drying up streams has to be illegal. How can anyone have the right to destroy such a fundamental part of the landscape? In outrage and frustration I begin shooting a film.

"It's just a small structure where we take the water out."
—Homestake project manager

The subject matter is obvious: beautiful streams being swallowed up in giant tubes, the barren banks of fluctuating reservoirs, wasteful sprinklers on Denver lawns creating small rivers in the streets, seemingly endless Front Range subdivisions, urban air pollution.

The more I film and travel around the state, the more I discover how bad the situation really is. I talk to people who have been forced to sell their land under threat of condemnation. I interview a woman whose well has dried up as a result of a nearby diversion. Others tell me about fish dying in depleted streams. It is a grim picture. Worst of all I discover that the law encourages, even forces, all of these things to happen.

Perhaps the most telling interview we do was with the Homestake Project manager. He is giving several of us a tour of their diversions on the edge of what is to later become the Holy Cross Wilderness.

Project manager, "You're looking at the main part of the Homestake Project in the Homestake Dam and Reservoir itself, here. At the present time we catch the east fork of the Homestake Creek which is right around here and you saw the pipeline coming around this end of the dam. On the far side you see the Missouri Creek tunnel where we pick up four streams on the west side of the mountain range: Missouri, Sopris, Fancy, and French creeks—and bring them through a series of pipelines up to this tunnel and into the reservoir. Future developments include the Cross Creek area, which will take another five-mile tunnel through the mountains into the Cross Creek watershed and Fall Creek and the other creeks where we have water rights. Of course, it won't be much of a dam: just a small structure where we take the water out."

I ask Ed Browning, Forest Service District Ranger, what he thinks.

"Our position is to control how it's done and to do it with minimum impact."

I ask the manager, "Does Colorado Springs have any plans to improve the environment of this place here, bury these pipes, or put any water back in the dry creeks?"

He answers, "Not to my knowledge."

I ask, "How do you feel about the three streams that you've totally dried up and the fish population and so forth?"

His answer, "I can't really say because I don't know how much fish population was there before."

My question, "There are fish in puddles there now doing quite well."

He responds with pride."Yeah, of course there's some seepage, I suppose, past the diversion structure and some springs and little streams that feed in there and give water to that. But if you noticed, when we crossed the east fork of Homestake down below where we stopped, it was totally dry at that area."

"How do you think the people of Colorado Springs feel about drying up creeks and the zero water flows?"

"I don't know if they know about it."

"How do you think they would feel about it if they did?"

"Depends on how bad they want to drink and how bad they don't as far as that goes," he chuckles.

"Did Colorado Springs ever think about restricting its growth because of a lack of water?"

"This I do not know."

Opposite page—

Clockwise: a natural stream, The place they suck it out, the pipes that carry it away, the Homestake Reservoir.

"With water we will dry up the world." —Bob Fulton.

I narrate the film at this point:

> "Homestake looks like a bomb crater. There is a hole with water in the bottom. People who use this dam for fishing tend to make it more of a mess. Why should a guy pick up a beer can if he's walking through a garbage pit?"

Most of the atrocities are occurring in rural countryside. Very few people in the urban areas of the state have any idea about what is going on. Films take time to make, so I begin writing articles for the *Vail Trail* newspaper as an interim measure. I figure others might get upset if they know the facts. I am right.

Water law is complex and, as far as I can see, water lawyers want to keep it that way. I think they sense that if the public ever understands what is really going on they will never put up with it. One of my first articles, "A Realistic Look at the Water Problem," is as follows:

> All the water must be removed from all the streams. That's the law in Colorado, believe it or not.
>
> If those of us who wish to save any of the natural, full flowing wild streams in Colorado hope to succeed, we must ultimately change the basic state water laws. Until the laws are changed we can only hope to postpone the destruction which will eventually occur.
>
> Colorado water law is solidly based on the doctrine of prior appropriation. The State Constitution, originally drawn up in the late 1800s reads as follows:
>
> "SECTION 5, ARTICLE XVI. The water of every natural stream, not heretofore appropriated, within the state of Colorado, is hereby declared to be the property of the public and the same is dedicated to the use of the people of the state, subject to appropriation as hereinafter provided. . . .

"SECTION 6, ARTICLE XVI, The right to divert the unappropriated waters of any natural stream to beneficial use shall never be denied."

What this means is that the water must be diverted in order to be placed in beneficial use. Since every stream is dedicated to beneficial use, if you follow the laws to their illogical conclusions, then all the water in all the streams has to be removed and put to beneficial use. There is no provision in Colorado law for leaving any of the water in the stream except to allow it to reach downstream users. The water cannot be appropriated in the stream. Recreation, fishing, the riparian environment, or simply the presence of a natural full flowing stream, are not considered "beneficial."

A particular kind of quasi-private-public agency has evolved out of these water laws—the City Water Board. On the public side, they have the power to do things like condemn land. They are exempt from federal laws like the Wilderness Act. In effect they are accountable to no one, not even the state government. On the private enterprise side, these water boards have the right to sell water outside of their own city and even county boundaries.

City water boards compete with each other in a completely uncontrolled manner. For instance four different water boards have water rights on the relatively small Upper Eagle River drainage. The result is that each board is going to build its own individual collection system, on top of, around, and next to the other systems. The city of Pueblo has an open ditch near Tennessee Pass, the Colorado and Aurora Association has a dam and several enclosed pipelines on Homestake Creek, and they plan a tunnel under the Mount of the Holy Cross in order to tap Cross Creek. The Colorado River Water Conservation District plans a dam and a hydroelectric plant lower down on the Homestake. The water dammed by the CRWCD will go to service Rifle on the Western Slope. A dam could be built nearer to Rifle, storing Colorado River water there, and leaving the Upper Eagle River natural flowing, but here again the design of the law forces them to exercise their water rights where they own them, not where they need them. The Denver Water Board plans two dams, several tunnels, and an enclosed ditch on the streams flowing off the west side of the Gore Range.

Almost all of the water in Colorado is over appropriated. What this means very simply is that more claims exist on the water than there is water to satisfy those claims. So each water board is going to take water out according to the seniority of the rights it holds, leaving in the stream only what is necessary to satisfy older downstream rights. As the cities grow and their water demands increase, they are going to become more and more desperate. The water collection systems are all designed to handle more water than the cities have a right to. Obviously, when a giant city starts to dry up, it is not going to concern itself much with a hand full of downstream ranchers, or a few small villages. Legal battles cost money and one thing a water board has is money. That's where the expression "water flows uphill to money" comes from. So the picture is bleak.

The Denver Water Board manager, Jim Ogilvie, comes to Vail to let the citizens know about the diversions they plan to build in the Gore Range north of town. He may have expected some resistance, but the Denver Water Board has never been stopped before and they don't expect to be stopped now. After all, water is a property right. They have filed for it first, so the courts are completely on their side. Jim isn't in Vail asking for the water, he is asking for cooperation in removing it.

I am too naïve to consider playing by their rules. To me it is a moral issue, not a legal one, so I push ahead with a campaign of public outrage. I put together a petition and, with the help of many others in Vail who are becoming aware of the problem, collect 375 signatures. That is just about everybody in the town. The petition read as follows:

> Let it be known on this 12th day of July 1971, that we, the people of Vail, do oppose the plans of the Denver Water Board to remove for any purpose whatever, any water from the Piney and Upper Eagle River drainages (including Gore Creek and its tributaries).
>
> We, the people of Vail, do believe that the laws under which the Denver Water Board plans to confiscate the above mentioned water are both unethical and immoral. What right does one city have to destroy Nature's design on federal Lands that belong to all the people of the United States? What right does one already overcrowded city have to develop its future growth potential at the expense of many towns and cities which are still small and have healthy growth potential, cities which would not destroy the natural flow of the water by using it?
>
> Since Vail depends almost entirely upon tourism for its income, the value of our scenery and the value of a natural, full flowing Gore Creek cannot be over estimated. We believe there is no way, under any ecological disguise program, that the Denver Water Board can proceed with its plans without causing great harm to our village, to the Colorado West Slope and to the natural heritage of our nation.
>
> We do ask the State of Colorado, the City of Denver, and the Denver Water Board to do the following before it proceeds any further in its plans to divert the water of the Piney and Upper Eagle Valley drainage's.
>
> ONE, meter all water users in Denver and those other towns that the Denver Water Board supplies water to.
>
> TWO, recycle all of (or as much as is feasible considering the state of technology of recycling) the water now being used by the city of Denver for continual use by the city of Denver.
>
> THREE, discount lawn watering as an essential water use. Lawn watering is a recreational use which can only be weighed equally with recreational values of the natural flowing water of the West Slope.
>
> FOUR, eliminate all of the overgrowth problems which are evident in Denver mainly pollution (air and otherwise) and crime to a level which is equal to or better than the most healthy cities in the nation that are of Denver's size.
>
> FIVE, publicly seek the opinion of the entire nation in order to determine if they would prefer a larger Denver over natural free flowing streams on federal lands.
>
> Once Denver has achieved these goals and answered these questions, we, the people of Vail, would be willing to reconsider our opposition to the Denver Water Board's water diversion plans in the Piney and Upper Eagle Valley drainages.

The people of Vail really pull together, holding events like the Walk for Water in which they raise $4,000. Tam Scott, the son of Fitzhugh Scott, one of Vail's original architects, signs on as the head of the Eagle Piney Water Protection Association. His legal background is very valuable when it comes to figuring out

Reprinted from: THE Vail TRAIL

Vail, Colorado — Friday, October 19, 1973

official plans call for taking just the spring run-off.

"I have no desire to see the water in pipes here or in Denver. *The water should go to California," he said in answer to charges by the DWB that opposition to the plan is from others who want the water.

Brown maintains the DWB is not concerned

*(This statement was made by Roger Brown, leader in the anti-Denver water faction.)

"THE WATER (DENVER'S) SHOULD GO TO CALIFORNIA."

So demands a leading spokesman of the claque opposing Water for Denver. Some demand!

Our reply:

We're not about to give up Denver's dwindling water supply to California.

Not when Denver faces critical water shortages.

Not when this water belongs to the people of Denver.

In fact, not now or ever do we want any more of Denver's water flowing into California.

Let the swimming pools in Los Angeles get along without us.

Why keep California green with Denver's water?

Let the outsiders worry about Los Angeles.

Our concern is Denver.

VOTE "FOR" DENVER WATER. ON NOV. 6.

DO IT FOR DENVER!

DO IT FOR OURSELVES!

TOGETHER WE CAN!

Water for Denver Citizens Committee
G. M. Wallace, Chairman

Ad appearing in The Denver Post.

how to change the laws. George Knox, affectionately known as the Skipper and the editor owner of the *Vail Trail* newspaper, gives the issue front page attention. My wife, Monika, knowing full well I am burning up our savings, never complains but works just as hard as I do to fire up the community. Chuck Ogilby, a developer with a conscience, carries on the fight long after I have to go back to making a living shooting sports adventure films. I am really proud to be a member of the Vail community at this time. The town has its heart in the right place.

Fortunately for us, there are a number of people in Denver who feel the same way we do, the most important being then State Representative Dick Lamm (Denver area). Dick is worried about the decay of the inner city that is occurring, as the rapidly-growing suburbs suck businesses away from Denver's center. I'm sure he also agrees with us about growth in general and how it is destroying the quality of life in Colorado, although politically he can't take a no growth position.

Our next task is to try to get a Denver Water Board bond issue defeated, which will create the funds to build the Eagle Piney Project. We work quietly and closely with Dick Lamm on this, finding money in Vail to help finance the anti bond issue campaign in Denver. My film, *The Water Plan* (which points out there is no water plan for the state), airs on Denver television. As a result of Dick's efforts and the film, the Denver Water Board receives its first bond issue election defeat in forty years. They try again, successfully, a few years later using scare tactics about greatly increased water rates. But the cat is out of the bag, and most of the state is against them.

Less than a year after the bond issue defeat the Colorado Legislature passes Senate Bill 97, the minimum stream flow law—the first law in the Rocky Mountains to give a free-flowing stream a legal right to exist. For me this is the crowning achievement of a difficult battle that leaves me tired and broke but grateful for having had a chance to make a difference.

We have one additional piece of extremely good luck. Shortly after Jerry Ford replaces Richard Nixon as President, the Eagles Nest Wilderness Bill comes up for final authorization. Ford is a part-time Vail resident and knows the story. I had taken him on a helicopter tour of the Gore Range and the Homestake project a few years earlier when he was the House Minority Leader and I had shown him the diversions and dry creeks at Homestake. I also flew with him over to Piney Lake and along the west side of the Gore. Others, particularly Sheika Gramshammer, keep him informed on the importance of the issue to Vail.

In spite of tremendous pressure from Republican developers and politicians from the Denver area, Ford signs the Eagles Nest Wilderness Bill that includes the larger, rather than the smaller, boundaries. Certainly the primary benefit of these boundaries is the additional forested terrain that is set aside, but Ford's decision also means that the Denver Water Board will have to get a Presidential exemption to build diversions in the Gore Range high enough to have a gravity feed system into the Dillon reservoir. Without the exemption they will have to install expensive pumps on lower diversion sites to move the water up over Vail Pass. The larger boundaries also preclude the construction of a large storage reservoir at Piney Lake that is needed to make the project viable.

A Presidential exemption is a hard thing to get on such a controversial issue but there is a scare when James Watt become Secretary of Interior under Reagan. Watt is trying to get Reagan to sign off on the Eagles Nest water diversion exemption but is forced to resign before it happens.

The Denver Water Board will never give up. Vail will have to stay on its guard for the foreseeable future.

Postscript

In the 1980s, as Vail and the Upper Eagle Valley became urbanized beyond what any us ever imagined, I became bitter about the water fight. Obviously we had not saved the water for the stream, we had saved it for development. Instead of going into pipes in Denver it was going into pipes in Vail, Eagle Vail, and Avon.

Locally used water is in-basin use, as opposed to a transmountain diversion which is an out-basin use, so there isn't as much of a net loss in the Vail area, but the Eagle isn't the same river it was in the 1960s and 1970s. The sewer plants, as well designed as they are, still pollute the river, and they handle more and more effluent every year. Vail and Beaver Creek snowmaking has pulled Gore Creek and Beaver Creek down below critical winter water levels for fish habit, or very close to it. In spite of dozens of studies and clean up efforts, the Eagle is dying. It is hard to realize it was a commercial fishery at one point, supplying the miners in Leadville.

"If you want to make a small fortune go into ranching. You start with a big fortune and make it small."

—Anonymous Rancher

Chapter 7

The Burns Hole Cowboys

Above: Roundup, Flat Tops.

Previous spread: Roundup below Dome Peak, Flat Tops.

NOVEMBER 2000. A WAY OF LIFE IS PASSING in the Rockies. The ranchers are selling out to developers. The worst example of this is right here where I live in the Eagle River Valley. There are only a few working ranches left and their days are numbered. How long can the ranchers hold out against such low cattle prices and high land values? Just in the time I have been in the Gypsum Creek Valley, land prices have gone from a $1,000 or $1,200 an acre to $6,000 or $8,000. The ranchers have a strong attachment to the land and really don't know what they will do if they sell except to look for another ranch that isn't in the I-70 corridor. I don't know any of them who are dancing for joy at the prospect of all that money. Their children and grandchildren are different. Like many young people the money looks pretty good to many of them.

There is still one unspoiled ranching area in Eagle County—the Burns Hole. It lies about thirty miles north of Dotsero on the Colorado River Road. Basalt cliffs wall-in the river above Burns, cutting off the view of the broad mesas stretching back from the cliffs up to the Flat Tops Wilderness. The Derby Mesa Loop Road climbs precipitously up from Burns, crosses the upper mesas, and swings back down to the River Road again a few miles north of Burns.

Derby Creek has three branches, the south, middle, and north forks. The ranchers built elaborate irrigation systems a hundred years ago for capturing the water from these streams, using it to turn the dry stoney hillsides into lush

Above: Winter feeding on horse-drawn sled.

meadows. The big lumpy Flat Top Mountains rise up on the skyline to the west. A few scattered log homesteads sit inconspicuously in the trees.

The famous Western writer Zane Gray based one of his novels, *The Mysterious Rider*, on the Benton family who owned the biggest ranch in the Burns Hole until recently. Owner John Benton was killed in a small plane crash, and none of his children wanted to take over the ranch, so it went up for sale and was purchased by Bill Nottingham. Bill's family owned the ranch that eventually became the Beaver Creek Ski Resort. He purchased a ranch along the Colorado River Road—the Benton Ranch, and other ranch lands in the Burns Hole—with the money from land sales in the Vail/Avon area. The Nottinghams are ranchers at heart. They don't like what's happened in the Eagle River Valley but they have obviously made the best of it. Susan Nottingham is married to Vern Albertson. Vern's family is one of the other big land holding clans on the Derby Mesa. His brother's family owns a big chunk of the Gypsum Creek Valley. The Wurtsmith, the Gates, and the Schlegel families also have large holdings in the Burns area.

Once in a while you get a chance to do something you know is "right." It may involve risks, not necessarily to your life but perhaps to your future if you choose to go against the grain of established conventional thinking, the thinking of people who have been your clients in the past. This is what son Nick and I did when we went to work on behalf of the cowboys and then the loggers.

Below: Roger and Nick defend the cowboys. Illustration by Nick Brown.

Orris Albertson and great granddaughter.

Western Ranching: Culture in Crisis

Above: Ben Wurtsmith and Nick Brown working on "Western Ranching: Culture in Crisis."

It's strange how you can go through your whole life living near some people without ever understanding them. I have lived in Vail since 1962, quite content in that world of skiers and celebrities, all the time thinking I am in tune with the land because I ski, hunt, fish, and otherwise enjoy the mountains and rivers, not just around Vail but all over the world. But the only people I really get to know well are a few simpatico souls in town, some kayaking buddies, the film crews I assemble, and the adventure sports athletes who perform in our films.

I have always admired the cowboys so when the town of Vail asks me to do a summer promotional film I want to include them in it. I manage to get some great shots of a high country roundup, but the contact is brief and superficial. Then, in 1993, I receive a call from Bud Gates, an old time rancher and county commissioner from the Burns Hole area. He is upset.

Bud: "They are going to put us out of business."

Me: "Who?"

"The environmentalists. They want to get us off the federal lands." Bud has sent me newspaper clippings on the grazing issue but I haven't paid much attention. I am almost completely out of touch with the environmental movement that occupied so much of my time in the 1970s.

But still thinking of myself as a pretty serious environmentalist I say, "Oh, that's just a few radicals, Bud, don't worry about them."

"There are more of them than you think, and they are serious. They are going to get the grazing fee raised and we can't afford it. Can you help us, take some film?"

"Let me look into it, Bud. I'll see what I can do." I am noncommittal. I really think he is worried about nothing.

A day or so later I turn on my television set, which I almost never do, and there is a documentary playing called *The New Range Wars*. It is sponsored by the Audubon Society. I can't believe what I am seeing. It is an unrestrained attack on Western ranchers, claiming they are overgrazing the federal range lands. The filmmakers have been manipulative, using images of deserts, suggesting that cows have destroyed all the vegetation. I knew better because I live on the edge of a desert. Deserts exist primarily because of a lack of moisture. The ranches in this part of the country, on the other hand, are very green because of irrigation. The ranchers divert the streams coming out of the high mountains and soak their fields, creating pastures that otherwise would be dry sagebrush flats. They move their cows up on the higher federal lands in the summer months so they can grow hay on these irrigated meadows to feed the animals when they bring them back down for the winter.

I can see that Bud is right, it is the established environmental organizations, not just the radicals, that are after the ranchers. They are disseminating inaccurate information to the large urban centers of the country. The image of the great American cowboy as a hero is being attacked. I know I have to help. I have to make that film Bud has asked me for. Nick also becomes interested, and we begin traveling around the West, meeting and working with these unpretentious cattlemen (and women) who are so much a part of the landscape. Nick and I find hard-working, self-reliant, family people who live by standards most of America lost thirty years ago. Some are stubborn and ornery, and I know a few

Above: Desertification expert Allan Savory with man-eating lion he killed.

Right: Allan Savory in a captured guerrilla camp.

who only put up with us because we are trying to help them, but all in all I count them among my closest friends.

What do we learn?

The Science

The range lands of the West have always been grazed by large ungulates and need grazing, as well as the dung and urine from these animals, in order to be healthy. The obvious comparison is a lawn. If you don't cut the lawn and fertilize it, it will grow tall and rank and eventually choke on itself.

The idea that a cow is that different from a buffalo or an elk is mostly nonsense. The grass can't tell the difference. The important thing is how the animals manage themselves or are managed. Predators, such as wolves, keep the elk and buffalo moving so they won't overgraze one area. The cowboy has to do the same thing—keep his cows moving so they graze enough but not too much.

Many of the Western range lands are undergrazed, not overgrazed, because some land owners and managers refuse to recognize these facts. For a long time the U.S. Department of Interior Bureau of Land Management had a policy of scattering cows over vast landscapes in order to avoid overgrazing. In some places in Wyoming they only allow one cow and her calf on every 120 acres. The cows just sat there, undisturbed, not breaking up the crusted soil and planting the seeds with their hooves. In fact they have no real impact on the land at all. The plants, which evolved over millenniums of periodic heavy grazing by buffalo and other ungulates, died and the ecology changed as a result.

For me these revelations are rude shocks. I can suddenly see that the big urban based environmental organizations, and even the federal government, are not only pursuing policies that will hurt the ranchers, but also the land.

Of course my son Nick and I don't know any of this until we are well into the shooting of *Western Ranching: Culture in Crisis.* It is Dr. Wayne Burkhart who points out the history of the range lands to us and the famous desertification expert, Allan Savory, who shows us specific examples of how the land can be improved with more animals on it, not less.

Allan is from Zimbabwe (formerly Rhodesia) in Africa. He grew up with the large animals of Africa and began working in park management at a young age. At various points in his career he was a "man-eater" hunter and guerrilla fighter. His very life has depended on his powers of observation. One out-of-place blade of grass could be the sign that could save him from an ambush by a lion or a man.

While Allan was with the Rhodesian Park Service they decided to move local tribal people off the land along the Zambezi River so a national park could be established there. Allan soon discovered that without the villagers to drive the elephants and other large animals away from their gardens along the banks of the Zambezi River, there was nothing to stop the animals from moving in and overgrazing. The river banks soon collapsed and seriously compromised the park. After several experiences like this, Allan realized that there are no simple or final answers to land management, that he would have to respond continuously to an ever-changing dynamic.

Left to right—

Top row: Joe Albertson, Bud Gates, Vern Albertson

Middle row: Bill and Jill Schlegel, Keith Scott

Bottom row: Orris Albertson and Curtis Scott, Dale Albertson

Today Allan probably understands the relationship between the soil, the vegetation , the grazing animals, and the predators, better than anyone in the world, but he has been ignored in some circles.

It is incredibly frustrating for me as a filmmaker to see endless exciting wildlife action films coming out of Africa that do not address the deep underlying problems of ecosystem degradation. I believe Allan and his organization, Holistic Management (based in Albuquerque, New Mexico), are our last best hope for saving the range lands and the wild megafauna inhabiting them.

The Cowboys

"If you want to make a small fortune go into ranching. You start with a big fortune and make it small." Allan Savory is quoting a rancher he works with. "I've made all the money I can afford," says another weather-beaten, smiling cowboy. Most ranchers who haven't given up this difficult occupation will tell you it's the work and the lifestyle that is the reward, not the money. The average federal lands ranching family earns less than $30,000 a year.

Very few people have any idea what cowboys really do and the movie industry hasn't helped. Yes, many cowboys are as clear eyed and honest as they have been portrayed, but, no, they don't have endless romances the way, say, a ski instructor might. Most of them marry early and have families to whom they are totally dedicated. The ranching families we filmed have been on the same land for several generations. Their grandparents usually live with them, not in old-age homes unless they are physically debilitated. We meet several eighty-plus-year-old cowboys who still ride in the roundups. Ranching is a seven-days-week, ten-hour day occupation. Orris Albertson still rides with two replaced hips.

Burns Hole, Colorado, cattleman Ben Wurtsmith says:

> "I've put most of my life in doing what I like to do which is ranching, but with my family in mind. I wanted my kids to have the good life I have had, and now it's my grandkids. The decision to stay on the land will be up to them, but that's what I've worked for all these years."

Kathleen Sun, who has one of the biggest ranches in Wyoming, tells her story:

> "We practically ran our two boys off with a stick because we thought they should do something where they could make a little more money and have a little better life. And they both worked elsewhere for ten or fifteen years and then they came back because they like the life. They feel they are accomplishing something, that it's a worthwhile occupation. They both agree that if you don't wake up at four in the morning, anxious to get started on your work, you're in the wrong business."

Burns Hole rancher Jill Schlegel (Ben Wurtsmith's daughter) sums it up:

> "The biggest pressure to leave ranching is because you don't have enough money. You live from day to day, you're happy with what you have, but you don't get extra things to go on vacation or to buy something that's extra, that you don't use every day. You might buy a new tractor because you have to keep the ranch going, but you don't spend frivolous."

COW CAMP

Opposite page: Cowcamp, Flat Tops.

Top: Haying on the Derby Mesa.

Bottom left: Starting 'em young.

Bottom right: Vern Albertson.

Cowboys spend a lot of time by themselves, on the back of a horse, working in a landscape that urban environmentalists only get a chance to read about or see on television. Their sensibilities are based on doing primarily one thing for an entire lifetime. They know the animals, domestic and wild, that depend on the lands they oversee. They seldom kill anything without a very good reason.

Most of the ranching people we meet are soft spoken and independent. They are not argumentative; they won't confront you when you are shooting your mouth off about "saving the West." But don't underestimate their intelligence, and don't be fooled by their "country talk." As in many rural cultures, a slang has developed. But it's a good idea to listen carefully. The way something is said, the tone, is often more important than the words. We found cattlemen usually mean what they say. A handshake is as good as a contract. They have never disappointed us, and I hope we haven't disappointed them.

When we start the film project I'm sure the cowboys think, with our display of hyper enthusiasm for their problems, that we are trying to sell them some kind of snake oil. It is only when they see some of the film sequences that they begin to trust us. Nick and I are very fortunate in this regard because we create friendships in a few months that might take decades to develop otherwise.

Generally the cattlemen we meet are land rich and cash poor. Their lands are more and less beautiful. The mountain and southwestern desert ranches, for me, are the most striking. The prairie is less dramatic but equally beautiful in more subtle ways. The older ranch buildings belong in the landscape as do the fences and the irrigated meadows. Without them the views would be far less friendly. Even the double-wide trailers, which many of the biggest ranchers we meet live in, do not seem out of place because they are functional, just as every other manmade ranch structure is.

Perhaps it is the beauty of the rancher's land and the romance surrounding the culture that are the ranchers worst enemies. Wealthy urban business people fall in love with the ranches and buy them, not really knowing what they are getting into. They hire ranch managers who are often capable, but when pressured into making a profit, do not always do what is in the best interest of the land. A cowboy whose family has owned the ranch for several generations and wants his children to follow in his footsteps will usually take the best care of the land.

Ralph Lauren and Ted Turner (and former wife Jane Fonda) are classic examples of people who have tried to use money to substitute for lifetimes of hard work on the land. Ralph Lauren, rags-to-riches necktie salesman turned clothing designer, has a magnificent ranch on the east side of Dallas Divide near Ridgeway, Colorado. Many of the longtime citizens of Ridgeway seem to feel he believes he owns the entire town. Turner is determined to prove that buffalo are better than cows, and you can prove anything if you throw enough money at it. We film one buffalo ranch and are not impressed with their manageability. We hear horror stories of buffalo goring horses out from under cowboys and jumping eight-foot-high fences or just going through them. When they want to vaccinate a buffalo against disease they don't corral him in a pen, they shoot him with a dart gun. Buffalo are wild and they need careful and intense management. I'm not sure why we want to undo thousands of years of animal domestication. Maybe it's because, as Ted Turner said, "buffalo have prettier asses than cows."

The most tragic loss of ranches is to developers. There is nothing more disheartening for me than seeing a beautiful ranch turned into a collection of nonfunctional trophy homes, owned by people who have a lot of money and no connection to the land. These monuments to the ego are most evident around the ski resorts of Aspen, Vail, Telluride, Jackson Hole, and Sun Valley. More about this later.

Unfortunately, the ranchers have never learned much about public relations. They are too busy working to have much time for politics, they are too few in numbers, and they are scattered over vast territories. You have to go out of your way to get to know a genuine cowboy. The film projects are our introduction, otherwise we might still be oblivious to what is happening.

I ask myself a few questions these days when I think about supporting an environmental group. Does the organization really want to solve problems or just fan the flames of conflict? The way to raise money seems to be to find, or create, a crisis. Does the chief executive sitting in Washington, D.C., or San Francisco really know more about the environment than the people living and working in it every day? Would somebody really want to destroy the very thing that has maintained them for generations?

Actor Lee Horsley hosted our *Western Ranching: Culture in Crisis* documentary. This was one of my good Hollywood experiences. Lee is a cowboy at heart and Tinsel Town hasn't been able to corrupt him.

"The community maintains itself through the association of the old and the young."

—Wendell Berry

Chapter 8

Old Timers

Above: Freda Orgish.

Previous spread: Old ranch cabin (left) and Pond on the Million Dollar Highway between Ouray and Silverton (right).

I WOULD LIKE TO INTRODUCE A FEW FOLKS who, for lack of a better description, I will call "Colorado originals." These people are pure country: kind, modest, polite, unassuming, but in their own unique way quite extraordinary. No fancy education gets in the way of clear vision.

The Orgish Family

Freda Orgish adopted us when we moved from Vail to Gypsum. She and Paul lived in a house on the corner of Valley Road and Cottonwood Pass Road about a mile-and-a-half from us. She introduced us to what country people in these parts call "neighboring."

When Freda and Paul would thin out their raspberries or yellow rose bushes or yellow lilies, they would give me the extra plants. Later, when I got a bumper crop of raspberries from these plants I would invite them over to pick a few gallons. I also shared my apples with them.

Freda was always smiling, polite, and grateful when I took the time to stop and "neighbor." I would drink an obligatory cup of tea and nibble on a cookie or two and pass the time of day. One day Paul showed me his arrowhead collection, another time some fossil bones and a saddle he claimed belonged to Poncho Villa. He collected about everything and anything that was interesting and could be picked up off the ground without going to jail.

Paul invited me elk hunting in the Flat Tops one fall. I'm not sure who was honoring whom, him the wise old hunter or me the famous filmmaker—but off we went. We took his big canvas tent that had space for two bunks, a stove, and a kitchen table. Paul was fastidious in the way he set up and managed the details. Everything had to be in its place. I felt like a school kid getting my first lesson in camp etiquette.

It snowed pretty good on us one night, there was almost a foot on the ground when we woke up that morning. We agreed that I would track while Paul would take a stand on the edge of a big meadow. It didn't take long for me to find tracks but the elk took me on a long slog through several aspen forests, away from the meadow where we were camped. They were always enough ahead to be out of my view. After an hour or so the elk turned back and headed straight for the meadow where Paul was waiting. I wondered why I didn't hear shots. When I got to Paul he was sound asleep and very embarrassed when I woke him up. I was a little upset but tried not to show it. I should have understood that Paul was old and his heart was tired. He died a few years later, and Freda died a year or so after him. I miss them.

Their son Billy Orgish lived down in Mancos in the southwest part of the state, but he used to visit his folks every so often. A year or so after they died he moved into their house.

Like his dad, Billy is "witcher" and a healer. Water "witching" or "dousing" is an accepted practice in this country. Certain people have the ability to locate water using a freshly cut forked willow stick which turns down when there is water in the ground below it. Billy Orgish is one of the more respected witchers in the area. Billy is married to Anne Gibbons, a former counterculture woman who has been in Gypsum for at least thirty years. Both Anne and Billy are massage therapists and healers.

I call Billy and he comes up to the house. It is late in the day so we don't waste time, quickly walking to the ground on the high north side of the property near where I pipe in the water from the spring down by Gypsum Creek.

Billy holds the forks of the thin, green willow branch in both hands, fingers facing down. He grips it lightly so that it can pivot easily. The single part of the branch points straight ahead, level with the ground. Then suddenly it shifts sharply downward. He takes a few more steps, locating the margins of the ground water. After more tests and measuring out distances he tells me how much water he thinks there is and how deep.

We move further west, and the stick goes down again and then back up as he takes more steps.

"Did you find water?" I ask.

"No, that was a grave."

"You can find graves with that thing?"

"I've found over a hundred gravesites down along the road between Slaughter's and my place."

The Gypsum Creek Valley was inhabited by Indians for thousands of years before the first white man showed up in the early 1800s. The Indians were hunters and gatherers. Obviously many died over the years and their bodies had to be disposed of. In the winter the bodies were wrapped in skins and hung in cedar or pinyon trees, but in the summer they could be buried.

Billy Orgish with ancient buffalo skull.

This is really interesting, I think, that these old bones can send off a signal that Billy can pick up with his willow stick. I am skeptical, so I decide to give him a test. Three hundred yards west of my house is an Indian campsite where I've found a few points, some flint, and pottery which is very rare in Eagle County.

"There is this site I want you to see, Billy. It's over this way." We hike along my fence line and run into a big flat rock. Billy's twig points down.

"There's a grave here," he says. I lift the rock which has been horizontally split in two. Three rocks keep the slab halves apart like little burgers in a big bun. It has obviously been assembled by humans. I have lived here for over twenty years and have never noticed this rock before.

Left: Nepalese shaman.

Below: Billy Orgish.

We move further south to where Anne Helene and I found the pottery. I don't say anything, but when he gets to the sagebrush where the pottery was his stick goes down. He points out three gravesites within a few feet of the brush. I'm amazed. Could it be a coincidence? Maybe the stick does work.

May 5, 2002. The developer of Chatfield Corners moves two trailers onto the land today. He places them in front of Billy Orgish's house. Lot markers are scattered across the hay fields. The whole ugly business of destroying this agricultural land is beginning. Why can't the developers build on the nearby barren hillsides, I ask myself, but it's a rhetorical question. Everyone knows it's cheaper to build on flat land, and the cows are gone anyway. No thought is given to the idea that this fertile land might be needed for other crops sometime in the future.

June 10, 2002. There are big backhoes on the Chatfield property, removing soil from a strip of land along the fence that has water under it. The water is only about four feet down. As they dig, a long pond develops. There are sedge grasses in several places on the land, an indication that water is near the surface. The development seems to be largely on a swamp. And this is the driest year on record in Colorado. It's a place where Billy says there are several graves.

June 19, 2002. The water drillers arrive and set up their rig near the west boundary of my hillside farm. Clouds of dust fly when the drilling starts, and it stays dusty until a small amount of water is hit at around seventy feet. At ninety feet more water shows up. I cut off the drilling at 110 feet. I have no indication from Billy that there is anything below ninety feet and they have found it right where Billy said it would be. The drillers guess the water is flowing at about five gallons a minute, but it might be more. We can hear the water gurgling in the pipe. There's a little underground stream down there, coming from the hill above and entering the other flows on the valley floor.

Billy comes up the next day and drops a line down the drill hole. It gets wet seventy-six feet down which means the water has pushed fourteen feet up the pipe. This kind of pressure is a good sign. We dip out a little water which tastes good in spite of the dirt that accumulated when the small plastic bottle scraped against the pipe. Everyone—the drillers and Billy—tells me I have a nice little well; not a huge amount of water, but plenty for the domestic use allowed by law.

In a tribal society Billy Orgish would be recognized as a shaman, but here he is on his own. I have traveled with shamans in Nepal and seen them in Mexico, Bolivia, and Sarawak. They are well known and respected in their villages. But here in the United States there are very few viable teachers who could possibly pass on the ancient knowledge to Billy, and there are not many believers who might be willing to follow his lead if he did have knowledge of the rituals. So Billy wanders around with these feelings in him, finding underground water, occasionally healing people, giving advice about diet and medicinal plants, but never reaching the status that would be accorded him in the high valleys of the Himalayas or the Andes.

June 28, 2004. Billy Orgish died at 3:00 A.M. last night from a heart attack. Some days later I ask his wife, Annie, how he felt about God and she smiles. Billy told her, "I belong to the round church. The devil can't catch me and the Lord can't corner me."

It was one of Billy's little jokes. He didn't spend time worrying about death in any case. He was much too busy living. I'm sure it was the Lord who got him.

Vail Finder Earl Eaton

I need a picture of Earl Eaton for this book, and I arrange to meet him at the Lion's Head gondola so we can go for a run and I can snap a few shots. Earl wears a Vail parka when he's on the mountain. It has a name tag on it that reads Earl Eaton, Vail founder. "It should read *finder*, not *founder*," he says. Earl is the man who discovered Vail.

I have forgotten how beautiful the ski mountain is. As we ride up out of the valley the Gore Range comes into full view. It seems close enough to be able to reach out and touch. When we step out of the upper terminal of the gondola building we look straight at the Mount of the Holy Cross off to the southwest. I have been looking at these views for over forty years now, but I never tire of them. They blow me away!

I am always more comfortable with a person who has a close connection to the land and to the other creatures that share this planet with us. I feel like I can trust someone who treats his or her working animals or pets well. So much the better if he or she is a hunter. A hunter learns to respect his prey and to value it. You can't be a good hunter without really caring for and understanding the animals you hunt. On farms and ranches the introduction to animals comes early, along with the knowledge of where food and clothing come from. Granted, it's a different kind of education and there are no diplomas in the end to hang on the wall, but to equate a person without a completed formal education with being dumb is a foolish mistake.

Earl Eaton, 1961.

Earl Eaton was born in a log cabin up Squaw Creek in 1922, not many miles from where Vail is now. His family farmed and logged and during the Prohibition Era they made illegal whiskey. There weren't many elk in the country then but he was fed a fair amount of buckskin (deer). By the time he was seven he was shooting his own deer. The Eaton family grew lettuce in the summer that ripened after the lettuce from lower altitudes had bolted and was no good. The lettuce was shipped by train to Denver.

Earl either had to walk or ride a horse to school, which was about four miles downhill from the family cabin. In the winter when the road was snow packed he could sled to school, but if the snow was soft and deep he needed to use either snow shoes or skis to stay on top. Snowshoes were too expensive, so his Dad decided to make skis for Earl and his brother. At first he built the skis out of pine but soon discovered that red spruce was tougher and has a natural curve at the base of the trunk that could be used for the upturned ski tips. Longer, wider skis stayed higher in the snow and went faster but were more difficult to turn. Earl would drag a single pole in the snow to slow down and to help with turns. The skis would tend to pivot around the pole, but mostly the skis didn't turn at all. Earl would run straight down the fall line and occasionally break his speed by sitting down on the pole when he got going too fast.

Earl dropped out of high school and joined the army where he worked as an engineer running supply depots during World War II. He was stationed in England and then traveled by train to France and then Austria. He talks about riding in a 40-and-8 boxcar and chuckles, saying it could either carry forty men or eight horses. The train moved so slowly the men would get out and walk beside it. He saw some action in what was called the Colimar Pocket in France, but he did not get as seriously wounded as his future partner Pete Siebert did in Italy.

View of the Gore Range from Vail Mountain.

After the war, Earl came back to Colorado and went over to Aspen where he hoped to be able to do a lot of skiing. He worked at various jobs: mining, ski patrolling, etc. Like many others in Aspen he had a dream about starting a ski area. The big difference was that he was a native and had hiked all over the Colorado mountains from an early age. He knew where the best terrain was. On the other hand, he had no formal education and no contacts for raising money.

One of Earl's favorite hikes was up Two Elk Creek south of Minturn and into what is now the back bowls of Vail. It was a spiritual place for Earl. He confided in me that he would have conversations with God while standing on the ridges looking at the Mount of the Holy Cross to the west. Then he said to me with a smile, "Well, there was no one else to talk to."

On one rainy day, at the end of a hike down the north side of the mountain, Earl was crossing Gore Creek on an old logging bridge when he looked up to see a big rainbow filling the end of the Gore Creek Valley. Two days later he stopped to see Pete Siebert at Loveland Ski Basin where Pete was the manager. He told Pete about Vail Mountain and the bowls, and Pete agreed to have a look. This was the beginning of his association with Pete, and Earl gives God credit for making it happen. Earl has no reservations about what has happened. He sees development as all good. "What would Eagle Country be without it?" he asks.

Earl Eaton, 2004.

Pete was impressed with the mountain and the bowls but they looked at other possibilities as well—Telluride, Ouray, etc. Earl tells the story of how the decision was finally made. He and Pete were having dinner in a cafe in Minturn, a town seven miles west of Vail, when the waitress overheard them talking about what is now Vail Mountain. She said to them, "Why, we get so much snow here it gets to be downhill to Leadville." Pete was impressed. Leadville is 2,000 feet higher than Minturn. Earl said he didn't pay the waitress for the remark but wanted to.

Earl never felt qualified to have a job in management because of his lack of a "proper" business education, but when the first lifts were being installed and the trails were being cut he was the all-round handyman who could make it happen. No one asked him about his degrees when he was adjusting the wheels on the chair lift towers.

When asked why he didn't make more money from the success of Vail, Earl replied simply that he didn't have any money to invest. Earl worked for Vail Associates in the maintenance department until he reached retirement age. You would think being one of the founders of Vail might have gone to his head or that

Earl Eaton at eighty-two on his skibob.

he might be angry about not making more money but if so, he certainly doesn't let it show. His health is fine. He shows few signs of stress and he still skis every chance he gets.

I run into Earl Eaton in City Market in Eagle. He informs me he is in the 2004 *Vail Undressed* calendar on his ski bob. "Did you really get completely nude for the shot?" I ask. "No," he says. "I wouldn't do it until they agreed to let me wear a helmet." He reminds me that the calendar is used to raise money for charity, then he says with a big smile that the calendars are sold out.

Earl has invented the ultimate sitski, otherwise known as a ski bob, or bike ski. His design tracks well in turns and can be folded so that it can ride in the ski rack on the gondola. The ski part of Earl's sitski slides under a chairlift seat while the seat rides on the lift chair, avoiding a situation where it might be dropped from the lift onto a skier's head. In spite of Earl's superior design no one has offered to help him start up a sitski manufacturing business. I would think that's the least Vail Resorts could do, considering he found the Vail Mountain in the first place.

Earl knows I'm a little upset about all the growth, so he says to me, "You know when we started Vail we didn't worry much about it getting too crowded because the valley is so narrow. What we forgot was how long the valley is." Right he is. There is an almost complete forty-five-mile strip city running from Vail to the Glenwood Canyon.

Ski patroller turned Vail Resorts executive Paul Testwuide asked Earl how he was going to make a living when he retired from the Vail Associates Maintenance Department.

Earl answered, "I'm going to make eleven-foot poles."

"Oh?" said Paul.

"Yep," said Earl. "I'm going to sell 'em to people who won't touch things with a ten-foot pole." Chuckle.

Even the old ranchers, who blame Earl in part for messing up their rural peaceful way of life, have no bad words to say about him.

"We are in a national sacrifice area."
— Randy Udall

Chapter Nine

Energy

Above: Russ Pearce and John McBride.

Previous spread: Roan Cliffs west of Rifle, Colorado., as seen from a Super Cub.

Fossil Fuels and Solar Deals

October 18, 2003, I have been talking to John McBride about using him and his airplane to shoot aerials for this book. We canceled a shoot a few days ago because of wind, but this Saturday morning is perfect, clear and windless. John calls me around 7:00 A.M. and says he will be at the Eagle Airport by 8:00. He brings the little Super Cub that he purchased from Les Streeter several years back before Les and his son Jake were killed in a plane crash.

I used to ski race against Les when he was at Middlebury College and I was at Dartmouth. In one of the slalom races I had a very good first run, placing second and ahead of Les, even though he was a U.S. Olympic team member. So when we were studying the slalom course for the second run Les said within earshot of me, "You know, I think I'm going to sneak that hairpin gate down the middle." I looked at it and thought the line was very risky but possible. In the race I tried it and fell. Les really set me up for that one. When you are ahead in your first run you don't mess with the second one. My career on the Dartmouth ski team never did quite recover. Of course, poor grades didn't help either. The dean of the college said I would have to make a choice between skiing and academics and put me on probation. Needless to say, I gave up racing.

So here we are now in Les's plane and all these memories are floating around in my mind. Jake Streeter helped me build my house in Gypsum. We cut small lodgepole pines up on Hardscrabble Mountain and used them to make the

Paonia Reservoir mudflats.

ceiling of the living room. Jake was a really nice kid and so was his father. Les never quite grew up. He always had a glint in his eye and a ready laugh. A good joke would make his day. John kept Les's Super Piper in Aspen so his wife Pia wouldn't know he had it. It was terrible loss when Les and Jake were killed. They were a much loved part of the Vail community. I used to run into Pia once in a while after that, and I could see the pain in her face from the hole in her life.

John flies us over to Paonia Reservoir, which is almost dry. Silt is accumulating rapidly. Sometime in the not too distant future, the reservoir will fill in and not hold water. I get pictures and then we head across Muddy Creek to Rifle.

Gas wells are invading some fine potential wilderness areas.
Left: Foul water from gas well.
Right: Gas well drilling.

We take pictures of some of the gas wells that are going in. There are hundreds of them. It looks like a cribbage board in a few places. The wells are set up on drilling pads with settling basins next to them to collect the foul water and sour gas that comes up before the natural gas. The smell reaches us a thousand feet up. It's not a pretty picture, the wells and pads are on what was once pastoral farm land. Energy expert Randy Udall calls these once quiet rural dream homes between the new gas wells "subdivisions from Hell."

I talk to an archaeologist friend who says her company has recently finished an archaeological survey for a company that plans to put 150 gas wells in the Piceance Basin west of Rifle. Apparently there's close to 100 trillion cubic feet of natural gas located in pockets in the William's Fork sandstone formation 6,000 and 10,000 feet below the surface.

There are 1,400 gas wells already in place in this energy belt. Fifty-five more applications for drilling have been approved in the last few months. In the next ten years several thousand wells are supposed to be drilled.

The Piceance Basin has a history of fossil fuel exploration and exploitation. I made a film here back in the early 1970s when the federal government subsidized a serious attempt to extract oil from the shale in the Piceance Basin. There is more oil there than in Saudi Arabia but it's locked in rock.

We put environmentalists Stella Leopold (Aldo's daughter) and Vim Wright up against the Colony Development manager in a debate to weigh the environmental impacts of the project against the the nation's need for oil. Arco, the company that owned Colony, was paying for the film so we had to make a fairly balanced documentary. On the other hand, we were looking at what was going to be the largest mining operation in the world, and a very messy operation. The spent shale (oil removed) expands to 110 percent of its original size, which means whole canyons would have to be filled with the stuff.

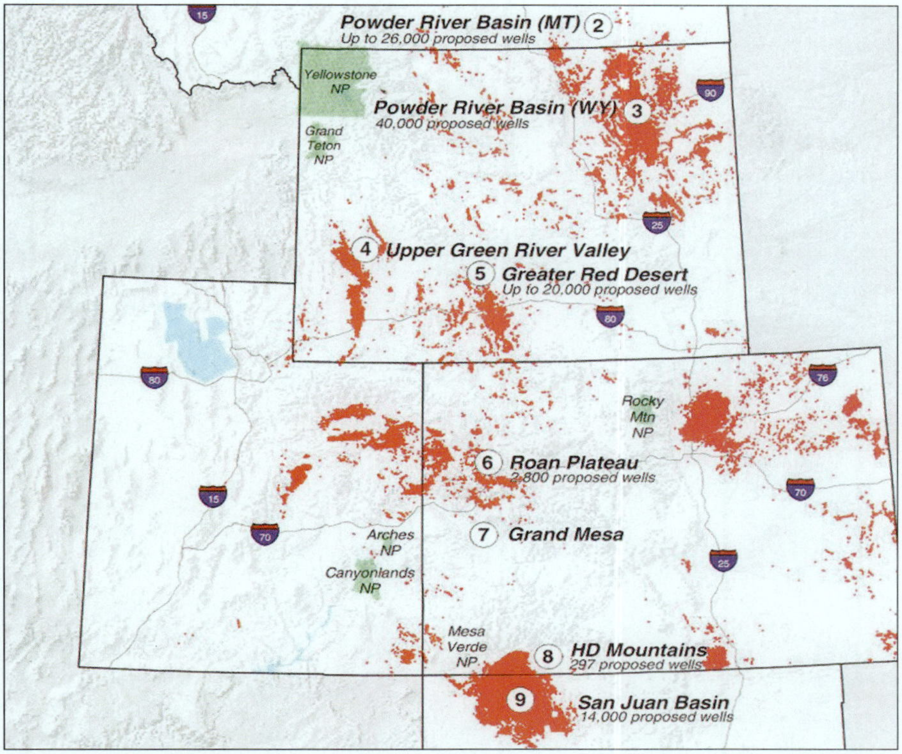

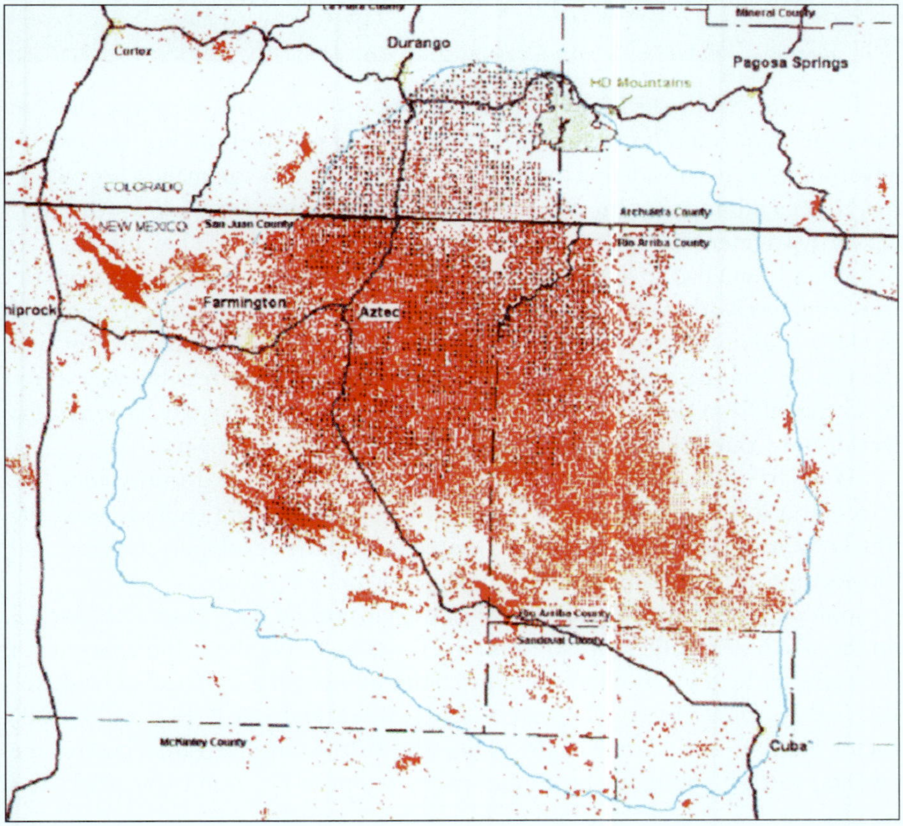

Top: Location of gas deposits in the Rocky Mountain region.

Bottom: Close up of region No. 9 in top map—the San Juan Basin.

The Colorado River near Rifle. I-70 and Highway 6, gravel pits and subdivisions—sometimes it's hard to remember what the river used to look like.

Facing page, top: A pristine section of the Colorado River near Rifle.

It became clear to us it was going to take more energy to remove the oil from the shale than could be recovered. It was a losing proposition, but the federal government kept subsidizing the effort, and eventually Exxon made a serious effort to get a mining operation going. They built a big company town for the miners on Battlement Mesa across from the town of Parachute. They hired 2,100 people and then had to let them all go in 1982 when it was clear that the operation wouldn't work. When Exxon finally gave up on extracting the oil, they sold the town and it was turned into a successful retirement community. I'm not sure the OPEC countries to this day understand there isn't any feasible way to recover the oil from the shale. They think we have more oil than any nation in the world, and I think this probably keeps them from blackmailing us.

After finishing the *Shale Oil: an Environmental Dialogue* documentary, we screened it in Denver. Gary Hart came to the screening and really panned the film because it was too balanced. He wanted to stop the developers. Later he had the nerve to ask us to support his campaign for the U.S. Senate.

John pulls the Super Cub up next to a DC 3 his friend Russ Pearce has parked on the side of the Rifle strip, so I take a few pictures. We shoot the breeze with Russ and some of his mechanic buddies. John points out a sign he had made for Russ's shop. It says, PRECISION AIRCRAFT MAINTENANCE, INC., A Non "P" Factor Shop. It seems some of the pilots who fly the fancy private jets (and the owners) can get pretty big heads and pushy tempers. "P" stands for prick, and

Russ is inclined not to work with these hot heads. This reminds me of a petroglyph I found on a wall along the San Juan River. It's Kokopelli, the Anazazi flute player, but he has a bit of anatomy not usually associated with him. I guess some of the Indians had pretty big opinions of themselves too.

Below: Kokopelli the Flute Player, a petroglyph from the San Juan River.

John and I visit his underground house on a ranch where he winters his cows. It's a beautiful spot right on the Colorado River. John has sold most of the property around the house under pressure from developers who have put in gravel pits nearby to supply road base to the gas well drillers. It's another thorn in John's side—one of many.

At lunch one of John's mechanic buddies, Jim, tells us how oil shale was discovered. Back in 1882 an early settler, Mike Callahan, built a log cabin at the foot of the Roan Cliffs and used the shale rock for his fireplace. When the cabin was finished he invited everyone from far and near to a house warming and gave new meaning to the concept. The rocks caught fire and burned the cabin down.

We get airborne again and head for the Roan Cliffs, the long, 3,000-foot high escarpment stretching from Rifle to Debeque along the north side of the Colorado River. The afternoon sun highlights the sharp ridges and rows of conifers clinging precariously to the rock walls. A scary, out-of-place dirt road runs along the top near the edge. I take several pictures.

I flew a similar route thirty years ago when we were making the oil shale film. We flew into side canyons with magnificent frozen waterfalls, an ice climber's par-

Gas well on farmland south of Rifle.

adise. The terrain is impossibly rugged, only suitable for elk, deer, and cougar. But I have a feeling if there is gas under there, someone will figure out a way to get it.

McBride suggests I meet with Randy Udall, director of CORE (Community Office for Resource Efficiency) to get a more comprehensive picture of the situation.

I arrive at Java Joe's Coffee Shop in Carbondale early and sit down with a latté. Young people wander in and out in a world of their own. I'm sure they are not thinking about where the fuel to heat their homes will come from in twenty years.

Randy is tall, craggy man in his fifties. Intense blue eyes peer out of a relaxed friendly face. "We are in a national sacrifice area," he says, matter-of-factly. He shows me a map. The Piceance Basin, northwest of Rifle, Colorado, is the middle of a gas rich energy belt stretching from Mexico to the Arctic. The Piceance contains a big part of the fossil fuel energy we have left in North America. It has to be used. Randy explains:

> "Half of all the natural gas in North America is gone. We are drilling as fast as we can but production is slipping relative to our demands. And we have made some mistakes, like building gas powered power plants without seriously considering the limitations of the gas supply."

Gas rates have doubled in just a year. Apparently I use a volume of gas equivalent to the interior space of my home each month during the winter. We turn the heat off every night and on most sunny days; and we burn a lot of wood, but the monthly bill still seems out of control. Maybe I'm mad because in 1978 I built a ninety percent solar heated house with a 1,000 square feet of air and glycol collectors on the roof. President Carter had introduced solar tax incentives that helped me justify the extra expense, but then Reagan came into office the incentives went away, as did many of the really inventive people who could design and fix the new solar systems. Eventually my active solar system broke down,

Above: coal vs. photovoltaic cells.

Right: Randy Udall in front of solar panels.

and I couldn't find anyone to repair it. I put in a gas burning heater but the guy who installed it couldn't figure out how to the loop in the solar air collectors that were still working. I've been waiting since then, hoping I can install photovoltaic cells where the air and glycol collectors are now, but the cells are still cost prohibitive. A lot of other people would be using photovoltaics if the government had provided the incentives to industry to develop them and reduce production costs but it didn't happen. The fossil fuel guys didn't like the competition, and they are heavy presidential campaign contributors.

The county has turned a blind eye to solar energy as well. I put in a 4' x 12' x 40' liquid heat holding tank in my basement. Can you imagine—the county called it a swimming pool and taxed it accordingly. They have no imagination.

Randy Udall has a different view of this. I get an ear- (I should say page-) full on photovoltaic cells—PVs as they are called. Randy has a small system on his house. It not only provides him with electricity but runs the Holy Cross Electric Company meter backwards on occasion, giving him a credit.

My first exposure to PVs was when we were filming the second ascent of Ama Dablam in Nepal in 1979. Climber cameraman Greg Lowe built a PV setup to charge our camera batteries. The PV panel was in a handy aluminum case that he opened to the sun. It worked even on cloudy days. The only problem I had was when a solar charged lithium battery self destructed in my tent one morning. The smell was unbelievable and probably quite poisonous although I suffered no ill effects. When we were in a remote village west of Mount Kailash in Tibet in 1999 we passed by a fellow who had some PVs in a box in front of his tent. It was revealing to see PVs so far from what we consider "civilization" while "civilization" seems to use so few.

Apparently off-the-grid homesteaders in New Mexico and California launched and refined these PV systems to help them grow illegal marijuana, and they worked very well. Mainstream America, which is on the energy grid, has done far less. At one point President Clinton promised PVs on millions of rooftops across the nation, but it didn't happen. So far Holy Cross Electric, here on the West Slope, has three dozen systems in place. To their credit, Holy Cross is doing a lot with wind power and recently announced they will provide photovoltaic cell incentives. Huge wind farms on Colorado's East Slope are making significant contributions to energy production. The problem with photovoltaic cells, however, seems to be cost.

Randy is angry:

> "When your wife is pregnant do you ask if the kid is going to be cost effective? Pay back is a mindless chant. Fossil fuel burning is stealing from our kids, solar isn't. You don't ask about the cost effectiveness of new SUV or a new couch in the living room."

Randy is right of course. Why should we question an investment that can keep us warm and functioning if the big energy grid fails? Why should we question an investment that will reduce the production of large quantities of greenhouse gases?

The PVs have a long life, about twenty-five years. Amortized over that time period they are cost effective. The government has invested in this technology for space vehicles and highway departments use them, but where are the incentives for homeowners? What are the governments waiting for?

Opposite page: Mt. Kenya, East Africa, 1976.

Left: This is the Diamond Couloir. It is gone now.

Resistance to change is there with automobiles as well. Randy says Colorado drivers on average put about 15,000 miles on their cars each year. A large SUV will use 1,000 gallons of gas to go this distance. A Subaru, which is a very popular car on the West Slope because it combines all wheel drive with good gas mileage, will use approximately 650 gallons to go 15,000 miles and save the driver about $650 a year over a SUV. The Subaru will produce 7,000 fewer pounds of carbon dioxide, the chief greenhouse gas according to the EPA.

There are much better cars than a Subaru. The Toyota electric Prius or the VW Jetta diesel only use about 300 gallons of gas in 15,000 miles. This will save the owner $1,000 in fuel costs and keep 14,000 pounds of CO2 out of the air.

Above: Glacier Bay, Alaska, 1997. The ice has retreated almost sixty miles in 200 years.

What about global warming? As I sit here in Gypsum, freezing in the coldest, snowiest January and February I can remember, it's easy to forget the last several unusually warm winters. For four years our fruit trees blossomed early and then froze, eliminating any harvest. The problem goes beyond our back yard, however. I'm not a climatologist, but it's obvious to me that bigger changes are taking place.

In 1976 we made a film about climbing a frozen ribbon of ice called the Diamond Couloir on Mt. Kenya in East Africa. The ice has completely disappeared now, and the snow on the top of Kilimanjaro, where I shot a film in 1971, is almost gone too.

In 1997 we filmed a sea kayaking adventure in Glacier Bay on the Alaskan coast. When Captain George Vancouver mapped the area 200 years before our visit, the Bay was a five-mile long inlet blocked off by 300-foot walls of ice. It has retreated almost sixty-five miles since then. Only the Johns Hopkins Glacier at the northern end of the Bay shows any signs of growing.

In 1998 I visited North Peary Land at the northern tip of Greenland. In spite of the fact that we were only 450 miles from the North Pole I filmed thriving populations of weasels, fox, musk ox, and various birds, flowers, and grasses.

In 2000 I was filming in Bolivia. My mountain guide friend Jose Carmalingi and I rolled out of our sleeping bags at dawn after a late night drive from La Paz to the Desaguadero River to gaze on Sajama, the highest peak in Bolivia. It looked like a melting ice cream cone on a hot summer day. Jose was sad. He told me the glaciers are disappearing all through the Andes.

Johns Hopkins Glacier—the only glacier I have heard of that is still growing.

I suppose all this could simply be a natural cycle similar to other periods between ice ages, but given the amounts of CO_2 and other gases that have been created in huge quantities since the start of the industrial revolution, I am inclined to believe we are responsible for global warming and that it's only going to get worse.

Randy paints a picture of short-sighted foolishness but also real solutions. He sympathizes with the tough energy situation President Bush has been handed, but I don't. We still aren't addressing the realities. The Bush Administration says boost the economy: consume, consume, consume! Very few of our politicians have been forthright with the public; they just hope "The Perfect (energy) Storm," as Randy calls it, doesn't occur on their watch. Perhaps those of us who live in western Colorado should try to shut the doors to more drilling until the federal government develops a serious alternative energy policy. Why should we have to pay such a big price in environmental degradation for irresponsible government energy policies? On the other hand, we don't want to freeze to death in the winter darkness.

Randy's observations should be on the front page of every newspaper and magazine in the nation, but I wonder if the public will pay attention. The competition is tough. Car bombs and earthquakes are more immediate and sensational.

The craziness has been going on for a long time. Many years ago an atomic bomb was blown up 7,000 feet under the ground near the town of Rulison. The idea was to set free the gas, but the gas turned out to be radioactive when they tapped into it. The blast shook plates off the shelves in my house in Vail, almost 100 miles away.

Energy companies are also drilling into coalbed methane, a gas trapped in coal beds in some parts of Colorado and other Western states. Large quantities of contaminated water are being pumped out in order to release the gas. The

Top: North Peary Land, 450 miles from the North Pole, 1998. Life abounds: Polar bear (below left) and musk oxen (below right).

question is what to do with the bad water. The Bush Administration has introduced an energy bill that will relax environmental standards and allow the dirty water to be deposited in dry gullies that, unfortunately, occasionally flash flood. These floods will carry the poisons into the Colorado River.

June 24, 2004. *The Citizen Telegram*, Rifle, Colorado: "Members of two groups are suing EnCana (a gas drilling company) to force them to get a permit under the federal Clean Water Act." Toxins from gas wells are seeping into aquifers, poisoning their drinking water.

All of the economically recoverable natural gas under the roadless areas of the White River National Forest would last the nation about fifty-six hours according to the Wilderness Society. This land qualifies for Wilderness Area designation until roads and other manmade structures change its character.

United States Geological Survey data says, "Unrestricted drilling on all federal lands would meet U.S. demand for oil for 222 days and gas demand for 1.7 years." This raises the question: Why isn't the government putting more money and effort into alternative energy sources like wind instead of tearing up pristine federal lands for such a short supply?

My heart is sick, seeing the big gravel pits replacing the riverine environment along the Colorado River, knowing the gravel will be used to build hundreds of miles of roads in the wilderness and pads for the gas wells. Bush and Cheney are oil people, all they see is oil and gas and the natural environment be damned.

McBride and I fly over the Rifle and Harvey Gap reservoirs that are more than half empty, just puddles of their former selves. Ironically we see a couple of lush green desert golf courses nearby. The people of Rifle and Silt have curious priorities.

The highway through the Glenwood Canyon is amazing from the air, an engineering marvel, more proof that the advance of American technology is unstoppable.

Below: Harvey Gap Reservoir is almost dry (left), but the nearby golf course is green (right).

Top left: Gravel pit above Eagle River near Edwards, Colorado.

Top right: Gravel pits and trailer park near Rifle.

Bottom: Wind turbine.

Campfires and Fireplaces

It's ironic that our government is spending millions thinning trees and using controlled burns to help prevent big forest fires, while our county administrators have created regulations to discourage wood-burning fireplaces because of air pollution. There are thousands of rural homes where pollution from wood fires wouldn't be significant and the local citizenry could help with the thinning in return for the firewood.

I don't understand the popularity of gas fireplaces. All they really offer is a clean convenient flame. There is no crackle, no smell, no ashes, no cutting, no splitting, and no carrying wood. They don't provide the same kind or intensity of heat. Each new log in a wood burning fireplace changes the whole arrangement of the fire, the way the flames leap and dance and pop, the way the heat comes blasting out, then quiets down to a steady warm flame until finally another log is needed. The coals in a wood fire glow and throb and turn to ash. The fake stuff in a gas fireplace stays the same. Gas is a finite fossil fuel, wood is renewable resource.

Roger at campfire.

A campfire is different. Cooking is the primary objective, so a small fire between some carefully set rocks works best. Sometimes after the cooking is done I build the fire up just for the heat, but only if there is a lot of wood to spare.

The smoke is usually a problem because the mountain breezes shift around and eventually put the smoke in your face no matter where you sit. It irritates the eyes for a moment. But the smoke also brings the smell that gets in your clothes and ends up going home with you and that's nice. I think pinyon wood has the nicest smell although any burning green pine needles remind me of the incense that is burned in the Himalayas. That's a memory-laden smell. I think of all those expeditions to the Third World, of being tired and hungry and cold which makes the heat warmer and the smells stronger and the food tastier.

The flames of a wood fire are mesmerizing and hypnotic, ever changing yet ever the same. Watching the fire, I discard more accumulated stress into those flames and forget it, than if I drank a case of wine or spent a week in the Caribbean.

Starting a fire on a wet evening in the high country can be tricky. I look for small dry twigs on the underside of a spruce tree and stack them in a pyramid between rocks that keep the wind out. If it's raining or snowing hard I build the fire under a tree and also use my body to shield the twigs until they get going. Then it's a mad scramble to get more dry stuff into the fire until it is underway and strong enough to burn against the moisture. I have failed to get a fire going on a few occasions while hunting elk in a snowstorm. I gave up because it seemed to make more sense to crawl into the sleeping bag in the tent than to get soaked struggling with a fire. It was a miserable night and the morning wasn't much better except for the increasing light. I didn't light a fire in the morning because I wanted to hunt in the first light when the elk are still moving and not bedded down.

Above all, each new fire awakens memories of hundreds of fires in wonderful places all over the world that I have enjoyed in the past.

What's the use of a house if you haven't got a tolerable planet to put it on?

—Henry David Thoreau

Chapter 10

Land Use Issues

MAY, 2000. I KNOW TIME IS RUNNING OUT. So much of what I have come to appreciate in my sixty-five years is gone or going. It is not just nostalgia that eats at me, it is physical loss: the loss of agricultural lands, the loss of natural landscapes big and small; the loss of quiet spaces where the lazy sun warms the aspen trees, the grass, and the soil, and where everything grows and blossoms, goes to sleep and wakes up again with each passing season, always changing but always the same. But now even the hidden places look dusty and trampled, and the clear streams and lakes aren't quite so clear.

There are fewer and fewer signs left of the ancient people. Most of the arrowheads, and even the discarded stone chips, have been picked up. Soon nobody will remember what used to be here, and I will go too and be forgotten. I am unsure about why I have been put on the planet. Everything seems meaningless in the face of the destruction. I resent having to bear witness to ever-increasing subdivisions, SUVs, golf courses, noisy motor bikes and snowmobiles, and all the other inventions that violate the land. It is all so nonfunctional and out of place.

I am part of a society that had created so much wealth and leisure time that it has lost its direction While the good citizens wallow in their excesses, much of the rest of the world is starving at the hands of corrupted governments made up of politicians who have embraced the American model. Most Americans only have the vaguest notion of what is happening beyond our borders. They are not involved; they feel little guilt when a bomb goes off somewhere killing and maiming a dozen or so people, as long as they aren't Americans.

Gypsum

The town of Gypsum sits at the western end of the Eagle River Valley, forty miles from the international ski resort of Vail. It's almost 2,000 feet lower than Vail and considered the banana belt by locals because of its warmer weather. Real estate in and around the town is less expensive than it is in the Upper Valley, and there is substantial amount of affordable housing. It's where much of the Vail and Beaver Creek labor force lives.

The Gypsum Town Council has been pro-growth for many years, anxious to increase its tax base and improve its facilities. A few years ago the town was able to build a big impressive town hall and library building.

Some of the council members are jealous of the affluent Upper Valley towns. They want their share of public access golf courses, shopping malls, and other urban amenities. They give lip service to open space but regularly approve developments that destroy it. Many in the town government see themselves as common folk, the core of what makes America strong. As a singer at a concert during a Gypsum Daze celebration said, "This is where the rubber meets the road." And it does, literally: dirt bikes, snowmobiles, big six-wheel pickups, ATVs, and SUVs sit in many backyards. The dust rises high on the Red Hill Road every weekend and many evenings when the locals go for a spin. Warriors all, the automatic weapons rattle: tat-tat-tat at the same time, giving one the sense of being near a war zone. Some of the seniors who have been in Gypsum all their lives are appalled by the rowdiness and the "growth at any cost" ethic, but they feel powerless to slow it down.

The Airport

A small-plane airport has existed on the edge of Gypsum for years. When the expansion minded principal owner of Vail Associates, George Gillette, looked around for a location for a larger airport in the 1980s, the Gypsum strip looked like the best possibility.

There were problems. First, the Town of Gypsum was too close to the strip. Almost all of Gypsum is in the FAA recommended low population density zone. Second, the flights would have to fly directly over the high school. The first problem couldn't be fixed so it was ignored. In order to solve the second problem the direction of the strip was moved slightly so the planes could miss going over the high school. An environmental impact study was produced but not easy to obtain because all these problems were obvious. Meanwhile the airport developers made deals with the town to stop any complaints except mine. I got letters from the head of the airport commission saying they were enlarging the airport to make it safer for small planes. A few years later the 737s began arriving. Then no night flights were promised in a Gypsum Town Meeting, but a year after that the night flights began. Then the County School Board approved the purchase of land for new schools that is located right under the adjusted flight path. These schools have been built. To add insult to injury, the town of Gypsum has approved high-density, low-cost housing that is right up against the strip, very close to the high impact zone in which high density is not just *not* recommended, it is *prohibited*. That housing has been built.

The airport is a big revenue-producer for the country, as well as a big boost for tourism traffic. It is fast becoming the major regional airport for the central Colorado Rockies. The county commissioners are very proud of the facility. Unfortunately, sooner or later a plane will probably go down, hit some building, and bring about a series of devastating lawsuits because so much of what has been built is marginally legal.

Top: Private jets at the Gypsum Airport.

Bottom: Housing next to the Gypsum Airport landing strips.

Snowmaking at Copper Mountain Ski Resort. This takes water out of the streams when they are at their lowest.

Water Problems

Water is the life-blood of all human activity. We drink it, bathe in it, grow crops with it, catch fish in it, flush away wastes with it, and simply admire it in our rivers and lakes. Without water life cannot exist. Without water in pipes no modern town or city can function. The problem is that much of the West is semi-arid—desert, if you like the word better. Water has always been scarce, but as the human population increases here in the mountains it is clear there simply isn't enough water to go around. This is complicated by old laws that set water up as a moveable property right. The water in the West is not tied to the land. So every entity from the big East Slope cities, such as Denver and Colorado Springs, to Western cities, such as Las Vegas and the mega cities of Los Angeles and Phoenix, are fighting over water originating here in the Rocky Mountains.

There is nothing ethical or morally correct about water laws or the water wars. It's a nasty race where everybody is trying to grab the water and use it before the next guy does. Usually the entity with the most money wins. Rivers and streams, per se, don't have money and can't hire lawyers so they often come out on the short end.

Gypsum is one of many towns in the Eagle River Valley struggling to acquire water rights for housing and commercial development. Their policy seems to be to approve development first and then go find the water to supply the needs of the new folks who move in.

The highest and best use of the water is open to debate. Some water uses, such as keeping golf courses green, are very consumptive considering the

Golf course subdivision in Carbondale, Colorado. An average golf course such as this uses approximately three million gallons of water a day in the summer months. They use about 180 pounds of pesticides a year.

semi-arid climate. There are twelve golf courses in the Eagle River drainage now, and several more are in the planning stages. The Colorado West Slope has close to fifty golf courses. Each course consumes around three million gallons of water a day during the summer months. Evaporation is high due to the short grass. An average of eighteeen pounds of pesticides is used on each acre of each course per year. If a golf course is 100 acres, then it is dumping 180 pounds of pesticides into the the ecosystem every year.

The Vail ski resort needs large amounts of water for snowmaking each fall. This is when stream flows are at a minimum, so the removal of any water can severely impact the ecology of the steam and the fish populations. Then folks ask what's gone wrong with the fishing, but it isn't hard to figure out when you add up all the different impacts.

Shenanigans abound in the water wars. Take Gypsum, for instance. Several years back the town annexed the Albertson Ranch at the south end of the Gypsum Creek Valley in order to obtain the ranch's senior water rights. They used the BLM land to get around sensible requirements that land be adjacent to the town in order to be annexed, claiming the road and federal land are adjacent to both. The result will be islands of development surrounded by rural agricultural land. The subdivisions and the golf courses that are planned threaten the water supplies of those of us who get our water from springs tributary to Gypsum Creek, and they threaten the quality of the water in Gypsum Creek, all the way to town and the confluence with the Eagle River.

Gypsum Creek flows out of the Red Table Mountains south of Gypsum several miles to the Eagle River on the north side of town. One of the development plans for the Albertson Ranch involves putting a water treatment plant next to the proposed subdivision and using the water that is flushed out of the treatment plant to satisfy the minimum stream flow requirements on Gypsum Creek below that point. This means the water in the creek through the valley will end up being little more than treated sewer water, or worse, there could be almost no water in the creek if the minimum stream flow requirements are not enforced. The Colorado

Department of Wildlife is politically controlled at the highest levels and is sometimes reluctant to insist on enforcement of a law that puts fish before people.

There has been a history of water problems in the valley. In the late 1970s the Upper Eagle Valley Water and Sanitation District managers convinced ranchers to let them spread sewer sludge on their hay meadows. The sanitation folks didn't know what they were doing and spread it several inches thick, some on fields less than fifty yards above the edge of the creek where my spring is located. I noticed the smell all the way up to my house a mile away but couldn't determine what it was until one of the water engineers called suggesting I check my spring for contamination. There was deadly *E. coli* bacteria in the water. I got pretty upset and started a loud and bitter protest which ended with the resignation of the sanitation district manager. They stopped putting down the waste material in the fields and I rebuilt my spring. It tested free of the *E. coli* about a year after that.

Ned Goldsmith is an rancher who owns a big chunk of the middle of the Gypsum Creek Valley and some of the oldest water rights in the area as well as the use of Lede Reservoir at the head of Gypsum Creek. The town of Gypsum, tired of negotiating with Ned, is trying to condemn Lede so it can be used to store water for the town. In the process the town hopes to pick up some of Ned's water rights under the "use it or lose it" principle of Western water law. But some of the water the town of Gypsum hopes to gain in the takeover process may already be lost to the neighboring town of Eagle. The Antoine's Cabin Creek ditch, one of the major sources of water for the Lede, has been leaking for years, possibly into the Brush Creek drainage, the town of Eagle's water supply.

Ned is fighting for his rights but it's not easy. It's hard to say how all these issues will be resolved. Water battles are esoteric legal matters, fought in the courts, and far too complicated for most of the public to understand. Generally, however, water flows uphill to money, and the town governments have more money than most of the ranchers.

Dancing Paper Water and the Reservoir Two-Step

Accumulations of water from rain and winter snowpacks vary greatly from year to year in the Rocky Mountains, so no one can predict exactly how much water is going to be available in the Colorado River Basin ahead of time. Recognizing this problem the legislators long ago set up a priority system of allocation—"first in time is first in right." The oldest rights holders take their share of the water first and others follow. Theoretically anyone can claim water in any stream or river in the West, but those with junior rights seldom, if ever, are able to take any water out. Many of the later claims are for spring flood waters that need to be captured in reservoirs.

This situation is complicated by other water users that are downstream from Colorado, Wyoming, New Mexico, and Utah. The lower basin states; Arizona, Nevada, and California, as well as Mexico, also require their legal share of the Colorado River water. This forces the State of Colorado to let much of the river water go beyond its borders. In recent years none of the Colorado River water has reached the sea of Cortez. It all gets used along the way.

The problem comes when municipalities approve developments that may have adequate water rights in a good year but not in a drought. The cities and counties make decisions according to water rights that seem to be adequate on paper but don't necessarily exist as water in the river system during dry years. This shortfall often isn't discovered until a subdivision is built out and the full water demand is in place. This may take several years.

This is when the water engineers and lawyers get creative. They have several options. Some are devious, such as creating bogus water claims on paper that probably can never be economically diverted into use. In my opinion, Gypsum's Eye Lake claim is one of these, a bargaining chip that the Town of Gypsum has developed to use in a trade, or as justification for condemnation, whatever gives them the best chance for getting additional water. I have walked the Eye Lake claim area (Eye Lake doesn't exist). Other than a tributary of Red Creek, which is spoken for, there is not enough water to fill much more than a big bathtub most of the time as far as I can see.

Another way for a town to get water is to buy it from existing reservoirs. For instance, Gypsum buys water located in Green Mountain Reservoir on the upper Colorado River that can be released to users west of Gypsum when needed to satisfy senior downstream rights (like the Shoshone Power Plant or the city of Glenwood Springs). This allows Gypsum to take more water out of the Eagle River, which joins the Colorado west of Gypsum. Unfortunately, when enough municipalities and other users (like Vail Resorts snowmaking operations) pull water out of the Eagle the flows in some sections of the river drop below the minimum required to support aquatic life.

All this juggling gives the temporary illusion, on paper, of having enough domestic water, but it's clearly marginal in terms of actual water and subject to delivery failure, particularly if the present drought conditions continue. Gypsum has been under water use restrictions off and on for several years now, but still they keep approving new subdivisions. There are approximately 18,000 approved (but not built) dwelling units in Eagle Country as of this writing. When built, these buildings will almost double the total number of units in the county. It's very hard to see where the water will come from to supply twice the population in Eagle County even if the Eagle River is sucked dry at certain times of the year.

The underlying problem is that all the water in the Colorado River is spoken for. It is perhaps the most used (overused) river in the world. Any new use is going to affect another use somewhere else. The river itself suffers the most.

Community Activities

There is also a lot to admire about the town. The Gypsum Lutheran Church, for instance, consistently demonstrates a generous community spirit, gathering donations for families with serious illnesses and other misfortunes. It seems like Pastor Jeff and his wife Laurie were always helping folks who are down on their luck for one reason or another. When Anne Helene and the kids come home from Sunday services, she is invariably uplifted and happy.

There are no chain stores in Gypsum, just small businesses. It's nice to be able to talk with the owners and know that they are involved members of the community.

There are excellent sports programs for kids. Our son, Christian, plays hockey in a new indoor ice arena and could join a dozen other activities if he had time.

Mesa Verde, one of the first Colorado housing developments.

Conservation Easements

The local citizens have not stood by to watch every piece of beautiful private land be developed in Eagle County. Brush Creek (now Sylvan Lake State Park) and the Bair Ranch are two notable land preservation success stories. Over 6,000 acres have been permanently preserved in their natural state. Briefly, the history is as follows.

Fred Kummer, a hospital and hotel developer from Saint Louis, purchased big chunks of land along East and West Brush Creek, south of the town of Eagle, back in the late 1960s and early 1970s. His plan was to build a ski resort similar to Beaver Creek on Adam's Rib Mountain. He planned several golf course subdivisions for the valley areas.

Fred is not known for his diplomacy or sensitivity to environmental issues. I remember several public meetings where he managed to alienate almost everyone. He said things like, "People only come to these mountain towns to shop in those fancy little boutiques." Or he would tell Bill Heicher, the District Wildlife Manager for the State of Colorado and whose job it was to manage wildlife on private as well as public land, "Keep your ass off my land."

When a representative from the Environmental Protection Agency came to review the Adam's Rib Ski Resort plans, Bob Young, the Adam's Rib manager, told her they planned to cut a huge notch through the several hundred foot high "Rib" moraine in order to join the village with the ski hill. It involved moving thousands of tons of earth. In disbelief the EPA rep blurted out, "You have to be shitting me." Finally, Forest Service District Ranger Ann Heibner, in Eagle at the time, told Fred he had a terrible project that was environmentally insensitive and would never get approved. Fred took her on her word and started making plans for trophy home subdivisions. Meanwhile various citizens groups, state agencies, and land trust organizations raised funds to buy 1,782 acres from Kummer. The price was high, fourteen million dollars, but when you drive the East and West Brush Creek roads you can see it's worth every nickel.

Dropping into Old Telluride.

The Bair Ranch sits largely inside the Glenwood Canyon. The rugged terrain is more suitable for sheep than cattle. Less than 200 acres is irrigated pasture. Craig Bair has been pursuing the conservation easement idea for several years. He sees it as a way to stay in the ranching business in hard times when many ranchers are giving up. The Eagle Valley Land Trust has been the lead group in this effort, fighting a major political battle with pro and con factions in the county arguing about whether or not county tax money should be used to preserve land that is private and has almost no public access. The preservationists have prevailed however. As with Sylvan Lake, State Park money has come from several sources: federal, state, and private.

Brush Creek and the Bair Ranch are western Eagle County preservation projects. A whole set of different but equally complex problems and needs face the towns on the east side of the county.

Beaver Creek, Cordillera, and Bachelor Gulch

One of our biggest problems here in Colorado, particularly in the mountains, is not poverty but wealth. Our ranches are being consumed by trophy home subdivisions. These are primarily second homes; big, energy inefficient, and socially exclusive to the point where they are not functioning parts of communities but escapes and entertainment centers for very wealthy people who may use them for only a few weeks a year. An average "casshole," as John McBride calls them, is about 10,000 square feet and has a market price of between one and two million dollars, but some houses have over 30,000 square feet of living space and eighteen million dollar price tags. Bachelor Gulch vacant lots go for one million dollars an acre. The

Top left: Beaver Creek, 1989.

Top right: Beaver Creek, 2003, built out.

Bottom left: Beaver Creek trophy homes.

Bottom right: Ridgetop condos at Bachelor Gulch.

owners of these monster buildings slip in and out on their private jets with little or no involvement in the town other than paying taxes. Perhaps the most ludicrous example of a trophy home is a 52,000 square foot house in Starwood (Aspen) built by Prince Bandar of Saudi Arabia. It has a complete British pub inside that doubles as a bomb shelter.

As Samuel Johnson said a long time ago about another form of wealth in British society, they are "ostentatious displays of conspicuous expenditure." These palaces accomplish few of the objectives of community living, and they waste incredible amounts of fuel. They are heated while empty and most have gas fireplaces as well as heated outdoor patios, sidewalks, and driveways. County building codes encourage this.

Beaver Creek, Cordillera, and Bachelor Gulch are classic examples of these recreational communities. No one who works there can afford to live there. It is a self imposed prison, automobile dependent, empty and lonely in the off seasons, without the laughter of children much of the time. Nor is there the diversity of jobs and incomes that gives normal towns much of their character. The condition can be compared to the feudal systems of the Middle Ages where lords were taken care of by vassals. A small army of Mexican immigrants drive up the mountain roads every day to clean up and then return home to their trailer parks at night. It is the opposite of Vail and Aspen in the 1960s and early 1970s when people of all walks of life lived and played together, and the primary motivation for being there was the fun of skiing and hiking in the mountains; not exclusivity, isolation, and the desire to make an impression.

Over seventy percent of the residences around Vail fall into the vacation home category.

John McBride and the North Forty

I first met John McBride in the early 1960s. He was living in Vail with his lovely bride Laurie, and their baby boy John. They built a *gemütlich* little house on Gore Creek in East Vail where my family and I attended occasional cookouts. John is from Chicago, a graduate of Princeton University and from an old midwestern family. His father never quite believed that John would stay in the West, and he used to ask him when he was coming back to Chicago to get a real job. This was not an unusual story. There were many sons and daughters of middle- and upper-class families and what we called "trust funders" coming out to the Colorado resorts in those years. But John didn't receive financial help from home. He had to make it on his own.

John got a job in investment banking in Chicago when he was right out of college but didn't like the work, so he got a job with Owens Corning that stationed him in Denver. From here, he found his way to Vail and his first independent venture which was a commercial building on Bridge Street. He had to contact dozens of banks before he found one willing to loan him the money to build what is now the well known Clock Tower Building. Like me, he occasionally shot wild game, ducks in his case, to help feed his family when things were tight.

John worked with me on a few of our early ski films. He had a creative mind and showed good promise as a filmmaker but soon realized there was very little

John McBride at the North Forty.

money to be made shooting promotional shows, and he had a family to support, so that didn't work out.

Bill Janss, a high minded developer who has left his mark on many ski resorts, hired John to work with him in developing a new ski resort called Snowmass not far from Aspen, so John moved his family to Aspen and settled down there. This is when he started the Aspen Business Center. John was a member of the 1961 National Hockey Team and has never lost interest in the sport. He found a way to get back onto the ice by developing and coaching in the Aspen junior hockey program.

In 1980 the McBrides purchased a 2,000-acre ranch near Old Snowmass where he and his family built their home. Friends said they "lost their marbles," selling valuable land in Aspen to buy a ranch several miles outside of town. As a result, the McBrides decided to call the ranch "Lost Marbles." John probably wouldn't say it if you asked him, but the ranch land is sacred to him, as is the old way of life it represents.

John and Laurie have been active in the Aspen community right from the beginning. One of their main interests has centered around creating forums that bring more important issues to the attention of the locals and VIPs that live in the town. This has developed into The State of the World Conference, which addresses issues in the state of Colorado, the nation, and the world.

The 1960s and 1970s were wonderful years in the Colorado ski resorts. Three basic kinds of people mixed together: the old timers, the new pioneers, and the visitors. The old timers had mixed feelings about what was going on, but it was exciting for them and not threatening. Many of the cowboys got winter jobs at the resorts, as lift operators or policemen or snowcat drivers, among other things. The new pioneers came in all shapes and sizes and levels of financial backing, but they were single minded in their enthusiasm for skiing and the lifestyle that came with it. The visitors usually made friends with the locals and, I think, felt like they were a part of an extended community. Many bought condominiums or built small second homes, but their primary lives were back in cities like Chicago, Cincinnati, and Denver. IBM's Tom Watson had a modest condo in Vail that he and his family used frequently. Irma and Fred Lazarus from the Sears Roebuck empire had a small house on Mill Creek Circle. Fred was a gourmet cook and used to bum a hunk of venison off me every winter when he arrived in town. These people had no thought of impressing anyone with their wealth, in fact just the opposite, they enjoyed anonymity. Their concern was simply to be happy and comfortable in the snow country with their families and friends.

As the resorts grew, however, they became more impersonal, and a new kind of high-powered second-homeowner arrived—a person with money who liked to show it off. Unfortunately these folks have driven the real estate costs out of sight. Aspen, like Vail, has priced itself out of existence as a viable community. The people who work there can't afford to live there.

Meanwhile, something interesting was happening at the Aspen Business Center. It was taking on the characteristics that Aspen was losing; it was becoming a community of like minded small business people with common goals. All that was lacking was enough reasonably priced housing. That's when John got the idea for the North Forty.

I ran into John in Glenwood Springs on a warm sunny afternoon. We both had time on our hands, so we walked the back streets where the small older homes are. There was a good feeling: friendly, intimate, unpretentious. John told me about a piece land he had next to the Aspen Business Center. "I want to build something like this in Aspen," he said. And sure enough he did—the North Forty.

Several things make the North Forty work:

- The lots are reasonably priced.
- The buyer and his architect design the house the way they want as long as it meets certain parameters that give the development its mountain mining town character. Pitkin County has cooperated by setting up guidelines and restrictions that screen out second home buyers and speculators.
- The buyer has to prove he is a permanent resident.
- The value of the home can only increase (for resale purposes) four percent a year.

The lots in the North Forty sold out quickly.

The North Forty is a walking village inspired by what John observed in European resort towns like Zermatt, Klosters, St. Antoine, and Lech. All of the homes in the North Forty are within a quarter-mile of each other and a bus stop. There is also a small grocery store, a bank, a daycare center, a liquor store, and a restaurant–bar within walking distance. Pete Siebert has this same vision for Vail and the old town is still this way, but urban sprawl up and down the valley hides the fact.

John points to three things that are making the North Forty a success: the creative energy of the residents, their cooperation with each other (they often barter building services like painting and plumbing), and the roots they put down. They are there to stay. Walking around in the North Forty everyone greets John and many strike up conversations. It reminds me of early Vail.

John introduces me to an older gal, Elli, who is thinking of selling her home in Starwood, a trophy home development on a hillside above Aspen, to move to the North Forty. Her reasoning is simple, "I want neighbors who are there that I can talk to and ask for help if I need it, and if they have children all the better." She is lonely.

In 1971 Safeway approached John about putting a 30,000-square-foot supermarket in the Aspen Business Center. The town of Aspen got wind of the idea and decided they were against having supermarket that far out of town. So John made an agreement with the city and the county governing boards. He wouldn't allow Safeway into his development if the town and county wouldn't let it happen elsewhere in the county. This is the main reason why there aren't any Big Boxes in Aspen today, and why a lot of little businesses aren't threatened.

Pitkin County continues to resist pressures to overdevelop. They recently passed an ordinance limiting new residential home size to a maximum of 5,750 square feet. It's possible to get an exception to this limitation through a TDR (transferred development right) that prohibits development on another parcel of land, usually thirty-five acres in size. The intent of this option is to encourage clustered growth near the resort centers and open space elsewhere.

McBride would like to go even further introducing a two percent county real estate transfer tax where the money would be earmarked for the purchase of open space.

Main Street vs. Strip City

I guess you know when you've arrived because the big boys begin to notice you. At first it was just MacDonald's, Safeway, and City Market, but then the heavy hitters noticed the demographics. The Eagle River Valley had one of the fastest growing populations in the nation and a lot of wealthy important folks as well. Vail had prestige. That's when Wal-Mart decided to put their big store in and Home Depot followed.

Vail was little more than a sheep pasture in 1962 when Pete Siebert and his friends started to build the ski lifts and the town. There were a few small old towns like Minturn (a railroad stop) and the mining towns of Red Cliff and Gilman. Going west, the next serious town is Eagle, the county seat. Gypsum is seven miles west of Eagle. Both were farming and ranching communities then and are mostly bedroom communities now. There were other whistlestops: Wolcott, Avon, etc., but these weren't towns.

Then Bud Palmer and his friends conceived a big golf course subdivision called Eagle Vail. It was successful and inspired more of the same. Singletree,

Home Depot and Wal-Mart at Avon, Colorado.

Arrowhead, and Cordillera built similar golf course housing developments. I remember Bud Palmer describing to me how the elk and deer would continue to graze in his idealistic mountain paradise and how the trout would thrive in the ponds. He was right, but they had to drive out the elk because they were destroying the golf course.

Next came Beaver Creek, which was going to be an Olympic Village before State Representative Dick Lamm led a successful effort to stop the Olympics from coming to Colorado. It was put to a vote and the people of Colorado, agreed with Dick that the Olympics would encourage irresponsible development, so they voted it out. These same people elected Lamm as Governor of Colorado for three terms before he retired.

Beaver Creek eventually was built but at a slower pace and more carefully. Concessions were made to the state government in regard to parking and other environmental issues. At the opening of the resort Governor Lamm, speaking along with Gerry Ford, called Beaver Creek the Cadillac, not the Ford, of ski resorts.

I asked Dick how he felt at the time and he said, "We didn't want more ski resorts along the I-70 corridor (between Denver and Eagle), but we were powerless to stop them."

By the mid-1980s Avon had grown into a good-sized base town for Beaver Creek and by the early 1990s all the little towns in the area grew together into a single strip city. There is still an undeveloped break between Wolcott and Eagle but it doesn't look like it will last long. On winter weekends I-70 gets completely clogged up with cars going to and from the ski resorts, forcing people to wait for hours in traffic jams. It's become so bad that a huge expensive monorail has been considered to move people between Denver and Vail and beyond.

EVERYTHING
STORE
Eagle
PHARMACY
EAGLE DRUG
TO NEARLY
EVERYTHING
IN 100 YEARS

Eagle Pharmacy vs. Wal-Mart

Opposite page: Broadway in Eagle, Colorado; 1918 (top) and 2004 (bottom).

The Hoza family moved from Colorado Springs to Eagle in the 1966. Al Hoza was working for Walgreens at the time and knew the drugstore business, so when he decided to leave that company and move to the mountains he looked for a small town drugstore that he could purchase. The Eagle Pharmacy turned out to be the perfect opportunity. One of the reasons for coming to Eagle was to become part of a small town community. The Hozas were not looking to make millions. On the other hand Al and Mary had eleven kids to feed, so they had to operate a reasonably successful business.

Vail was just opening up at that point and no one had any idea how successful it would be. The Hozas thought Vail might impact their business slightly but they didn't count on it.

When I walk into the Eagle Pharmacy I see familiar faces, the same faces I have been seeing in the store for twenty-five years, both employees and customers. When there is time we chat. I am forever embarrassed by the people I run into in the store whose names I have forgotten.

Al's health is poor these days so his daughter Annie Colby manages the store most of the time. Al believes in satisfying his customers, "Whatever someone wants we will get," he says. The sign in front of the store reads, "EAGLE PHARMACY, THE NEARLY EVERYTHING STORE." It comes close to filling the promise most of the time.

Big Boxes are not only cut-rate merchandisers, they are cut-throat competitors. When City Market went into Eagle they added an additional seventeen percent to the floor space and told the Hozas they did it just to be sure they would have the merchandise space to put Beasley's Market out of business. Of course this also was an implied threat to the Pharmacy. The Beasley family has been in Eagle for decades and were active members of the community. The money that the Hozas earn and Beasley earned (his store is gone now) stays in town for the most part. It isn't transferred to some distant corporate headquarters.

But there are bigger boxes than City Market. Wal-Mart opened a store in Avon that proved to be too small so they built a Super Wal-Mart nearby. It has 187,300 square feet of floor space. Avon also looked good to Home Depot. They built a store with 163,000 square feet of floor space. The new Avon Wal-Mart is carrying groceries and is hoping to take away City Market's business. What goes around comes around.

To get a sense of how big the Avon Wal-Mart and Home Depot are, I asked John McBride to give me the statistics on the Aspen Business Center that he started developing in 1969 and that is built out now. It has 292,000 square feet of floor space, 181 businesses, and 100 residences. Some of the businesses are quite large like Obermeyer Sports, a ski clothing manufacturer. Yet it is still 58,300 square feet smaller than the combined floor space of the Avon Wal-Mart and Home Depot stores.

The Hozas started out with 3,000 square feet and enlarged the store to 9,000 square feet in 1985. It's hard to get lost in there.

Wal-Mart drove a hard bargain with the town of Avon when they negotiated a contract. Avon agreed to defer the sales tax that should have been paid for twenty years at which time it comes up for negotiation again.

Why the town of Avon was so anxious to get the big Wal-Mart and Home Depot stores into town is a mystery to me. They willingly gutted much of the rest of the business communities up and down the Eagle River Valley. I guess the decision makers were romanced by money and power and the idea that "if you can't stop 'em join 'em."

The money I would spend driving to the Avon or Glenwood Springs Wal-Mart from Gypsum could never be made up with savings on merchandise, but developers want to put a Target or a similar Big Box in Eagle. I hope they don't count on my business. Making a purchase at the Eagle Pharmacy is the same as making an investment in the Eagle community. I like that.

Time Magazine, November 3, 2003, in the "Numbers" column, below a picture of a Wal-Wart sign with an American flag flying next to it reads, "Three hundred undocumented workers rounded up by federal officials during Operation Rollback at sixty-one Wal-Mart stores in twenty-one states. Two dollars daily the wage earned by the lowest paid of these janitors, illegal immigrants from Eastern Europe, Central America, and Asia."

June 22, 2004: 1.6 million women file a class action suit against Wal-Mart for sexual discrimination.

When I came to Vail in 1961 it was little more than the dream in the minds of a few people who wanted to build a ski resort, but there were numerous other functional towns in the nearby mountain valleys: Minturn, Eagle, Gypsum, Glenwood Springs, Carbondale, Aspen, Rifle, Leadville, and Grand Junction, to mention a few. Small, locally-owned businesses were operating along the main streets of these centers. The business owners were involved in some way or other in all of the community activities. In effect they were the community, but many of them have disappeared as chains and corporations have taken over and ownership has become less and less local. The implications of these changes bear careful examination.

Community

One of the biggest problems small communities face is in determining who the enemy really is. Small communities are constantly assaulted by proponents of growth. "Grow or die" is the battle cry. This opens the door to developers, who often are more interested in personal profit than the best interests of the community.

Many of the negative impacts of growth could be avoided if the citizens had a clear picture of what they want their community to be like. Some kinds of growth can obviously be beneficial, particularly if the growth is carefully designed from a holistic view.

Marty Strange, in his book *Whittler's Songs*, makes some important points. He is referring to small farming communities, but these ideas apply to our small, and not so small, Rocky Mountain communities as well.

Strange talks about that time when America was first settled and the European population was relatively small. Seemingly endless unused land stretched westward from the East Coast, and abundant natural resources like timber, minerals, and water were there for the taking. All one had to do was to push aside the native tribes, work diligently, and supply ever growing communities and markets

with whatever products they required. As time went on we learned how to mass produce things like nails, tools, wagons, and eventually automobiles. Growth was only good. Life became more and more comfortable.

Wolcott, Colorado, 1985. The barn is still here, but now it is surrounded by a golf course.

Strange observes:

> "We once practiced a blind faith that efficiency could and should be improved by increasing inputs in order to more than proportionally increase outputs. This idea was based on a world where both inputs and markets for outputs was inexhaustible. That world is gone."

Unfortunately the earth and its resources are finite. Now, 200 and some years after our nation's independence, we are running out of both space and natural resources. And we are not alone. It's a worldwide problem.

How does this situation manifest itself here in the Rocky Mountains? Obviously open space in our valleys is getting rapidly filled in. Yet developers are building like there is no tomorrow. It causes one to wonder when the second home markets will dry up because the real value of the product, a beautiful essentially rural environment, is turning urban? How can we continue to produce giant energy-inefficient second homes that wastefully consume a limited supply of natural gas? Does anyone make the connection between the Iraq War and and our energy consumption, our SUVs, and the dozens of other fuel-eaters we want but don't need?

Mountain village, New Mexico.

Strange goes on to say, ". . . we need to start taking a fuller accounting of these input costs . . . social costs can no longer be discounted even if markets are unable to price them."

There are numerous examples of problems that occur in a rapidly growing economy; pollution, congestion, increasing crime, etc., but for the moment let's just look at productive farm land. How do we put a value on and protect agricultural land when it is not needed to grow crops now but will be in future years?

Strange then addresses what is now called a holistic view. "It is easier to figure out how to do one thing best than it is to figure out how to do many things well. But there may be more efficiency in doing many things well than in doing one thing best." A small farm comes to mind here where the farmer is a carpenter, mechanic, driver, veterinarian, dad, boss, and as my father used to say, "chief cook and bottle washer." On a small farm everything is used: animals eat garden waste products and produce wastes of their own that go back into the soil that grows the garden that feeds us and the animals. We have a ranching system in the Rocky Mountains that makes very good use of the productivity of our federal lands, but it is being lost because the other half of the system, the fertile valleys, is being buried in subdivisions. We eat cattle shipped hundreds of miles, at great cost, to a slaughterhouse on the plains, when they could be butchered here if we had a packing house.

There are lessons here. A holistic view would give us incentives to save ranching and to save open space, but a false efficiency gets in the way. This efficiency is short term because it relies on cheap transportation costs which may soon end. Grapes from Chile, cheese from Switzerland, coffee from Columbia, etc., may become prohibitively expensive here in The United States.

This brings up another problem—"short term thinking." Let's take "sustainability" as an antonym for "short term thinking."

Strange says, " 'Sustainable' is a goal not a technology." And here he has an observation that gets at the core of a problem we have in the Rocky Mountains where our towns are becoming less and less connected to the use of the land and the resources the land offers.

> "The call for sustainability can be used by elitist environmentalists to deny the poor their opportunity to develop, and the call for development can be used by vested interests to deny their duty to future generations. Neither of these half loaves is good enough. The challenge is to pursue development strategies that are sustainable."

Strange goes on to say that this requires far more than technical choices. It involves moral judgments and political decisions, that it is "a messy, sweaty, ambiguous process, but that in a democracy at least we are joined by both brain and heart in the challenge of selecting our own course."

So many folks in Colorado are in the construction and real estate industries. They depend on growth and are reluctant to embrace anything that challenges growth, but they know that overdevelopment is threatening their reasons for living in the mountains.

Housing developments place demands on limited resources such as water, but you almost never hear anyone suggest that water should be used as a tool to control growth. In fact all the water here in the mountains was spoken for long ago. There isn't any water left; the Colorado River no longer reaches the sea. As a result, many people are uneasy but they seldom take a firm stand, and the powerful economic forces usually get their way. They find the water somewhere, usually from an already depleted source.

Strange turns the screw again when he quotes Norris Alfred, a home-grown philosopher from Polk, Nebraska:

> "That is what community means, common concerns, a reinforcement that provides form and substance for individual initiative. Community is inspired by our gregariousness which, in a psychological sense, means we are more content being together. We also feel more secure in a perceived hostile world. That perception is generated by competitiveness which, stripped of its disguise as a blessing in the marketplace, is the antithesis of contentment."

So how do we reconcile competition and contentment, growth and sustainability? Can they be reconciled or are we fooling ourselves? These are the questions everyone is afraid to answer.

The following observations and "rules," if you care to call them that, come from the agrarian philosopher Wendell Berry, and I have tailored them to fit the Rocky Mountain region. The principles he lays out are painfully obvious and neglected by our current society. It's like reading about another time on another planet. Berry speaks of the demise of the family farm, but it is much more than that. We are experiencing a "post small community world where boundless sprawl is homogenizing our towns." It is evidenced by malls, Big Boxes like Wal-Mart and Home Depot, massive subdivisions that are completely automobile dependent, and congested freeways. One would think this condition is only applicable to large cities but it is just as evident in our mountains along I-70 between Dillon and Rifle, between Aspen and Glenwood Springs, and it travels south from Grand Junction to Ridgeway.

To quote Berry,

> "We are now pretty obviously facing the possibility of a world that the supranational corporations, and the government and educational systems that serve them, will control entirely for their own enrichment—and, incidentally and inescapably, for the impoverishment of all of the rest of us. This will be a world in which cultures that preserve nature and rural life will simply be disallowed. It will be, as our experience already suggests, a post agricultural world. But as we now begin to see, you cannot have a post agricultural world that is also not post democratic, post religious, post natural—in other words, it will be post human, contrary to the best that we have meant by 'humanity.' "

I have observed this same phenomenon, this giant cancer as I see it, in many places in the Third World. Large cities in Asia and South America give the impression of success and wealth, but you don't have to travel very far to find the impoverished people who feed these monster cities but don't benefit from them. Globalization is a political rip off so far, governed primarily by graft and corruption. The rich get rich and the poor get poorer. Of course the country folks don't have a very loud voice and you don't hear much, at least not until the situation slips off the deep end and you get an Afghanistan.

American corporations have a legal mandate to consider social welfare but no one seems to enforce this part of corporate law. When corporations are doing well they can afford to be enlightened and altruistic, and many try, but what happens when things go wrong and the value of the stock drops? Will the stockholders allow enlightened management to continue exercising their social conscience at this point? Isn't the bottom line then going to be the determining factor?

Here are some of Wendell Berry's suggestions tailored to the Rocky Mountains.

1. Ask what proposed changes or innovations will do for the community? How will this affect common wealth? What do big boxes do for the community?
2. Include Nature—the land, the water, the air, the native creatures—within the membership of the community.

   Demands for water in Colorado are pulling many mountain streams and rivers below minimum flows, seriously damaging the ecology. Snowmaking at the ski resorts is one of the big culprits but the Department. of Wildlife seems reluctant to exercise its rights. Critical winter habitat for deer and elk is being lost to subdivisions. We give lip service to this problem but seldom let wildlife stand in the way of development.
3. Ask if local needs can be supplied from local resources, including help from neighbors. Develop value adding industries for local products to ensure that

the community does not become a colony of the national or global economy. Small scale industries and businesses can be developed from the local farm and forest economies. Make an effort to increase earnings within the community and decrease expenditures outside the community.

Big Boxes like Wal-Mart, with corporate headquarters hundreds of miles away, do not pump their profits back into the local community. Much of the money leaves town.

We import most if not all of the beef, lamb, potatoes, and other vegetables that could be provided by local sources but aren't for the most part. Our cows and sheep are shipped to distant slaughterhouses and the meat may or may not find its way back.

The Colorado mountain valleys not only produce cattle, but in years past produced large quantities of potatoes, lettuce, and other cool weather crops. The Gypsum Creek Valley, for instance, produced fifty train car loads of potatoes a year. High country lettuce filled demands for that crop when lower elevation lettuce bolted. Other specific crops that do well are rhubarb, asparagus, strawberries, raspberries, and some strains of apples. Of course in Grand Junction, Delta, Montrose, and Paonia most vegetable and fruit crops do well. They even have wineries. But they only supply a small part of what is consumed in western Colorado.

4. Understand the wrongness of the industrial doctrine of "labor saving" if that results in poor work, unemployment, or any kind of pollution or contamination.

   In Colorado we employ large numbers of illegal immigrants to do menial labor at low wages, bringing a good part of the rest of the labor force to a subsistence level .

   A West Slope co-op slaughterhouse would be of great benefit to our ranchers. Sheep ranching could offer the basis for wool product manufacturing, but the dumping of cheap wool into the United States from New Zealand would have to be curtailed. There is room for more wool product industries like sweater manufacturing.

   Tourism was a small scale industry and could be again if semi-monopolies like Vail Resorts were not in control. Small ski areas operated by the towns could offer skiing to those who otherwise cannot afford it. This would eventually generate more skiers in a sport that is growing very slowly, if at all. If condominiums and entertainment center homes are discouraged the hotel business will certainly improve. Hotels use resources far more efficiently since they seldom sit idle the way second homes do.

5. Try to produce as much of the communities' own energy as possible.

   An abundance of cheap firewood (our high forests are plugged with dead wood ready to burn) is available but air pollution problems would have to be addressed and legislation changed to encourage wood burning. Right now wood burning fireplaces are discouraged. People put in gas burning fake fireplaces instead. So a renewable resource has been replaced by a non renewable resource. Hanging laundry outside is also discouraged or forbidden in some towns so people have to use a clothes dryer which runs on gas or electricity. One of my favorite high water kayaking runs is on the

Cloud walkers, north Peary Land, Greenland.

Eagle River through Minturn. Not only is the white-water intense, the laundry is hanging out behind the homes. It feels like I'm in Mexico or Bolivia. Photographers love laundry, it's colorful, personal, and real. Unfortunately some uptight Minturn Town Council members seem to want to keep it out of sight. Occasional early bird sun bathers don't hurt the view behind Minturn either.

Solar and wind energy are obvious answers in our semi-arid Western mountains. I built a solar energy house in Gypsum during President Carter's term, but Reagan removed the incentives when he came into office so the active parts of the system have been hard to maintain. The passive system still works well. I remember asking Jack Marshall, one of the developer/designers of Beaver Creek, if he was going to use solar panels on the buildings. He looked at me like I had a few screws loose.

6. Make sure the community can invest in itself, maintain its properties, keep itself clean (without dirtying some other place), care for its old people, and teach its children. The old and the young should be able to take care of one another. The young learn from the old and not always in school. Institutionalized "child care" and "homes for the aged" should be a last resort. The community maintains its continuity through the association of old and young. The cowboys live by this rule.

7. Take into account hidden hard-to-recognize costs. Debit these costs against monetary income.

   What do we pay for the loss of our rural lifestyles as we urbanize? Do we lose business as we become like those places people are trying to escape?

   Pollution, traffic congestion, increased crime, substance abuse, etc., all those problems associated with rapid growth often are not addressed adequately until it is too late. These problems have increased exponentially in Eagle County in the last few years.

8. Be aware of the economic value of neighborly acts. Cooperate with nearby towns. The costs of living are greatly increased with the loss of neighborhood because people are left to to face their calamities alone.

   Second home communities should be discouraged since they are "neighborless" much of the time.

   Cooperation and exchanges with neighboring towns is happening. For example produce from the Grand Junction and Paonia areas is being sold by small venders throughout the mountains on a seasonal basis, but much more could be done to promote in season dishes at restaurants. Glenwood Springs has a Strawberry Days and Carbondale has a Potato Festival. What about a Silt Asparagus Days or the promotion of Colorado range-fed beef in restaurants? Colorado rancher Mel Coleman has done a excellent job of promoting "natural meat," but that's just a beginning.

It sounds like the enemy is capitalism but it is not. The free market system has worked very well for more than two centuries, but we could and should do much more with anti-trust legislation. It would be nice to stop the process where the big get bigger and the little get lost. People need to understand the real value of small locally owned businesses where the profits stay in town and the owners contribute time and money to making their town a better place to live.

"We find that the spiritual actions we undertake, which are motivated not by narrow self interest but out of our concern for others, actually benefit ourselves. . . . and they make our lives meaningful."

—THE DALAI LAMA

Chapter 11

State of the World

Above: Cowboy wedding in Burns, Colorado: Brooke Schlegel and Josh Fitzsimmons, June 20, 2003.

Below: Indian paintbrush.

Previous spread: La Paz, Bolivia.

Sometimes seemingly unrelated events come together in meaningful ways. Or maybe it's just my age and the fact that everything seems to be interconnected these days.

Son Nick and I filmed Brooke Schlegel for our *Western Ranching: Culture in Crisis* documentary. She was a young teenager then, the apple in her granddaddy Ben's eye: pretty, idealistic, able to talk clearly about the cowgirl life. That was in the early 1990s. Now, ten years later, June 20, 2003, she is entering into marriage with Josh Fitzsimmons. We are invited to the wedding.

Brooke comes from several generations of ranchers. She is the daughter of Jill and Bill Schlegel and granddaughter of Ben and Mildred Wurtsmith. Ben is part of the Gates family who settled in the Burns Hole back before the turn of the last century. Brooke teaches school in Gypsum, as does her Aunt Betsi who is Ben and Mildred's youngest daughter.

Josh is the son of Carol and Corky Fitzsimmons. They are early Vail people who moved down-valley to Gypsum and now live in a cabin on forty acres up Gypsum Creek. Corky was on the Vail ski patrol and later got into other businesses: a garden nursery, firewood, a gas station and laundromat, and log house construction.

Many of the ranchers in Eagle County have worked at other jobs to make ends meet. Ben Wurtsmith was a policeman in Vail for a while, Vern Albertson worked in the mines. Susan Nottingham taught skiing. Bud Gates was a county commissioner. Now any of them could become millionaires by selling their land. Except for the Nottinghams, who made a lot of money selling the land that is now Beaver Creek and Avon, the ranchers are land rich and cash poor. Amazingly they hang onto their land, believing their way of life is more important than a lot of money.

Anne Helene and I leave Gypsum for Derby Mesa around mid-morning. It's a beautiful Colorado blue sky day, a little breezy and not too hot. I can feel the pressures of the urbanized Eagle River Valley peeling away as we turn off I-70 and head north along the Colorado River Road. Every rancher for miles around is at the wedding when we arrive. You would never know from the congeniality and the smiles that some of them are long time adversaries with serious differences over issues like irrigation water rights, past land deals, etc. To those outside the ranching community they appear to be a well knit tribe of cowboys, mostly of one mind.

For me it's like coming home. Everyone looks a little older, but the warmth is still there even though I haven't seen some of them for several years. Once you are accepted by these people you can count on their friendship. We have different views on some land use issues, but they know where I stand and trust me when it comes to trying to protect the cowboy way of life. When they first met Anne Helene I'm sure they wondered what I was doing with such a beautiful woman so much younger than me, but when they found out she came from a farming background in rural Norway they accepted her as well. Her strong-minded Viking ways confirmed that she is a woman to be reckoned with. The cowboy culture is full of strong-minded women, used to hard work and no nonsense. Anne Helene fits right in.

I have decided to video the wedding and we are late, so I go to work immediately. The bride and bridesmaids arrive on a horse-drawn wagon. I am warned that one of the horses pulling the wagon has a colt with her and not to spook the colt or the wedding might turn into a runaway chase over the surrounding fields. As soon as the bride and her entourage leave the wagon I run around to the front of the seated guests to catch the party coming up the aisle.

There is a big, well-dressed fellow with a baseball cap turned backwards on his head, taking stills. It's a while before I realize he is Dayna, Jill's brother. Dayna is a complex man, bachelor, cowboy, bow hunter, and photographer. He came to our house once when we were editing *Western Ranching*, hoping to get involved in filmmaking. I'm afraid we turned him off to the idea and I'm sorry. He is a kind person who deserves only the best treatment. A few years back the tractor he was running rolled over on him and cut him up badly, damaging internal organs. The recovery was long and difficult. He is lucky to be alive. But tractor accidents are not unusual, nor are horse accidents. Ranching is hard, often dangerous work, and it takes a terrible toll on the body. Hips wear out, arthritis is common. Old age is painful, and many of these folks live to very old ages.

I get chatting with Vern Albertson and Susan Nottingham. Vern's uncle, Orris, and father, Joe, have died since we were elk hunting a couple of years ago. Now Vern is the family elder. He has a daughter who is a doctor but no offspring who want to ranch. And he is getting older and tired. He's not sure how much longer he can do the work. Susan feels the same way. Her parents are pushing their eighties. One of her brother's sons shows interest but he is young and untested. She is tired as well. My God, I think, this couple is, or soon will be, in control of almost 30,000 acres of the most beautiful land in the West and they are not sure what they are going to do with it. What a tragedy if it falls into the hands of developers. These are good friends but they have strong negative experiences with environmentalists and little or no faith in those folks who work with land conservation trusts. I don't know what to say, but I know the land should stay in ranching and I feel very passionately about it. We don't need more trophy homes cluttering up the landscape and destroying the functional uses of the land. We will want all the agricultural land we can get someday, and we will want people in our society with the strength of character that is developed doing ranch work.

Interestingly, this wedding is in the middle of the John McBride's State of the World Conference in Aspen. John and more recently his daughter, Kate, have been holding conferences on population and environmental issues for years, trying to give Aspen residents, and anyone else who wants to attend, a broader viewpoint on the big issues facing the world. So I attend the conference on Friday, miss Saturday for the wedding, and come back to the conference on Sunday. As a result my head is being pumped full of issues like global warming, genetic engineering, overpopulation, water and land conservation, etc. before and after the wedding ceremony. The conference seems very far away from the Burns Hole. These cowboys don't know how lucky they are to live in what is surely one of the great secluded paradises left on Earth. Few realize how valuable this piece of the Old West is. I wonder how many speakers would trade their lifestyles for this one if they could? More than a few, I think, if they understood where and what it is.

The Burns Hole is a tangible reality, an example of what the Conference is fighting for. But most of the speakers are caught up in the Washington Beltway view that ranching is bad for the land because of overgrazing. Only Ed Marston, former publisher of *High Country News*, and John McBride, who owns a ranch, seem to fully understand the value of the ranchers and open spaces they protect. They both touch on the subject at the Conference, but it falls on the largely deaf ears of the urban based World Watch folks and their followers. Never mind, they all have their own vitally important axes to grind. A few differences have to be expected.

Many of the lectures sounded like old songs, stuff I have heard before, issues I have given hundreds of hours to over the years. Unfortunately it also all sounds a little late. So much has been lost that I sometimes get the feeling there isn't anything left to save.

David Getches talks about the Colorado water law and the dammed West; past, present, and future. I am reminded of the battle I fought with the Denver Water Board in 1971.

The struggle has never stopped. East Slope cities keep growing and demanding more water from the West Slope. There is seldom any mention of the only realistic solution to the limited water supply, restricting growth. That's too obvious and painful for a people who have always been able to exploit the land. Colorado has had one big land development scheme going on since the Europeans arrived in the mid 1800s. First it was mining, then agriculture, then municipalities. Now the powers in the Colorado Legislature realize they can't suck more water off the top of the Rockies to water the East Slope so they want to put in a huge pipeline that goes all the way from the Utah border to the mega strip city that runs from Fort Collins to Pueblo. It's appropriately called "the Big Straw Project." California, Arizona, and the Nevada haven't said much so far but it's not hard to guess how they feel. Lake Powell is drying up and with it, much of their water supply.

Writer Hal Clifford described how the ski resort business has gone from lifting skiers up mountains to making money on real estate sales and shopping. The big companies like Vail Resorts look at Aspen, Breckenridge, Vail, etc. as big landlocked cruise ships. They try to own all the associated businesses and capture most of the money being spent, but the problem with skiing goes much deeper than that.

The ski industry people have lost sight of the fact that skiing is nothing more than enjoying a ride down a slippery slope on about any device that will slide and hopefully turn. Thousands of dollars in high fashion clothing, sophisticated equipment, luxury lodging, and lift tickets are not essential, just nice to have if you can afford them. But the industry has largely forgotten the low end, the poor folks that still might enjoy the basic joys of the sport. Skiing is now primarily for the rich. A few fifty-vertical-foot hills with rope tows, run by the parks and recreation people in towns that have snow, could go a long way toward revitalizing the sport and more importantly, give skiing to kids who really need it.

I have been sitting between ranchers and ski resorts for forty years. I have come to see them as nurturers and exploiters. Let me quote from the agrarian philosopher Wendell Berry so you can catch my drift. Ranchers are essentially farmers, nurturers of the land and what it produces. Berry compares this way of life to that of a business executive in an exploitative company like Vail Resorts:

> "The exploiter is a specialist, an expert; the nurturer is not, The standard of the exploiter is efficiency, the standard of the nurturer is care. The exploiter's goal is money, profit, the nurturer's goal is health—his land's health, his own, his family's, his community's, his country's. . . . The exploiter thinks in terms of numbers, quantities, 'hard facts'; the nurturer in terms of character, condition, quality, and kind."

Ed Marston talks about the need to get along with the cowboys. He has come a long way since the days when he was editor of the *High Country News* and suggested he might help the cowboys if they would just embrace the land use regulations the federal government and other enviro groups had in mind for them—nit picking regulations that were designed in part to put them out of business. Most of the cowboys I know take good care of their land. They have to since it provides them with their livelihood and has for generations. Of course there are a few bad operators that hurt the other's reputations. That's the same in any business.

But Ed's heart is in the right place. He is an intellectual in a working man's environment struggling with complex issues that no one has the answers for. "A modern de Tocqueville from Brooklyn, living in the West" is the way Stewart Udall describes him.

Mike Dombeck, former head of the BLM and Forest Service under President Clinton, talks about forestry and fire suppression among other things. He says pretty much what we have said in our film *The Forest Wars*. Forests need to managed and can be managed in a way that supplies much of our need for wood products AND beautiful forests as well. I think this can be accomplished fairly easily if the greedy tendencies of the big timber companies can be controlled. They all know how to manage forests but some of the better practices cut into their profits so they ignore them.

It was good to see Steward Udall again. I interviewed him for a documentary about oil shale back in the mid-1970s. The only change I can see is his white hair. His mind and his sensibilities are the same—sharp and true. He is a giant, a worthy leader we all respected and loved during the early days of the environmental movement. I leave the Conference completely uplifted after listening to him.

One of the most interesting doors is opened by Gary Gardner from the World Watch Institute. He speaks about possible alliances between environmental and religious groups, and offers some amazing and disheartening graphs while discussing his

Girl and her cow in Kathmandu, Nepal.

position. There has never been a wider gap between the rich and poor in the world than there is today, for instance. The idea of connecting environmental groups with religious and spiritual organizations gets a very good response from the audience.

For me, the environmental movement has always been a spiritual one. I have only been able to participate because of a love for the natural world. Contrary to some, I believe humans are part of the natural environment and can live in harmony with nature if we learn to behave. Unfortunately that is not the case right now. I have never experienced a more anti-natural environment attitude than exists in the Bush Administration.

Gary does not get into the specifics of what ethical behavior is according to various religious groups, nor does he address in any detail how they handle environmental issues. He has less than an hour for his presentation, and it would take several hours to adequately cover these subjects. But I can take it a bit further here.

The greatest living spiritual leader of our time, in my opinion, is the Dalai Lama who defines religion and spirituality this way:

> "Religion I take to be concerned with faith in the claims to salvation of one faith tradition or another, an aspect of which is acceptance of some form of metaphysical or supernatural reality, including perhaps an idea of heaven or nirvana. Connected to this are dogma, ritual, prayer, and so on. Spirituality I take to be concerned with those qualities of the human spirit, such as love, compassion, patience tolerance, forgiveness, contentment, a sense of responsibility, a sense of harmony—which bring happiness to both self and others."

Using this definition, the Bush Administration's connection to spirituality through the Christian Right is clearly thin or nonexistent. They have decided to prop up the American way of life and standard of living at the expense of the rest of the world. They encourage unlimited material consumption at a time when much of the world is starving and the natural environment is disintegrating at an accelerating, near terminal, rate. They are willing to start unilateral wars to assure a stable and cheap supply of oil. All Americans are created equal, but all humans are obviously not in their view. In effect, they have not only declared war on Iraq but on the Third World and the natural environment as well. And we are becoming the most feared and hated people on the planet in the process.

I don't think this means we have to sink to the level of the Third World's poor, but spending more money on appropriate foreign aid and less on the military would certainly improve international relations. There is also much we can do to help the situation without significantly impacting our basic standard of living. We don't have to embrace SUVs and all those gas-guzzling toys tearing up the fragile federal lands. Even better if we can implement a basic change in attitude that substantially affects our consumption habits and the choice of those jobs we are willing to do.

As the Dalai Lama says, "The problem is not materialism as such. Rather it is underlying assumption that full satisfaction can arise from gratifying the senses alone."

It is also a matter of thoughtfulness and asking the right questions. What are the consequences of my actions? Does my success cause the suffering of others? Am I profiting from something that pollutes the environment?

Above: Sheep herder in the Bolivian Andes.

Below: Callawaya farmer near Charasani, Bolivia.

State of the World Conference organizers Kate and John McBride.

Again, the Dalai Lama:

"We find that the spiritual actions we undertake, which are motivated not by narrow self interest but out of our concern for others, actually benefit ourselves. . . . and they make our lives meaningful."

Fifth State of the World Conference in Aspen, Colorado, July 2004

It's been clear right from the time I started putting this book together and flying around with John McBride to get aerial photographs that he has been more than a little upset with the neo-conservatives of the Bush Administration. What I didn't know was how far he and Kate would be willing to take the State of the World Conference in order to expose failed and failing government policies.

In previous years the State of the World Conference has been mostly concerned with environmental issues, but this year the overwhelming focus is politics. The presentations, delivered by counterterrorism Czar Richard Clark and Ambassador Joe Wilson, go from tough to vitriolic. These men paint a grim picture of where the neo-conservatives are taking the nation. We have squandered lives and resources in Iraq where there has been little if any real threat to our national security, while neglecting much needed security programs here at home. We are, in fact, creating terrorists because of our occupation.

When Ambassador Joe Wilson, who was stationed in Africa, refused to support rumors that Iraq was trying to obtain yellowcake uranium ore from Niger, the vengeful Bush Administration leaked the fact that Wilson's wife was a CIA operative and put her life in serious danger.

Kurt Gottfried, founder of Concerned Scientists, revealed how politicians have been trying to manipulate scientific facts to suit their political agendas. "The Bush people feel they have a right to their own facts," he said. Both Gottfried and Wilson suggested that the Bush Administration was being governed by "creationist" beliefs (a literal interpretation of the Bible), not scientifically based evolutionary theory.

Joe Cirincione, director of non-proliferation efforts for the Carnegie Institute, spelled out the threats posed by unaccounted-for stores of nuclear materials and rogue weapons programs. He said that we invaded the wrong country, that Iran, not Iraq, was well along the road to producing a nuclear bomb. Worse still—Pakistan, which has bombs, is unstable and ripe for a takeover.

Amy Goodman, radio commentator for *Democracy Now*, made a highly-charged, emotional presentation about corporate media takeovers and how independent journalists are being silenced. The government has successfully pressured corporations to tow the ruling party line. "You are with us or against us, and if you are against us you better shut up." The Fox Network has been publicly accused of being a mouthpiece for the neo-conservatives.

Several speakers talked about efforts being made to set aside basic rights set forth in the Constitution. The USA PATRIOT Act is an example. One could conclude from the evidence presented that we are on the brink of a Fascist takeover by the neo-conservatives.

Lester Brown, founder of the World Watch Institute, shifted our thoughts to what he feels will soon be the biggest issue—worldwide hunger. He explained how China and India are quickly becoming bigger consumer nations than the United States and that they are in a position, along with the United States, to strain the world's resources beyond what is sustainable. Global warming will exacerbate this problem, reducing yields of wheat and other crops in many places.

Norwegian Øystein Dahle spoke with inverted optimism saying, "This is good. The situation is so grim people are finally waking up." He called for a fundamental reordering of priorities and pointed out that if we consume less we won't need as much money, so we can work less and enjoy life more.

Øystein Dahle, President of the World Watch Institute.

Dick Lamm pulled a lot of the environmental, social, and political pieces together in an overview that made it clear there isn't much time left. We are well along "the Hubbard Curve" and it's complete chaos on the down side.

All of the State of the World Conferences have had depressing information but none have carried messages as urgent and frightening as this one. A strange kind of comfort comes from sitting in a packed auditorium where everyone is reacting in the same way to one terrible message after another. You get the feeling that with all these brilliant speakers on the warpath the necessary changes will come about. Then, after regurgitating the material for a few days, a cold reality sinks in. The world is indeed broken, as the conference points out, and fixing it may not be possible.

Dick Lamm used to be referred to as "Governor Doom" for laying out painful truths before the public. I think the McBrides have also earned this honor. We got a three-day dose of bitter medicine, but just maybe events like this will fire people up to the point where necessary changes will be made.

The State of the World Conferences are also about the state of the Nation and the state of the State of Colorado. They are wonderful gifts from the McBrides to those of us who care about where we are going. When you look at the Rocky Mountains in the perspectives developed at the conferences you begin to understand how blessed we are and why should protect our remaining farm and ranch lands, save our wilderness areas, conserve our water and our fossil fuel, and develop the solar and wind power that are so abundant here. If we act now, we can assure ourselves of a comfortable future in a pleasing environment. If we don't, we will become victims of our shortsightedness and sink to level of many of the more crowded and impoverished nations of the world.

I hope we have learned a few lessons. The war in Iraq has been a huge mistake and will be a problem for the world for years to come. It may have been a good idea to remove Saddam Hussein from power, but we have had to pay a terrible price in lives and money, and our purpose has not been achieved. We are creating terrorists faster than we are eliminating them.

We cannot solve the world's problems alone. We need to regain the support of the rest of the world if we hope to defeat the terrorists in the long term.

Recreational development is a job not of building roads into lovely country, but building receptivity into the still unlovely human mind."

—Aldo Leopold

Chapter 12

The Adventure Sports

"It would appear, in short, that the rudimentary grades of outdoor recreation consume their resource-base; the higher grades, at least to a degree, create their own satisfactions with little or no attrition of land and life . . ."

—Aldo Leopold

Opposite page: Bill Kerig jumping Vail Pass cliffs.

Previous spread— Kayakers on the Santo Domingo River, Chiapas, Mexico (left) and Doug Ammons, Falls Six, Agua Azul, Mexico (right).

Adventure sports are a significant force in the Rocky Mountain West. The mountain towns are full of climbers, kayakers, bikers, extreme skiers, and the like, people who may work at odd jobs but whose first love is out there doing their "sport" thing. These activities are practiced primarily by kids in their early twenties, the same age I was when I came to the Vail Valley. But the scene is very different now.

I think the evolution of adventure sports is worth examining because it is indicative of the larger problems facing the West. I will recount my own experiences to give historical perspective.

In the mid 1970s we produced a feature film called *The Edge*. It is about a young cinematographer who makes a documentary about six adventure sports: climbing, kayaking, hang gliding, scuba diving, surfing, and extreme skiing. In many ways it marks the beginning of the "extreme sports" movement. John Wilcox, then executive producer for the *ABC American Sportman* television series, sees *The Edge* and begins hiring me to do adventure films all over the world.

Unfortunately *The Edge* is a financial disaster. We are defeated by the Hollywood distribution system. *The Edge* gets excellent reviews and big audiences where it plays, but we have trouble booking the theaters in the bigger cities where we can make serious money.

One booking cancelation in particular is damaging. Even though the Denver based Cooper Highland Theater chain has invested in *The Edge*, they bump us out of their Minneapolis theater on Thanksgiving Day weekend when Warner Brothers threatens to pull *The Last Tycoon* out of all of their theaters if they can't have Minneapolis. We have already purchased the advertising. Thanksgiving is traditionally one of the most profitable moviegoer weeks, and Minneapolis is big sports town. Losing the revenues from that booking breaks us.

Subsequently I try to sell *The Edge* to Disney. They show interest, but ultimately the deal falls through. It is painful knowing we have a commercially viable film, watching it die for reasons beyond our control, reasons that have nothing to do with the quality of the picture. What hurts most of all is losing the investor's money. I don't have any desire to try producing another feature.

Barry and I split up. My marriage is a mess. It seems a whole lot easier to shoot and direct for other people than to move to Los Angeles or New York and become executive producer within the film business establishment. I don't know it at the time, but I have committed myself to a life on location—traveling the world instead of becoming a businessman and possibly becoming financially successful.

It is a time, too, when the lid is being put on the creative energies unleashed in the 1960s. People are disillusioned with the liberal Democrats who seem more supportive of the counterculture than the ordinary working people. Reagan introduces the aphorism, "Government isn't the answer, it's the problem." Corrupted idealism is being replaced by the profit motive. For me this is a clear signal that I will not have the freedom to be whimsical about my film projects.

The powers are going to want their whiskey straight. No more poetic dances on a boundless stage, just straight tourism promotions or death defying adventure documentaries.

The new attitude is clear in Vail where the bottom line becomes far more important than any subjective idealism about the skiing experience. Founder of Vail and 10th Mountain Infantry veteran Pete Seibert has been fired and replaced by a series of business managers and wealthy owners who understand financial matters but not much about the soul of the sport they are selling. Vail is a wonderful mountain and it has survived, but the spirit that was there in the beginning has largely disappeared. Siebert lived pretty much out of sight for several years until he had his autobiography written and printed and briefly became a hero before dying of cancer. The other founder of Vail, country boy Earl Eaton, retires without making a nickel from Vail's success. He lives in Eagle, thirty miles west of Vail and has been even more obscure than Pete. I think the present managers of Vail have been quite happy to ignore much of Vail's early days, because the new "industrial strength resort" stands up so poorly to what Vail was in its first ten years. Adam Aron, the CEO of Vail Resorts hosts a 40th Anniversary party for the old timers, but most of what he talks about in his speech are the plans the Mark Marriot Hotel has for expansion and other matters of financial interest. He can't address the spirit of early Vail because he wasn't there. Paul Testwuide, an early ski patroller turned corporate executive, gets a little tipsy and applauds Vail's rampant no-holds-barred expansion, much to Adam Aron's pleasure, but there are many old timers in the crowd who see it differently.

I continue to do more kayaking television shows: a first descent of the Jatate River in Mexico that was fun because I work out of a kayak and have to run the drops with the experts, a rafting show with adventure travel guru and writer Rich Bangs on Waghi Tua Purari River system in New Guinea, a show on the Grand Canyon of the Stikine in Northern British Columbia, and the first descent of the Zambezi River in Africa. My reputation as an adventure shooter and helicopter cameraman also gets me into directing and shooting national commercials.

I am up to my ears in a process that commercializes adventure.

When I arrive in Vail in 1961 skiing is not only a sport, it is our livelihood. My work is primarily making promotional films for ski related industries. Hunting, trout fishing, and climbing provide off season fun, and a lot of people own horses, but these activities are not businesses, they are recreation.

I introduce my kids to all the sports, and they go on occasional film shooting assignments with me. There is no thought of turning them into sports adventure filmmakers in the beginning. That doesn't happen until the 1980s when they are old enough to starting thinking about a career. By this time I am doing sports adventure films for national television. I'm traveling all over the world doing these shows and taking the boys along every chance I get. They are learning the skills of the trade.

My children go through continuous Outward Bound School experiences: first in the Rocky Mountains, then in mountains, jungles, rivers, oceans, and deserts all over the globe—learning to work and survive in sometimes very difficult conditions.

One of the hardest taskmasters for me, and the boys, proves to be kayaking.

John Paris in Gore Canyon on the Colorado River.

Kayaking

When I start kayaking in 1976 it embodies the same spirit that climbing and skiing did in the 1950s. Everyone is in it primarily for fun. Kayaking has the exploration aspect of climbing and the adrenaline rush you get from a rapid descent through the unknown.

The currents constantly change in a river as the water rises and falls. Some runs have a low water volume and lots of rocks to maneuver through, others are big and powerful with huge waves. Many river canyons can only be explored from the water as the vertical walls prevent hiking. In these situations kayaking becomes a wilderness adventure. On the down side, kayaking can be a cold sport and dangerous if your skills aren't up to the technical difficulty of the river.

After getting a taste of kayaking in the Grand Canyon while shooting *The Edge,* I pursue the sport with a passion. I am forty-two years old at this point, so I know I can never become what we call today an "extreme kayaker," but I get good enough to kayak on some filming expeditions, to have an enormous amount of fun boating the rivers in Colorado, and to introduce my sons to the sport.

Learning a roll is critical. You can't kayak white-water without a roll (a roll is the maneuver you use to get back upright after you have been tipped upside down). It does not come easy to me, I spend hours and hours in the Intermountain Pool in Vail working on my roll and teaching the boys how to roll as well. The roll comes a lot easier to them than me.

During the first few years of pursuing the sport my roll isn't very good, so I do a lot of swimming. Friends I boat with, particularly Vail based expert kayak-

Nick Brown in Endo Hole on the Arkansas River.

ers Steve Boyd and Jack Carnie, rescue me dozens of times. I swim through almost all the Numbers rapids on the Arkansas, some them several times. I swim in Gore Creek, the Eagle River, and numerous places on the Colorado; particularly the Shoshone Power Plant Run and West Water Canyon. I swim in the Lower Box on the Rio Grande in New Mexico. One of my worst swims is in the Slaughterhouse run on the Roaring Fork River near Aspen. I get used to banging on rocks, holding my breath for long periods of time, and getting relaxed about chasing my boat and paddle down the river. But I have to muster my courage sometimes. I get almost physically sick on my way to the more difficult

Gordon Brown starts Christian kayaking, 2004. Tor Erik will be next.

rivers just thinking about the swims I am sure I will take. On the other hand, there are those wonderful moments when I do things right and stay up in the tough drops or roll back up just before dropping into some big hole. The rewards are worth the fear and the pain.

There are more similarities to skiing: you head down, you're moving fast, you have to size up what's ahead, you have to react quickly, you have to accept the fact that you are going get knocked over occasionally and can get hurt.

If you want to push the limits you need to spend a lot of time training, improving your skills and strength in small increments until you know you're ready. If you take the macho attitude that "you might just be able to get away with it," too often you can die. In recent years a lot of very good boaters have been killed getting pinned on logs and stuck in bad holes in sections of rivers that, in my opinion, never should be boated. "Being the first to do the toughest" can come with a terrible price.

Introducing Michael, Gordon, and Nick to kayaking in a pool makes a lot of sense. In my opinion, that's where all kids should start if they can because it's safe, warm, and not intimidating. But I take them on the rivers too quickly. They all have scary swims although only a few are dangerous.

One time Gordie flips over in the Eagle River right next to a wading trout fisherman. He is frightened even though he is in less than three feet of slow moving water. Another time he goes down West Water Canyon with us. Walt Blackadar, a surgeon from Salmon, Idaho, is along. He is a famous big water kayaker even though he is in his fifties; he is also a featured kayaker in many of our television shows. Walt encourages Gordon to run everything, even the hardest drops. Gordon keeps getting knocked over and rolling up. It is a situation where his roll is too good because we never pick up on the fact that he is frightened out of wits. Finally he swims, and when he is pulled into the raft he vomits with fear.

In time Gordon gets past being afraid and begins to scare me with his fearlessness. He is only thirteen when I take him with me to Alaska and down the Susitna to the top of Devil's Gorge. All the way down he keeps paddling off by himself, and I have to follow him. Finally we get into some big standing wave trains and his fear returns. We stop on a sandbar full of iron pyrite which looks like gold. This keeps his interest until one of the rafts come by and he gets on board. I am very relieved to have him out of the kayak. I don't know when we might come around a corner into something bad that he won't know how to avoid.

Son Michael also has some scary experiences when he starts kayaking. I take him into The Numbers on the Arkansas before he is ready. He swims the falls at Rapid Five which is not that bad but it makes him tired. In Rapid Six he tips over right at the top and has to get out of his boat. Six is a long rough rocky rapid with a few nasty holes at the bottom. Friend and doctor Phil Freedman comes to Mike's rescue. He grabs Phil's stern loop and puts his hand through and can't pull it out. The drag of his body pulls Phil back into a hole and Mike is pushed underwater, Phil can't paddle out with the extra weight, Mike can't let go, and he is held under a long time. This experience turns him off. Later, on a shoot in Mexico. Jeff Snyder lets Mike try his Ducky (a Ducky is an inflatable kayak that cannot be rolled easily but is very stable in white-water). Mike quickly masters the Ducky and starts doing class three, four, and even five, drops without much trouble. In subsequent years he goes on to Ducky paddle more dicey runs in Mexico and Bhutan. Now he is relearning how to paddle a hard shell kayak. His roll is almost bomb proof, so it is coming easy to him.

Nick takes a bad swim on the Eagle River near Wolcott. He gets knocked over in a rapid we call Tressels because of a railroad bridge that crosses the river there. He floats straight for a big log jam where the water is going under the debris. Fortunately I get to him in time.

Years later, when I am fifty-nine, Nick and I kayak the Grand Canyon. I do all the rapids without swimming. It's the highlight of all my kayaking experiences

Gordon gets into sea kayaking while living in Half Moon Bay, California. Michael Powers, photojournalist and captain in the Tsunami Rangers, introduces him to surf zone kayaking, an edgy sport in which they kayak in breaking waves and occasionally explore sea caves.

January 13, 2004. Gordon calls me from somewhere in the middle of Ethiopia. He is making a first descent of the Blue Nile River with an IMAX film crew. He says they are through most of the big white-water and that he has been attacked but not bitten by crocodiles, stoned and then shot at by angry villagers. Fortunately they have two rebel sharpshooters with them who have repelled the attackers. They are now through the Sudan and struggling with Egyptian security.

On March 28 Gordon calls again to say they have completed the first descent of the Blue Nile. He has kayaked and rafted a total of 5,247 kilometers, a feat the British and others have been trying accomplish for over a hundred years. This is a man who had a serious brain tumor five years and was given very little chance of surviving..

Pinned

The word "pinned" sends a chill through any kayaker. It's probably the most common cause of death in the sport. Usually the obstruction is a tree, but it can be an undercut ledge or a rock in the middle of the river as it was in my case. When the kayaker is pinned with his head underwater and the force of the current is too strong for him to break loose, he can't last long. This was not the situation in my case, my head was above water, but it was not a nice position to be in.

Phil Freedman and I are doing a run the Eagle River near Arrowhead west of Vail. It is May 30, and the water is murky and cold. It's a fast rocky class four stretch at high water. There are lots of holes but they are easy to miss. Earlier, perhaps in April or back in October, there were heavy equipment operators in the river putting in a sewer line. Someone must have missed the survey marks because there are cement cisterns right in the middle of the river. The contractors have left a lot of big loose rocks that have been dislodged from the bottom. They are not quite moving but not secure either.

Both Phil and I are pretty relaxed. An eddy catches me and turns me upstream. I take a few lazy strokes to get straight again and slip up against a boulder sideways. I expect to bounce off, but I don't. I lean downstream to avoid having to roll upstream, and suddenly I find part of the big loose boulder in the cockpit with me.

The force of the water presses against the bow and stern of the boat and bends it around the rock. My chest is against the rock that now is in the cockpit with me. I push hard backwards so that I can breathe. I try to move the boat forward and then back but the force of the water is too strong. I can't move. I can't get out of the boat. My hands get numb in the freezing water.

Phil looks back to see my dilemma. He paddles to shore, walks up the bank, and wades out, trying to reach me. I throw him my paddle and try to free myself again, but I still don't move. Phil keeps wading out, carefully in the fast current, moving closer until he can grab the stern of my boat. He pulls and lifts me enough that I can pop loose my jammed spray skirt. I start to get out but now the rock is pressing against the boat where my knees are, bending them back the way they don't bend. I yell in pain, and Phil gives another big tug. I get past the rock and out of the boat and half crawl, half swim to shore. Phil tries to pull the boat to shore, but it is full of water and heavy and he has to let it go. We find it later in an eddy about a mile downstream and continue our run.

Town of Vail Search and Rescue guys meet us when we pull out below the Edwards Bridge. They are looking for some canoeists who had drowned here a few days before. Apparently the men had been drinking and put in at 7:00 P.M. at night without wet suits or life jackets. Suicide.

I remember my first run through this stretch of water in 1976. I am just back from shooting *The Edge* in the Grand Canyon. I have a boat and a paddle, but no wet suit and almost no experience. I put several layers of wool clothes on thinking this will be enough. I tip over under the Edwards Bridge, and I didn't know how to roll so I have to swim. By the time I reach the shore a hundred yards downstream, my lower body is completely numb. I tug myself out of the water by grabbing some willows and pulling with my arms. I don't regain feeling in my legs for at least ten minutes. After that I spend a lot of time in a warm pool learn-

Dr. Phil Freedman on a clff trail high above Karnali River in northwestern Nepal.

ing how to roll, and I purchase a wet suit. I do a lot more swimming. In fact it seems to me I swim most of the major rivers in the Central Rockies, but I have the right equipment and a lot of dumb determination. Finally, after a year or so, my roll starts to work and the swims become less frequent.

Today the rivers are stuffed with kayakers, and nothing is off limits. The boaters are jumping into places we never considered, like a set of waterfalls on the Crystal River that I can only compare to a meatgrinder, or into a small creek like the Piney River where dozens of log jams act like sieves, catching every floating object that comes down and sucking it under. The kayakers are dying, not just the beginners but also the experts. I fail to see the point.

Showdown on the San Miguel

July 1994. He and his horse are like one, bearing down on us, deliberate and unflinching. This is no Ralph Lauren cowboy, this is the genuine article. And he is angry.

I am reminded of my preservationist roots while kayaking down the San Miguel with two friends. The San Miguel is a neglected river because it has no class four rapids to tell hairy stories about (at least not down to the point where we left the river), and it only runs high enough for raft and kayak travel for a month or so a year. More significantly, however, much of the river runs through private land.

We put in at 7:00 P.M., planning to go about five miles before we camp. The river runs west and the sunlight is low and directly in our eyes, but there is still much to see. Aside from a cattle fence that crosses the river, the inner canyon is a pristine wilderness. Giant ponderosa and flat-limbed blue spruce grace the lower slopes and bottom land. Grass covered openings look like manicured city parks. Sandstone cliffs rise up in tiers, adding to the isolation. We surprise two golden eagles eating a rabbit on a beach. For us, sitting in a kayak a few yards away, their size is overwhelming. They back away reluctantly as we approach, but they don't fly; perhaps the younger one has not yet learned how. We camp by a side stream that yields two trout for our dinner, and my friends give me an astrology lesson when it gets dark. In the morning we catch a few more trout and hike the nearby slopes. Stone chips tell us the Indians had liked this spot as well. A bull elk left last season's antlers in a meadow for us to trip over.

Certainly this is a place I want to see untouched. On the other hand, I wouldn't mind having a little cabin in one the meadows. I'm sure others would share my contradictions. It is both a nice place to live and to leave alone. I suppose I could look into the situation, see what is private property, try to get the Nature Conservancy involved, and rally the "wilderness" advocates.

But no, I'm afraid my serious preservationist days are over. I'm not even sure preserving things is a good idea anymore. Yes, you can set large tracts of land aside but who is going to protect it? Owners protect things, broke governments aren't quite so good at it. Think of how easy it is to start a fire on a dry windy day. If police can't control crime in the relatively small confines of a city how they going to patrol millions of acres of public land with thousands of points of access? And how are we going to pay for these police which most people don't want anyway?

If you look at the projections it's not hard to see why every little piece of fertile land like this will be occupied. There are approximately five billion people on Earth right now. There will be ten billion, more or less, by the year 2037. Double. One-third of the population today lives on a dollar a day or less. And this misery isn't just confined to poverty. The killing going on in Bosnia, Rwanda, and other regions is so grotesque that our American minds cannot accept it. Few of us are really able to let these atrocities into our psyches, if we do, we suppress them into a kind of subconscious fiction.

Almost all species expand their numbers naturally, claiming new territory and filling voids, until other species or forces cut them back. The cutback process has always been harsh, but here in the United States we have been lucky. No war has touched our shores in any of our lifetimes. Our first hand experiences, other than for those who have fought overseas, has been relatively gentle. The violence in our cities is tragic and senseless but not happening on a massive scale.

I wonder, as we try to preserve more and more, cutting off access to resources we consume while putting good people out of work, when the American revolt will take place? How different are we from the Bosnians and the Serbs or the Tutsi and the Hutu when the chips are down? Nothing will probably happen in my lifetime but what about my sons' lifetimes?

My friends and I beach our kayaks in order to stretch our cramped legs.

"That's a great-looking old cabin."

"Let's have a look."

The cabin is full of rodent droppings and chewed apart cushions. Old newspapers cover the interior walls. They are from the turn of the last century when most of the nation was employed in agriculture. There were far fewer people on Earth then, but they still found their way into this remote valley.

We return to the river and prepare to enter the water again.

The old cowboy seems to come out of nowhere. He is like John Wayne on the track of an outlaw. He towers above us on his big horse as he draws closer. He slaps a braided leather crop (whip) in the palm of his hand. I am full of admiration for this character, but I know we are in trouble.

"Don't you know this is private property?"

"No, sir." I am glad he didn't see us at the cabin.

"Don't you have any maps?"

"No, sir, we left them in the car. We didn't want to get them wet."

He has heard enough nonsense. "Get off of here, and don't set foot on this land again or you'll be in real trouble. And I mean it."

"Yes, sir," we respond in unison. He rides off with the same fluid grace. Talk about being close to Nature, how many of us will ever become part of an animal the way he is on that horse.

"Phew! Gone. What a relief."

Now I think I really understand what inspired Lynn Jacobs to write the anti-cowboy book, *Waste of the West.*

"Let's get out of here."

I wonder how then Vice President Gore or then Secretary Babbitt might have viewed this encounter. This man doesn't have a badge but he is certainly protecting the land, at least from us. Here we are, three men clad in purple, blue,

Aspens.

and black neoprene suits, spray skirts hanging from our waists like oversized New Guinea penis gourds, long, sharp-bladed paddles in our hands. Are we any match for this old leather chapped warrior on his perfectly disciplined horse? It doesn't matter. None of us, least of all him, have the slightest intention of spilling any blood. We have courts to do that for us. I can try to create legislation that will put him out of business and get him off the land; he can take me to court and get me fined for trespassing. Of course, he is not a litigious person and neither am I. The courts and the politicians and endless studies have worn everyone down. We are both tired of being angry. We are ready for workable solutions.

The Bosnians, Serbs, Hutus, and Tutsis also have their justice systems. Why are their legal institutions failing while our institutions still work? Is it just tribal conflict, or is there another reason? Could it be that they have run out of space? Are there too few resources for too many people? Overpopulation? Is Rwanda a mirror of our future?

The world is finite, but our capacity to reproduce doesn't seem to be. Many people are still operating on instincts and traditions that were developed as a result of a high child mortality rate. In New Guinea, for instance, they still don't give a child a name until he or she is four years old. They don't want to get too attached.

That old cowboy and I, if we live long enough, are going to have to get used to having a lot more people around. He can kick them off his property and I can fight for more wilderness until we are both blue in the face.When it comes down to not enough room and to survival, people are going to take what they need, and no one can stop them.

There is a possibility for a solution. Some of that money we are spending in the courts trying to protect owls, property rights, old growth trees, and the like, could be redirected into education so that Third World folks can avoid the cycles causing them to produce so many children. Better yet, more sustainable agricultural and forestry methods could be used in this country, rather than simply trying to shut down the ranching and logging industries.

Ignorance and poverty are the real enemies of mankind. Overpopulation is only one of the results. If we really want to save those wild places and things we love so much, we are going to have to pay more attention to the poor and desperate.

I'll bet if that old cowboy and I could sit down over a beer and talk, we would agree on a lot of things. I might say give women more power and hand out condoms, and he might say improve the irrigation systems to create more food, but our long range goals would probably be the same. He doesn't want to see his ranch overrun with ever-increasing numbers of unwelcomed tourists. I don't want to see the last wild areas trampled into dust. With too many people, it seems sure to happen.

Commercializing Adventure Sports

Adventure sports, like so many other activities, have fallen victim to what I will call, for lack of a better word, "professionalism." The root causes of the problem are straightforward enough: competition, the need for recognition, and the desire to earn money doing what was previously done just for fun. Two of the early adventure sports—climbing and kayaking—were initially pursued simply for the sheer joy of doing. No thought was given to earning a living at it unless the ath-

letes signed on as guides. The next step was probably when someone wrote a book on their adventures and it sold well.

Hang glider pilot John Heiney starting into a loop near Mt. Cook, New Zealand.

As the sports grew and gained a following, manufacturers discovered they could sell products endorsed by the top athletes in the sports. Here the adventure sports people took their cue from baseball, football, and basketball. This is when competition entered into the picture; it provided a measure of proof as to who was the best. The best got the recognition, contracts, and money.

Some adventure sports have developed competitive venues: climbing walls, slalom courses, obstacle courses, races (when mountain bikers entered the scene), and judged events like freestyle skiing. The joy of doing is taking a back seat to prize money. Many of the athletes have forgotten the origins of the sport and its basic purpose in their lives.

As television producers, we have supported this process. After an athlete is seen by millions of people on television, his or her career is more liable to take off, or at least they think it will take off.

Two sports—adventure kayaking and freestyle skiing—illustrate the point.

A Helicopter Rescue in Cross Mountain Gorge

I do an interview with a state trooper on the highway to the Yampa River. He is a big man, the kind of guy you don't argue with when he decides to give you a ticket. We tell him about our plans to film a kayaking descent of Cross Mountain Gorge.

"Would you like to try it?" I ask.

"That sounds like fun," he says, "but I have this back problem."

"Oh, what's wrong?"

"Well, I have a big yellow stripe running down the middle of it."

A huge "keeper" hole forms at the top of Cross Mountain Gorge during high water. It spans the entire width of the river. It is called Mammoth Falls. "Keeper" means just what is says. The hole will hold any floating object that comes into it. The only way for a kayaker to get through a hole like this is to get out of his boat and dive down to where he can hopefully catch deeper currents that are passing through near the bottom of the river.

It is May. It's been a good snow year and the Yampa River is running over 8,000 cfs. We are at Cross Mountain Gorge, not far above Dinosaur National Park, to make a television show for the *ABC American Sportsman* series. We have a strong team of kayakers: world champion Norbert Sattler from Austria; seven-times national champion Eric Evans; expedition kayakers Cully Erdman, John Wasson, Rob Lesser, Kirk Baker, and Matt Gaines.

John Wilcox, the executive producer of *Sportsman* is with us, as well as several cameramen and soundmen. The show is my idea. Originally Walt Blackadar was going to run the gorge with us, but he died in a kayaking accident a few months ago. I will be the helicopter cameraman and action director. John is producing and directing the interviews.

We camped here last night so everyone has had a chance to look at the falls. It's a violent, perfectly-formed, giant wave that folds back on itself and runs from shore to shore. It's not a subtle problem and there is not much room for discussion, but it's easy to become hypnotized by the symmetry of the waves. Norbert Sattler decides to portage around. Eric and Cully want to run it. The others want to see what happens to Eric and Cully.

I get in the air, fly out over the river, and radio down that I'm ready when they are. Eric pushes off. He heads straight in, paddling hard, hoping to punch through the hole. He almost makes it but then slips back when he is about through, and gets violently recycled in a series of back and front endos and rolls. Finally he gets out of his boat, swims down to the bottom, pops up below the hole, and is quickly rescued by the safety boaters.

After seeing Eric's run I radio down to the others, "Don't run. There's no way through! It's too dangerous." But my message doesn't get through. I see Cully pushing off and heading for the far right side of the hole. He seems almost motionless on the smooth water above the drop, but the current is moving faster and faster, gaining speed from the pull of the giant hole. He must paddle hard enough to go faster than the water that is carrying him. What can he be thinking? This river does not know he is there. It will show no mercy. Oh, shit. He hugs the far right bank, trying to sneak by and almost does, but then the current sucks him in like a thirsty kid taking down a cold Coke on a hot summer day. He slides to the center, to the bottom of the trough, is turned sideways, and gets thrashed unmercifully, over and over, just

as Eric did. He separates from his boat and goes down under. But he doesn't come to the surface where we expect him, and when he does appear he is well below the rescue boaters. They can't see him from water level.

Father and son in handmade tin kayak, Largo Oruro, Bolivia.

I follow Cully in the helicopter. His thin life jacket doesn't give him enough flotation. He keeps disappearing and coming up again. The gorge is continuous rapids for two miles. Also, he is in a shorty wetsuit, which is not warm enough to protect him from the near freezing water for very long.

Cully is out in the middle of the river for the first half-mile, but as it takes a right bend he drifts to the edge and is just barely able to grab onto a log jam piled up behind a rock. He holds on, but he doesn't have the strength to pull himself out.

I scream to the helicopter pilot, "You've got to land. I have to get to him before he lets go!"

There are no flat spots; the steep banks come straight to the river's edge and they are 600 feet high.

The pilot shouts back, "There's no place to land."

"Can you hover above that rock? I can jump down."

"I can't have that camera mount floating around in the ship without you. It's too windy. It will bounce around and knock me out of the air."

"You've got to. He's gonna die. I've already locked the mount arm in place."

Jeff Snyder, Agua Azul, Chiapas, Mexico. Beautiful insanity.

Reluctantly, "OK!"

The pilot drops down above a large, flat, top rock. When he is as close as he dares to get, I jump.

I scramble over to Cully as quickly as I can, grab his arms, and pull him out. He is very blue and wet. Something is wrong with his chest and his legs don't work. He is just barely conscious. He is seriously hypothermic. I strip off his wet gear and put my dry clothes on him. For what seems a very long time, probably over half an hour, he doesn't move. Then, slowly feeling starts to come back. He complains about his chest. And he finally starts to shiver, which is a good sign. I get him to stand up.

We find a place where the helicopter pilot can touch the skids down, load Cully aboard, and fly him to safety. After that, I get the camera mounted again and we finish the shoot without further mishap. Needless to say, no one else tries the hole.

We interview Cully back at the motel. He has broken ribs but is not otherwise seriously hurt.

The kayakers decide to celebrate. Cully hurts too much to drink, but Eric is up for a good time. "Eric the Hammer" he is called; nine times national slalom champion, now a struggling sportswriter living in Hanover, New Hampshire. The boaters start their celebration at the Cosgriff Hotel, then move on to a cowboy bar. They are drinking tequila shots with beer chasers. Norbert puts down about seven, and Eric drinks even more.

Cully's girlfriend Jo Jo recalls the scene:

> "The first strange thing I notice is when Eric starts eating a ballpoint pen. His face turns blue. Then he gets up and walks over to a table of cowboys, looks them straight in the eyes and says, 'I know why you guys wear those big hats. It's to hide your pinheads.'
>
> "One cowboy, a big, well built fellow, white-knuckles the edge of the table and starts to get up. His friends grab him while Kirk and Cully hustle Eric out the door. Eric and Norbert get in the back of the pickup truck and start a wrestling match. When they get to the motel Eric starts kicking on the doors, one after another, never stopping to see the reaction. Some of the guests get pretty upset."

The next morning there are denials, red eyes, and big headaches. Eric heads back to New England. Some of us head to Cataract Canyon for a high water run down to Lake Powell.

When we get to Moab, Utah, Norbert meets Joy Ungritch—a famous, young, woman rafter noted for her strength. After various challenges only given to world champions, Norbert proceeds to take her pants off in the Sidewinder parking lot, right in front of everyone. This delights all the crew, male and female. Joy is "butt-naked," but she laughs. Her eyes are blazing. It's clear she is plotting some kind of revenge.

On the river, Norbert gives me lots of pointers on paddle strokes and rolls. He is firm believer in rolling with your body forward so you don't smash your face on the bottom. Walt Blackadar liked to roll with his body back, because there is less water resistance and it's easier to come up. I do whatever seems easier and quicker at the time. Norbert keeps emphasizing follow through in my paddle stroke. Use the whole stroke. Where have I heard this before? Shooting a shotgun, swinging a tennis racket, turning skis, living life. The complete turn, the smooth arc, the graceful thought that flows without doubt—these actions become the moments treasured.

I run the big drops without any problems. There's plenty of room to dodge the bad holes. The most fun is at the narrows before the the river enters the lake, where huge standing waves form in rows like a long roller coaster. At first they are intimidating but as I experience their benevolence they become pure joy.

The fun wild days finally come to an end, but not the memories or the repercussions.

The *Cross Mountain Gorge* film plays on the *ABC American Sportsman* series. The editors in New York focus on the swims of Eric Evans and Cully Erdman. Pam Miller at *Adventure Travel Magazine* writes a feature called, "Action Films: Is the View True?" in which she is critical of the athletes, the film, and network television's handling of adventure sports in general.

Eric Evan's response to Miller is classic, one of the best defenses of media-inspired extreme sports I've ever seen. Here is some of what he says:

> "As one of the ego hungry experts willing to prostitute themselves and their sports for cold, hard cash who was verbally rapped on the knuckles in your magazine, I have managed to recover enough feelings to respond. Let me say that in my experiences with *American Sportsman* producer John Wilcox and director Roger Brown I have never been directly pressured to run a dangerous rapid . . ."

In the late 1970s extreme kayaking was only a small part of the sport, and class five and six white-water running was considered a marginal activity. *Adventure Travel Magazine* said that "the filming of the boaters running wild white-water in kayaks misrepresents the sport." To this question Evans asked:

> "Whose sport is kayaking anyway? The last time I checked there were many different ways to use a kayak; big water river running, kayaking, camping on a fishing trip, lake paddling, sea kayaking, paddling down a local stream, etc. The ABC show happened to focused on big water, but I don't feel they misrepresented big water river running. It was being done long before television got involved."

The point *Adventure Travel Magazine* was trying to make was that the general public's view of the sport of kayaking was warped because people only see big water river running on television. Evans responded, remarking that he gives the public more credit than that:

> "The only skiing I see on television is Franz Klammer or some other crazed downhill racer rocketing down a mountain slope at eighty miles an hour. But watching that doesn't warp my impression of skiing in general, because I realize that I'm not required to do likewise when I go skiing. The only hockey I see on television is the bruising, body jamming game exhibited by the Boston Bruins, but this doesn't deter me from participating in a no checking, no lifting shinny game of hockey on a weekend."

The magazine asks, "Does TV get in the way, that is, do the participants risk more than they would without a television camera present to capture the action?" Here Evans says he has to agree:

"There's no way I would have run the top hole on the Yampa during the ABC shoot without the accompanying chorus of television cameras. Why then? Yes, the evil specter of ego does raise its ugly head. I wanted to be seen running that rapid, not only for the camera, but also by the expert boaters in attendance to reinforce my position as one of the sport's best big water kayakers."

"But there is a point that is missed. Are people watching a kayaking show or are they watching a show depicting individuals extending the limits of of their ability under stress? And is kayaking just a medium in this exercise? And if the presence of television creates an unnatural setting, can this be likened, say, to miler Steve Ovett running the mile in world record time, spurred on by a large crowd, other able milers, and television cameras? Could he have run that fast alone in an empty stadium?"

Evans admits his motives are both egotistical and commercial at times, but then he asks:

"Don't we all compromise these activities we love so much when we publicize them? Don't the adventure sports performers and writers essentially invite the viewers and readers to participate, and doesn't this eventually result in damage to these wild areas where these activities take place?"

Evans winds up his remarks, "Yes, many of us make all or some of our living by 'exploiting' the outdoors in a variety of ways. So perhaps we should be careful about critizing others who do the same."

In defense of television, I quote from a *Time* magazine article introducing the 2000 Olympics in Australia:

"Sport at its highest level is a pure rush to the edge of human capability. How often do we get to watch mankind at its absolute best? We hear a composer's symphony or see the scar from a brilliant surgeon's operation, but we seldom see these men and women at the moment of supreme achievement. Sport provides one of the rare theaters where these moments can be glimpsed. . . "

A year or so later Cully, Eric, and I go off to explore the Jatate River in the jungles of Chiapas, Mexico. I run into Joy Ungritch again when I'm filming the first descent of the Zambezi River, below Victoria Falls in Africa. Later I hear she has died of cancer. It's hard to believe. The Grim Reaper does not just harvest in wild rivers and on dangerous mountains. Joy was so full of life and happy and healthy. I'm glad she had so many good times before the cancer got her.

Freestyle Skiing, a Brief History

Our films, particularly *Ski the Outer Limits* and *The Moebius Flip,* inspire young skiers everywhere. Kids start flying off bumps, bashing the moguls, and doing tricks at all the ski resorts. A few prominent ski industry people, particularly Tom Corcoran, owner of Waterville Valley, and Doug Pfeiffer, editor of *Skiing Magazine*, see the excitement and the promotional potential of the freestyle phenomenon. Tom and Doug hold one of the first events at Waterville Valley. It isn't long before three competitive venues emerge: aerials, moguls, and ballet. One of the first freestyle competitions is at Waterville Valley, then Vail and other ski areas soon follow.

Unfortunately few people realize the potential danger of the aerial acrobatics until it is too late. When we are filming Scott Magrino in Vail, he lands his jump

BRECKENRIDGE
SKI CORPORATION

wrong and breaks his back. A lawsuit follows, and many ski areas start banning any kind of aerial acrobatics, in or out of competitions. But skiers are irrepressible, and the craziness just keeps increasing.

One problem can be traced to the fact that each skier reshapes the jump to suit the kind of stunt he wants to do. A back flip and a front flip jump need completely different shapes. If the shape is wrong, the skier can end up landing on the back of his neck. This is what happens to Scott.

More events are held, and more accidents occur. Over time, however, the skiers create rules and begin to control the the jump building. Finally the Federation International de Ski, a worldwide governing body for ski competition, gets involved and the serious accidents diminish to almost zero. The competitors push to have the events accepted in the Olympics. After a demonstration in Calgary, the aerial acrobatics become an Olympic event and the moguls soon follow. The ballet never makes it.

Fall 1978. After seeing *The Edge* in a Salt Lake City theater, a lawyer named Curtis Oberhansley calls me about making a freestyle feature documentary for theatrical distribution. Curtis is trying to organize a professional freestyle skiers' union of sorts and make money selling television rights to the events. He thinks a documentary feature about the freestyle scene can be profitable. I start writing a treatment and shooting preliminary material.

Opposite page: Aerial acrobatics, Breckenrige, Colorado, 1990.

The Treatment

Freestyle the phenomenon—sport, art form, competition, exhibition, and road show. Springing from gymnastics, diving, figure skating, ballet, and skiing, of course. Sometimes it's hard to remember the skiing part of it.

A unique movement, freestyle has been generated internally by the doers out of a desire to keep on doing. Imagination and organization have been the only deterrents. The skiers are not short on imagination, but they are amateurs when it comes to politics and business. Sophomore idealism mixes poorly with disguised self interest.

Madison Avenue, always impressed with wide open mountain country and rich resorts, has found a new game to play in the good old setting. And big business executives, always ready for a paid vacation, have poured themselves and the money in.

To really understand freestyle, one has to go back several years to the time when skiing was practiced by rugged lovers of the outdoors. In those days it was unselfconscious exercise. How you looked had little to do with how you felt.

Then German clothing manufacturers Willy and Maria Bogner introduced stretch pants. Ordinary, even flabby, bodies became graceful under the pressure of the new elastic fabric. The result was a tremendous ego boost for a lot of people, a sudden appreciation of self. "I am beautiful (or at least more beautiful than I was)." Now skiing is high fashion. Inhibitions have been peeled away, gray flannel men, stepping into lodge bedrooms, emerge moments later in fluorescent oranges and purples. Where else can a forty-five-year-old business executive run around looking like Superman or Buck Rogers (Darth Vadar today) and not feel

even a little bit foolish about it? Step right back there, Mr. America, into your adolescence. It's alright.

If skiing is the narcissistic indulgence of the decade, then freestylers are its vanguard, the showoffs of the century. "Look at me! I'm sexy, man, and watch me do these tricks."

The public eats it up. No question, the hot-doggers are really turning people on.

Beyond the narcissism there is doing it: the rush, syncing up to music, letting it all hang out in the bumps, getting air, going upside down. Performance still takes the highest points in the freestyle club. All the peripheral talk, the flash, the sex, and the drugs may be significant, but only as they relate to performance, out on the hill, in front of the crowd. Full funding for the freestyle feature film project never materializes and finally the project is aborted.

The freestyle movement was a lot more exciting in its early year, when it was essentially a bunch of naughty kids from the other side of the tracks doing their own thing, but it was too dangerous and had to change.

Opposite page: Herman Gollner and Tom LeRoy from the film, "Ski the Outer Limits." 1968.

Then and Now

In many ways other new sports such as snowboarding, climbing on the artificial climbing walls, rodeo kayaking, and the X Games have followed similar patterns. It's about young people trying to define themselves in a new way that separates them from older generations and about trying to make some money doing what they love to do most. These activities—"sports" is a stretch of the imagination—have gone from absurd to ridiculous.

Techno Trivializing

We have been struggling to survive on this planet for several million years, evolving, becoming smarter, improving our tools, until now we can be totally comfortable almost any place, doing almost anything. The only obstacle we haven't been able to overcome is age.

When I look back at all my experiences in the mountains, at how sports equipment and clothing have developed, and at the way we are now able to build our roads, homes, even towns in the most inhospitable places, I have to ask some basic questions. Are the mountains still a challenge for us as physical human beings here in Colorado or simply a beautiful, easy place to live? And is this what we want—a world where Nature's challenges have been eliminated?

Let's revisit the Glenwood Canyon for a moment and ask, "Was this an obstacle or a sanctuary before the roads were built?" We tried to treat it as both by putting in an elaborate graceful raised highway to match the grandeur of the canyon walls. Seen from a car it is a thirty-minute scenic orgy. If the speed limit is pushed, it becomes a mild driving thrill with all its nicely designed curves. But as a sanctuary it doesn't cut it. The Glenwood Canyon is no more than a blip in our hectic lives, an inspiring visual bite, soon forgotten in the rush to go nowhere.

When I was hiking with friends at the northern tip of Greenland, about 450 miles from the North Pole, everyone walked very fast, as if they wanted to prove how strong they were. There was a coastal hill that Dennis Schmidt was pretty sure no one had ever climbed, and he very badly wanted to be the first to the top.

Everyone embraced Dennis's goal except me. I walked much slower than the rest because I felt I was was already where wanted to be. A snowy owl flew over, fresh musk ox prints invited tracking, a fox watched me curiously as I watched him. Eventually group pressure prevailed, however, and I raced up the hill with the others to claim victory. Ole Jorgen Hammiken raised the Greenland flag in defiance of the Danes who subsidize him and the rest of the Greenland Eskimos. In the glory of our success I'm afraid we really missed the point. We had been rushing nowhere, at least nowhere significant. We had spent all this money on charter flights, food, cold weather gear, etc. and the perhaps the most valuable part of the experience was being overlooked. Who will ever give a damn about our first ascent?

If you are a hunter, the *Cabelas Catalog* is your equipment bible. Some of the most sophisticated military camouflage clothing, recognizance equipment, camping gear, cross bows, black powder rifles, and pistols, (everything but automatic weapons and armor piercing bullets) are available for purchase from the catalog. Once you've purchased all the latest stuff you may or may not need, you can buy an all terrain vehicle to help you to carry the paraphernalia into the woods with you. Unfortunately, or fortunately depending on how you look at it, the elk and other big game have not been able to improve their skills to match the new technology.

What is happening? So far, the elk are holding their own because of some difficult terrain where they can still hide, but it's only a matter of time before increasing numbers of hunters with increasingly sophisticated equipment will get into the last hidden spots and either wipe the game out or force the government to close the areas to hunting. Technology, it seems, will have won the battle but lost the war, at least as far as sports experiences go.

With enough money, anyone can build a road and a home on a remote mountainside and soak up scenery perviously only available as a result of hard work, hiking, climbing, and struggling against the elements. It's more than a little disappointing when you struggle up a rock face to the summit of a peak and find a road coming up the other side.

So what's left? Are we overwhelming everything that used to build character because it offered tough challenges? Are we making the sacred mundane? It would seem so. As I have mentioned before, it's no longer about whether or not we can do something, but whether or not we want to or need to. I don't think we want to tame every last bit of the natural world, but that's where we are headed. The only thing we can't seem to tame is ourselves.

It is clear that our technology has allowed us to cross a threshold into counter productive pursuits. It is the same problem that exists almost everywhere in the world with weapons. We did not exercise restraint when we designed, built, and sold weapons to folks that can't seem to be controlled or to control themselves, and so now they are murdering each other and us in unprecedented numbers for the thinnest of reasons. Our government claims war is necessary to achieve peace. Of course it is when all the middle eastern nations are armed to the teeth. And who armed them?

Perhaps I should reframe the problems facing The Rocky Mountains in terms of bad decisions, "techno trivialization," if you will. We have not seen the forest for the trees; we are destroying those places that give us the values we most cherish, writing them off to energy production, municipal water supplies, mass recreation, etc.; then turning what's left of our undeveloped agricultural lands into boring over-managed, trashed-out subdivisions, golf courses, and theme parks. Sad.

Perhaps the most obvious example of a destructive sport here on the West Slope, in terms of land damage, is dirt biking.

Force Your Trail: Off-road Vehicles

"FORCE YOUR TRAIL" reads a Nitto Tire ad. A picture of a tire on a jeep fills the page. It is grinding over a rock at an off angle. This is just one the milder pictures of various vehicles ripping up the terrain. Every picture shows some kind of off-road four-wheeler eating up the ground. Mud flies and dust obscure the view. In many shots the undercarriage looms as the vehicle rears up on its back wheels, plunging on through whatever is in its path.

But Peterson's *4Wheel* magazine is mild next to the stuff in *Dirt Bike*. The November 2003 issue has a feature called "Colorado's Rockies: Experiencing America's Mountainous Motorsports." The captions on the photos tell the story, "One minute you'll be above timberline, the next you'll be waste deep in a beaver pond. Colorado has surprises." The next shot is of a bike ripping through a high mountain stream, followed by a picture of a guy in riding armor fishing for trout in clear water. "National forests that welcome dirt bikes" reads another section of the article. Then it lists nineteen USFS district telephone numbers. In this way, the dirt bikers put pressure of the Forest Service to open up more terrain to the bikers or at least not close more.

Under "Tremendous Terrain" the article reads, "Colorado boasts more 14,000-foot peaks than any other state besides Alaska, but there are also beautiful buttes, mesas, valleys, alpine meadows, and scenery to recreate your own 'sound of music'." I'm not sure what music can be heard over the roar of the bikes.

When faced with criticism the author of the article, "Land Use Lump" he calls himself, claims timeshare condo owners ("newbies"), have forced the Forest Service to make illegal closures; tank traps, logs in the trails, etc., which he says are more environmentally damaging than the bikes. Land Use Lump doesn't mention the shredded forest floor, the missing corners on the trails where the bikers have taken short cuts, the archaeological sites that have been laid open with deep tire tracks, or the erosion gullies that have formed in the grooves the bikers left in some hillsides.

Jeep clubs have been using the old roads to mining ghost towns since before first I came to Colorado in 1958. I had a jeep for a while and did some exploring myself. We didn't leave the roads. Many ranchers I know, who for one reason or another can't ride a horse, use ATVs. These machines have been around since the 1980s. They have made cattle ranching a whole lot easier. But no rancher I know of would ever take any vehicle out in his fields or in the forest with the express purpose of tearing up the ground. In fact whatever support the ranchers gave to Wilderness Area designations thirty and forty years ago was because they were fed up with jeep and pickup folks ripping up the grazing lands, dumping trash, and leaving gates open.

Beaver pond.

The big problems for the land arise with the exponential increase in numbers of various off-road machines, their increasing power, traction, and performance, which the manufacturers promote because it sells more vehicles. The very phrase "off road" suggests man against the elements, conquering Nature, proving manhood. Magazines like *Outside*, normally environmentally responsible, say very little critically for fear of offending their big advertisers, primarily the car companies pushing gas guzzling SUVs.

Why do we need all these extreme events, races, and the like? We seem to be trying to achieve self-realization in competition instead of through contemplation and reflection. It is mindless and destructive, best practiced on race courses, not fragile wild lands. Nature often seems to be not much more than a stage prop for television shows.

These machines have long term health problems connected with them as well. I can trace many of the injuries troubling me now back to making promotional films for snowmobile manufacturers. Walking or running is a more natural, healthy form of exercise than hammering our backbones while bouncing along on, or in, a big, heavy, bucking, gas-guzzling machine. When I see six-year-olds on their own miniature versions of these machines I have to wonder when the crippling effects of the rough riding will show up in their lives.

This dilemma, which will ultimately destroy the land, boils down to the "consumer" ethic promoted by Bush Administration and others before them. More vehicles, more gas consumption, etc., means more manufacturing, more jobs, more growth. Everything is based on growth instead of sustainability. This begs the question: is "sustainable growth" an oxymoron, a placebo that keeps people from thinking too hard? We should probably think it is wrong thinking until we can demonstrate otherwise. The burden of proof is on us. The formula is self evident. Infinite consumption of finite resources can only be terminal. We will run out.

It's unfortunate that most of the unused land that might be available to rip up is either on the Moon or Mars; and it's too bad that American soldiers, Iraq civilians, and Muslim terrorists have to die over what is essentially a battle for the oil we Americans want in order to sustain our consumptive habits. It's not a leap of faith to correlate our use of motorized toys with life and death in other parts of the world. Better to address the changes we need to make now before the chaos of a failed economy eliminates our best options. War for peace obviously isn't working. Reduced consumption and alternative renewable sources of energy is where we have to go, and the sooner the better.

Scarlet gilia.

Friluftsliv

If I were to look for an opposite to dirt biking it would be *Friluftsliv*. *Friluftsliv* is a complex Norwegian word summing up a wilderness ethic. It means, among other things, to "touch the earth lightly," and to commune with Nature. It is not a new idea. Many years ago the famous Norwegian explorer Fritjof Nanson explained *Friluftsliv* as a partial return to an earlier form of existence, similar to the way ancient hunter-gatherers lived. His view is based on his experiences living with Inuit Eskimos in the Arctic.

Effort—"work" if you like the word better—using the muscles of the body, is a necessary part of *Friluftsliv*. Climbing a mountain on skis; paddling a lake, ocean, or river; cross country skiing; swimming; and hunting for food are examples. The effort is internally motivated, not dictated by any contest. Norwegian philosopher Arne Naess specifically rejects competition as a part of the experience. "*Friluftsliv* is not an elite activity that depends on defeating others," he says.

> "*Friluftsliv* requires a respect for the natural landscape and the life that inhabits it. Primitive unconfined solitude is primary condition. In this way the philosophy embraces the wilderness concepts laid down by John Muir, Aldo Leopold, David Brower, and others. Signs of human activity should not be noticeable. Each visitor should be able to feel as if he or she is the first or only person to be in one of these wild areas. Visitor centers, sign-posted nature trails, hotels, roads, etc., are not compatible with *Friluftsliv*."

High-tech equipment, which separates the participant from the rigors of the environment—be it for comfort, travel, hunting, etc.—should only be used sparingly. Natural fibers like wool are preferred over nylon, leather over plastic, and so on.

A knowledge of edible plants is encouraged but with this goes an understanding that their quantity are limited. If harvesting is excessive there won't be seed stock for the following years, therefore, the number of visitors to these wild areas needs to be limited.

Time is needed to adjust to wilderness conditions. It is a period when cell phones, computers, television sets, and the like, might be missed. On our filming expeditions it usually takes me a day or two to shift gears. Once the process starts

I seem to keep letting go, and I become more and more relaxed with each passing day. A Yampa River trip might last five days, but the best Grand Canyon trips run eighteen days or more. Slowly, an awareness of the natural surroundings increases, a slower pace is accepted, and entertainment becomes internally generated. What was overlooked in the beginning becomes central: reflections in the water, waves, moving clouds, mossy rocks, cliffs, driftwood, the flashing colors of a jumping trout, the snap of a twig broken by a frightened deer, the incessant buzzing of cicadas.

Noise, even the roar of a rapid, becomes subdued and restful because it belongs. Cold and heat are welcomed confirmations of being alive. The upside down world slowly rolls and rights itself. Balance is regained.

Ridiculous Adventures

October 2002. The hypocrisy of my filmmaking career is just beginning to dawn on me. I have gotten away with murder.

I created a formula with the feature film I did in 1976 called *The Edge*. It was based on maximum visual excitement. We climbed, we kayaked and rafted, we did some hang gliding, skiing, and scuba diving. We explored the extreme in each of these sports before "extreme" was a popular concept.

Usually one sport wasn't enough for John Wilcox at American Adventure Productions. If the show was primarily kayaking, I would still try to throw in a climbing or a caving sequence. Any additional hair-raising idea would help to sell the show, John saw everything in terms of adrenaline based entertainment, and he was pragmatic about it. The more near death events the better.

"Firsts"—first ascents of cliffs and big mountains, first descents of remote whitewater rivers, first to bike a trail across the Andes or through the Sarawak jungle, etc. It was a competitive thing. Get there "first " before someone else beats us to it. And our talent competed among themselves. Who has the guts to be first off that big waterfall, for instance? This competition fostered extreme aggressiveness. The place— the mountain, the river—became a background or disposable Hollywood set for the performer. Who cares what happens to the place, who will visit after we leave? None of us plan to come back.

So this was the magic formula: putting together the most exiting sport adventures I could think of in the most exotic locations possible with the most daring, if not crazy, athletes I could find, doing firsts. Of course, I always picked the location I wanted to visit. It was a very self-indulgent process, but nobody seemed to mind.

I enjoyed the athlete's performances, which were often beautiful and exciting, but I found some of their egotistical, single-minded personalities boring. Of course their were exceptions such as Doug Ammons, whose broad interests and inquisitive mind invariably resulted in interesting conversations. Doug would bring his guitar along and play classic pieces at camp in the evening.

In some cases I had to think like a psychiatrist, nursing fragile egos, coaxing, mediating, doing whatever was necessary to keep harmony in the group and performances good. Doug was also very skilled at nurturing egos because he was respected and liked by almost everyone.

Catayaks on Uyuni Salt Flats, Bolivia. They float, sail, roll, and divide in two.

Then there is the whole "high-tech" issue. Our athletes always used the latest high performance gear, sometimes different boats for difference kinds of water, different climbing gear for rock, ice, or high altitude mountaineering. The manufacturers not only gave us the gear, they paid the athletes to use it. Then photos of the athletes using the gear would show up in magazine advertising. The advertising industry became fully aware of the value of the exciting images and started using pictures of the athletes in all kinds of situations; next to or unloading SUVs (Fords, Toyotas, Blazers, etc.) The idea is that the cars are as powerful and aggressive as the athletes, able to conquer the toughest terrain Nature has to offer. Now it's 350-hp engines, spinning wheels through the dirt and mud of the back country and the fragile topsoil of the wilderness.

The various sports industries feed on themselves. The snowmobilers, dirt bikers, hunting, fishing, and clothing companies all focus on equipment performance, comfort, ease of travel, etc., that increase sales. But they all forget one thing: the countries and terrain where all this takes place are limited and fragile—beautiful because they are remote and unspoiled by visitors.

My primary happiness through all these experiences has come from simply being in some exotic location, seeing it for the first time, seeing the flowers and smelling the damp forest or the dry dust of the high desert, hearing the roar of a waterfall, or the wind from an approaching storm. And I invariably took a liking to the local people whose lives often seemed more real than those of myself or

Opposite page: Rafting down Glenwood Canyon (top) and Glenwood Hot Springs pool (bottom).

my crew. My regret is that the encounters with Third World cultures were so brief. We worked with the locals in the sense that they were guides and porters, but only in a few instances did they become the central subjects of our films. I seldom had a chance to truly experience the rhythms of village life over extended periods of time. So I only caught a glimpse, usually a romantic image, that missed many painful realities.

I can see now that the fragile indigenous cultures we have visited are being impacted by a rush of adventure tourism that follows our filming exploits. In fact this has been the Sobek Adventure Travel Company objective, to open up an area for tourism by getting films made that promote these areas. So it's not just the land that is being impacted, it's the cultures as well. The commercial rafting run below Victoria Falls on the Zambezi River is an example of this.

I am guilty. I have been promoting many of these activities for several years. My only redemption now is to go against the current and the the forces I helped to put in motion, to urge restraint or total abstinence. There are some places we should stay out of.

Recreation Future: Glenwood Canyon

From a recreational viewpoint a vision of what the future holds can be seen in Glenwood Canyon area today. Here is a beautifully constructed super highway through a magnificent canyon. Its convenience outweighs any pollution concerns about the adjacent highway. There is a bike path that is crowded with bikers, walkers, rollerbladers, etc. Moms have kids in tow in various carrying devices. The river is stuffed with rafts and kayaks. The interstate itself is heavily used by trucks. At the east end of the canyon various roads lead into the Flat Tops and the Cottonwood Pass area where ATVs, motorbikes, mountain bikes, etc., hammer the semi-arid high desert and sub-Alpine lands. This area is supposedly managed, but not controlled, by the Department of the Interior Bureau of Land Management and U.S. Department of Agriculture Forest Service. These agencies don't have the money for management personnel.

The Glenwood Hot Springs pool serves as a mountain substitute for an ocean beach. In spite of the fact that it is one of the largest hot springs in the world, and has ample grounds it is approaching a standing room only condition in and out of the water on some days. And in truth the crowd seems to thrive on the human density. These are "people people," showing off their bodies, tanning in the sun, picnicking, flirting, and, there is no other word for it "re-creating."

Of course Glenwood Springs and the local businesses depend on tourism and want more. The national outdoor industries depend on more and more boaters as well. I talk to three Dagger Kayak reps on their way to a trade show in Salt Lake City who have stopped for a quick run down the Shoshone rapids. They had a truck and a trailer loaded with boats. "How many boats do you sell a year?" I ask. "Around 40,000," they answer. These are very durable plastic boats that last for years. That's 400,000 boats in ten years and Dagger isn't as big as the Perception Kayak Company. If a 100,000 new kayakers are hitting the rivers every year and no one is making any new rivers, what will it be like?

The Grand Canyon from Dutton Point.

The fact is the boatable rivers are diminishing because of other demands for the water as well. And the same problem exists with fishing. I talk to Buffy, an expert kayaker who had been teaching kayaking above State Bridge on the upper Colorado River. She says the water is quite low this year and subsequently very warm. She finds dead fish in the eddies on a regular basis. This area has been one of the state's prime trout fisheries. At the headwaters of the Colorado River around Granby the reservoirs are almost empty, as well. Yes, it's a drought year, but the situation is bad regardless. A few wet years will not solve the problem if the East Slope cities keep growing and demanding more water.

Wilderness Rivers

There are several rivers in national parks, wilderness areas, and other federal and state lands that have restricted access. The government policy makers and managers have determined how much use these areas can handle without destroying the riverbanks and the quality of the experience for visitors. The rafters and kayakers who get permits must be self-contained and carry everything out, including human waste. The policy works quite well. Most of the campsites are clean when you get to them. The groups of rafters and kayakers are scheduled so that they only run into each other occasionally. Most of the time you feel like you and your friends have the river to yourselves. The permits are rationed between commercial operations and private trips. The permits are hard to get, the waiting period for the Grand Canyon is several years.

The Yampa Green River run is one place in the West where the word "requiem" doesn't apply. So far it has escaped serious impacts from dams, gas exploration, and overuse.

In the future wilderness areas may have to be handled the same way the rivers are, with permits so that they don't become overcrowded. The Western rivers are extraordinary treasures.

The Canyon is a spiritual place; giant spaces enclosed
by sculptured walls, reflected light turning water into
molton gold, delicate vegetation growing out of moist
cracks in an otherwise desert environment, rocks of every
imaginable color. Comforting contradictions: I feel
enormously expanded and at the same time very small and
temporal when I am in the canyon, I know I do and don't belong.
I want to be and not be there. So much is taken and given,
absorbed and released. My body wakes up, my mind rests.
I am in balance

The Yampa–Green River Run

The finest workers in stone are not copper or steel tools, but the gentle touches of air and water working at their leisure with a liberal allowance of time."
—Henry David Thoreau

June 7, 2003. In spite of the fact that this may be the most spectacularly beautiful river canyon in the United States, if not in the world, it seems to occupy a sleepy place in my mind. I don't think about the Dinosaur Run unless someone gives me a call about doing it. This is probably because the white-water isn't that interesting, at least not compared to the Grand Canyon. But the geology is beyond the imagination. Uplifted beds of different periods of sandstone slope in all directions, broken and twisted like wooden blocks in an angry child's sandbox. In other places the river has carved vertical walls that rise hundreds of feet straight above the water, smooth, and stained by dripping water from a million rains. Labyrinths of side canyons, too rugged to enter casually, invite exploration if only there were more time, ropes, and climbing gear available. Each time I visit I promise myself I will plan for this on the next trip, but I never do. The folks I run this river with are usually not even big hikers, much less climbers.

An old river running friend, Bill Gray, gives me a call. Dick Gilbert. a former accountant for Summit Films, has a permit for the Yampa. Dick knows how to get permits. The last time I went down the Grand Canyon was on his permit.

In any case I'm just off my fourth trip and thinking I would like to make the Yampa Green an annual event for the rest of my active life. There's plenty of excite-

Steamboat Rock, Echo Park, Green River.

ment if the water is high and lots of holes to jump into if I'm feeling up to it. But it is the giant sheer sandstone walls, rising almost straight up from the water, that get me. Here are some of Nature's finest sculptures, as grand as Yosemite or Zion.

I have been having neck problems for about a year now, compressed disks, bone spurs, etc. A chiropractor took a poor x-ray and claimed my upper back was in terrible shape, the bones of a hundred-year-old man hidden in a lot of muscle, which is why I still function. After listening to him I figure I will be in a wheelchair in a few months. At this point I decide to see Dr. Raub, an orthopedics guy, who takes an MRI and sees that my nerve channels are getting restricted, particularly on my right side. He says the problem is too deep for an operation and sends me to a physical therapist. She helps me regain some mobility and gives me some strengthening exercises to do. Meanwhile, I do a few sessions with Billy Orgish. He taps into knotted, seized-up muscles and breaks them loose so they will function again. I suffer terrible pain during the next few days, but know I will be able to heal. He also gives me some herbal medicines to take, which I believe have helped.

I can't turn down a trip on the Yampa Green. It's a perfect chance to introduce Christian to Western river running, and it's a beautiful trip even if I only sit in a raft and look at the scenery. I call oldest son Gordon, and he has time to join us. I'm on the fence about taking my kayak. It will probably aggravate my back problems and then the boat will have to be carried on a raft. When Gordon arrives in Gypsum he convinces me to at least try kayaking. This turns out to be a good decision. The kayak rejuvenates me. Near the end of the trip I do a combat

roll in some squirrelly, big waves and brace through a big hole. I'm boating the way I did several years ago. And my back doesn't hurt.

Gordon Brown with camera in Little Joe Rapid, Yampa River.

River rats (I'm not sure they like to be called that) come from all walks of life. Bill Gray is business entrepreneur with his feet in the very different worlds of real estate and television and he works with New Age thinkers such as Barbara Hubbard. Professor and anthropologist Dr. Peter Skafte doesn't teach but travels around the world visiting out-of-the-way places and people. He and I have visited shamans in Nepal and nomads in Tibet, and we did a trip to the ice-bound coast of Northern Greenland. Accountant Dick Gilbert, affectionately called Captain Big Dick, is a large jovial disorganized organizer. There are building contractors, dads with their kids, photographers, moviemakers like my son and me, and other assorted characters noted mainly for their unique, occasionally difficult, personalities. Some of the men are married, others are single with girlfriends, and some are alone. These people have one common interest—the river.

There are qualifications and rules. First, it's a good idea to own a raft and all the necessary rigging. We get invited because we are kayakers, but we depend on the rafters to carry some of our gear. Everyone is expected to take a turn at cooking, potty duty, and other necessary tasks. If you don't pitch in, you don't get invited back.

Gordon, Christian, and I see Mormon crickets all over the road as we drive from Gypsum to the put-in west of Maybell, Colorado. We find the crickets everywhere on our gear, on the boats, on us when we try to sleep. Their crackling

Gordon Brown dives off a cliff near Danger Cave, Yampa River, Dinosuar Monument.

sounds go on for what seems like most of the night. We see a garter snake climbing a bushes to eat them. It's a cricket year.

The rafts allow for a certain amount of luxury that kayaking trips don't offer because of storage space. Two-burner stoves and big iron skillets are an essential part of the gear. The rafters sometimes compete to see who can cook the most elaborate dinner. Setting up the boats and loading in the kitchen, tents, food, and personal gear in the morning is slow work, but after a few hours we finish and push off into the river.

Christian is still too young and small to kayak but he loves crashing through the waves on the raft and swimming in the flat stretches. He and Ned Cox's twelve-year-old son Keaton have a great time together. Keaton is struggling with cancer. Our hearts go out to him.

The thought of running the Yampa's rapids intimidates me until I stop and scout and realize that there is plenty of room for maneuvering around the bad places. I ride the raft for a few hours when I get muscle cramps in my arms and hands. Tepee, Little Joe, and Big Joe go by, reminding me of when I was here with Gordon several years back shooting an IMAX film with Greg MacGillivray. Gordon ran Big Joe with the heavy camera mounted to his bow. He made it through without serious problems.

We camp at Hardings Hole, across from Danger Cave, a well known Indian campsite. I am taken back by an eye to eye encounter with a bull snake. I had no idea they could climb trees until now. I sleep in the cool air on the river's edge to avoid the mosquitoes in the bushes. In the morning I cross the river for a hike. I go early and cover some distance before I see the others arriving on the beach. They find some big elk antlers dropped in the spring by some very large bulls that have been wintering on the flats. We push down the river the rest of the day until we get to Warm Springs.

I decide to walk around the Warm Springs rapid. It looks mean in the late afternoon backlight. Most of the water seems to be going into the big hole at the bottom of the rapid. When the rafts come down, however, it's clear that enough water is missing the hole on the right side to carry me out of trouble if I hit my line above there. But I will wait until morning and see how I feel then.

We are camped below the rapid. The last time I was camped here a big storm came through and blew my tent away. It went several yards before it stopped, but my memory is short and I make a foolish decision. Since the first two nights of our trip have been dry I tell Christian we don't need to bother with the tent.

Above: Anter "sheds."

Below: Bull snake.

Flash flood.

There are a few clouds around and one dry thunderhead rolls by but it seems to be clearing as we crawl in our bags to sleep.

About 4:00 a.m. I wake up to thunder and lightning. Then a few big rain drops hit, and it starts to pour. I struggle with the tent but it's impossible to place the wands in the right loops without light. I ask Christian to hold a flashlight but it doesn't give enough light, so I tell him to crawl under the tent rain fly while I keep trying to assemble the wands. I keep thinking the rain will stop but it doesn't. Eventually our bags become completely saturated.

Finally, as it starts to get light I get the tent up. We get inside with all our wet stuff and eventually fall asleep. Chistian has a pile jacket around him that is dry because it has been stored in a waterproof stuff sack. I wake up chilled and look for something warm and dry to put on. Gordon is also up. He sees I'm chilled and gives me his pile sweater for which I'm very grateful.

In spite of a tired feeling from being awake and cold a good part of the night, I decide to run Warm Springs. I have butterflies in my stomach walking up to my kayak, which is still beached at the top of the rapid. Another party of rafters has just arrived and are walking down the side of the rapid to scout the holes. Somehow they offer relief from what is now a lonely decision. I could have asked Gordon to run with me, but we have decided it's better if he is stationed in an eddy at the bottom in case I swim.

I squeeze myself into the spray skirt, wiggle into the boat, and slip the little foam brace behind my lower back. I am in tight, which is a good feeling. I know I have complete control over the boat. The butterflies leave as soon as I push off. I am surprised by the speed of the water. I am going to have to trust my instincts, there will be no time to think about my line, it has to be what I decided last night.

I paddle as hard as I can. It's better to be going a little faster than the water to maintain control. I want to be right of the big hole but not too far right as there are a few small messy holes that could turn me around if I hit them wrong. Then it's over. I'm past the big stuff and I am hardly even wet. I can't understand what I was worried about. It was a piece of cake.

There are lots of rapids and holes still to come, but I am relaxed now, and confident. The worst is behind me.

Down on S.O.B. Rapid Gordon decides to follow me with a mounted camera on the bow of his kayak. This means I can't be a wimp, I have to get into some of the big stuff. At one point I flip but my roll works perfectly and I am up again, facing upstream but in control. Gordon catches it on videotape. What fun. What a rejuvenating experience.

Humans are devouring the Earth's resources at a pace that is overwhelming the planet's capacity to support life."

—World Wildlife Fund

October 21, 2004

Chapter 13

The Environmental Movement

Spotted owl, Simpson Timber lands, Northern California.

Previous spread: Colorado high country.

"IT'S LIKE HAM AND EGGS. The chicken is involved but the pig is committed." Mark Ray, a forest products industry executive, is speaking at a meeting. He likens the folks working on the land to the pig and the environmentalists to the chicken. The natural resource workers have their livelihoods at stake. The environmentalists are concerned with relatively long term concepts like global warming or perhaps just about where to go on the weekend.

A struggle has existed between the preservationists and the conservationists from the beginning of the environmental movement. Many scholars have tried to define the difference, so I tip my hat to them and give you my personal analysis.

I would separate preservationists and conservationists by the degree to which they are willing to accept human intervention in Nature. At one end of the scale there are the Gaia followers who believe humans are just one of many species, and not necessarily a good one, like some big noxious weed the Earth would be better off without. At the other end of the scale, there are those who keep humans in the equation and believe Nature—the forests, oceans, soils,etc.—should be used for the benefit of man as long as it is done in a sustainable way.

I think most urban people think of themselves as environmentalists because they want clean air and water, green belts, parks, flower gardens, bike paths, wilderness areas, and so on.

Mountain goat.

In rural parts of America, and particularly here in the West, "environmentalist" is a dirty word with some people. It describes a person or group trying to put loggers, cowboys, and miners out of business. The environmental groups are accused of using endangered species as surrogates to tie up land and stop development. I think in some cases this is true. We filmed spotted owls on Simpson Timber lands in the Northwest and found them living in small patches of mature timber and feeding on rats in clearcuts. They were thriving. We also filmed the red cockaided woodpecker in the South. Their situation improved substantially when the timber companies left enough dead standing timber where the birds

Flamingos in Bolivia.

could nest. Allan Savory points out that the desert tortoise has an easier time feeding in cow pastures because the new shoots of grass that spring up after grazing are more accessible to the tortoise than the high, old, rank vegetation clogging ungrazed areas. The cows help the tortoises more than they hurt them. So the resource workers have a point.

On the other hand, there are many "endangered species" clearly needing protection, and these species are indicators of the overall health of the natural environment in many places. Hundreds of creatures and plants are becoming extinct every year because of habitat loss, chemical pollution, and the like. So both sides are right.

In the early years of the environmental movement the message was clear, positive, and undeniable. It was articulated well in the battle to save Dinosaur Monument from dams. Olaus Murie, president of the Wilderness Society summed it up. Wilderness is essential "for our happiness, our spiritual welfare, for our success in dealing with the confusions of a materialistic and sophisticated civilization."

Howard Zahniser went further:

> "We deeply need the humility to know ourselves as the dependent members of the great community of life. . . . to know the wilderness is to know a profound humility, to recognize one's littleness, to sense dependence and interdependence, indebtedness, and responsibility."

Dozens of environmental organizations grew out of these ideals, designed to protect land and species worldwide. Offices were established in most of the major "Westernized" nations around the world. Power and money for the causes concentrated in cities like Washington, D. C., San Francisco, and London. There was a concerted effort to "save what was left of the natural world."

Unfortunately, here in the United States the movement was almost too successful. Congress and some presidents listened and acted, sometimes arrogantly without adequately considering the local folks who lived on the land. The bubble burst in the West when the Clinton Administration started restricting and otherwise locking up large tracts of federal timber and grazing lands, and eventually a huge chunk of the desert in southern Utah. Secretary of Interior Bruce Babbitt, in spite of his Arizona ranching background, came off as an Ivy League Eastern intellectual, irritating and discouraging ranchers like the Sun family who sold their million-acre operation north of Rawlins, Wyoming, to the Mormon Church rather than struggle with more federal interference. The Suns were responsible ranchers who had been on the land since the West was settled. This was a tragic loss to the Wyoming ranching community.

One amusing case in point: when Bill Clinton and Al Gore attended the the 1993 Forest Summit in Portland, Oregon, they both said, "Once the old growth is gone, it's gone forever." Then Buzz Eades, a gypo logger from northern California, spoke. He talked about job losses due to forests being closed and then looked to Clinton and said, "You know, you'll be old growth too someday, Mr. President." Clinton had to laugh, but the point was made. Trees live and die. Old growth is only a matter of time. If you leave a forest alone long enough, and it doesn't burn, it will become old growth and die anyway. A forest that might be lost for our lifetimes will grow back eventually. Of course, some trees such as sequoia or redwood, might take several centuries to become old growth.

Grassroots movements like People for the West appeared and started getting organized politically. They were energetic and angry, as only folks being put out of work can get. I attended their meetings in Salt Lake, Albuquerque, and Washington, D.C. Bright, sincere, young people like Bruce Vincent, a logger from Libby, Montana, spoke passionately about injustices to working folks occurring in the name of the environment. But there were also some other less sincere forces at work. Oil and mining interests saw an opportunity and started giving People for the West financial support. Other special interest groups joined in: the off-road vehicle crowd, water and real estate developers, and people from the Washington-based conservative think tanks. So when George Bush and Dick Cheney (who is seen as a Wyoming boy), got the Republican Party nomination, the majority of the Western states jumped enthusiastically into their camp. The Bush Administration has been trying to undo almost every environmental law since the election. The federal lands are taking a terrible beating as a result.

Opposite page: Waterfall, Flat Tops.

Left: Cattle on the Flat Tops.

I don't think the environmental movement will be able to regain its power until it incorporate rural land users into its fold, or at least neutralizes their opposition. This may not be as difficult as it seems. Most cowboys and loggers I know have a strong land ethic based on the simple fact that they have been using the land for generations and understand when it's in good or bad shape.

The large corporations are the problem because, with a few exceptions, they put short term profits ahead of good long term land management decisions. And they will buy out the opposition if they can. The corporations operate behind the scenes, out of view of the public eye, but their employees know what's going on. The employees will usually make decisions in favor of what's right for the land if they are in a position to buck corporate policy. This means having locally based environmental organizations that don't threaten livelihoods and who listen to and care about small stakeholders. If the worker political base is strong enough the corporations will have to listen. They can fire one loudmouth but not all their employees.

In short the big urban based environmental organizations need to stop underestimating the intelligence and power of local "on the ground" populations, and have more faith in human nature to do what's right. Potential stewards should not necessarily be written off as the enemy. In Colorado the enemy is not the cowboys and small loggers, it is the big developers: the fossil fuel energy producers, the growth oriented East and West Slope water boards, and the off-road vehicle users who don't, in many cases, have a land ethic and see no problem in tearing up the fragile, semi-arid ground.

The land and what it produces are wonderful gifts,
and sacred, for if they fail
so will human civilization.

Chapter 14
Summing Up

I STARTED THIS BOOK WITH MORE THAN A LITTLE TREPIDATION. I am seen by many as an unrealistic, hard-nosed, no-growth advocate in Eagle County, Colorado, where I live. A lot of developers, real estate agents, Chamber of Commerce types, builders, and second-home owners are probably not going to be too happy about some of what is being said. These are people I have to live with on a day-to-day basis, people I like and care about, so I am uncomfortable. On the other hand, sometimes good medicine comes with a bitter taste. I hope those who disagree will come to see *Requiem for the West* in this light, as good medicine.

What I have discovered, much to my pleasure, is that a lot more folks than I thought do agree with me and are grateful that I have gone to the trouble of putting all these observations, experiences, and photographs together. A few have boldly contributed.

It's not just the older folks like me who are upset with what's been happening. Young people are also upset, but they realize despite its problems the Rocky Mountain West is still a fine place to plan a future.

I talk to Josh and Brooke Fitzsimmons. Theirs was the cowboy wedding we attended last June. Brooke teaches the sixth grade at Gypsum Middle School. Josh has a good business selling firewood to the second-home owners in Vail, but Josh and Brooke spend most of their weekends cowboying for Brooke's family. They are hopelessly hooked on ranching and cautiously optimistic about the future. Brooke is pregnant. She already worries about school for her child. She has seen signs of gangs and drugs in the schools, nothing severe, but she doesn't know where it will go in the future. They both have a healthy dislike for the resort lifestyle in Vail and the strip city that has spread down the Eagle River Valley, but seem confident they can be happy in Burns as long as it doesn't change too much. Brooke is like her mother—strong and strong-minded. She will make the best of whatever comes her way. I sense Josh is the same, easy-going on the surface but at the same time hard working. Josh and Brooke are connected, as are most ranchers who live from the land. Things in Burns change slowly. They have a happy future to look forward to, I'm sure.

Kara Klein came to the Rocky Mountains from Brooklyn, New York, about ten years ago. She is single and has a home in the North Forty subdivision in Aspen. Building and owning a house has been a struggle for her, however. She hired a contractor who blew her money away on crack cocaine. He was in such bad shape it wasn't worth suing him. Other builders came to her rescue, working for free, finding her fixtures from other buildings that were being torn down. Now the house is complete.

Kara's mortgage is substantial. She works two jobs: as a producer at a local television station during the week and as a guide for wilderness horse trips on the weekends. She has two roommates. Still, she hasn't any money to spare.

"Is it worth it?" I ask.

"Yes," she answers. "I can hike or ride into beautiful, wild country just a few minutes from my doorstep. I can attend music concerts or lectures that can only be found in big cities elsewhere. I have good friends that I met when I first got here, and they are still good friends." And it's a healthy lifestyle. Kara walks or bikes when she can, she is thin and fit. And she doesn't have television in spite of or maybe because of working at a television station.

Opposite page: Winter forest.

Above: Josh and Brooke Fitzsimmons on their wedding day.

Above: Kara Klein.

Kara likes the fact that Aspen is dynamic, that it isn't stuck in the past, that there is a steady influx of new ideas. "You can't hold on too tightly to the old ways," she says, "but you can't ignore the past either. Without traditions to follow we would all be floating."

When Kara travels she goes out of her way to find small town diners, bakeries, delis, and coffee shops, gathering places where people mingle freely and talk to each other. She places a lot of importance on eye contact and people who are comfortable "in their skins." In this sense she embraces the essence of traditional small community living. This is why the North Forty works so well for her.

Kara admits it is the wealthy second-home owners who provide much of the funding for the concerts and other events, so she doesn't get too upset about their trophy homes.

Other folks are standing up for what they believe in, working at jobs that encourage a sustainable future, living in modest energy efficient homes, supporting land trust efforts that preserve agriculture lands and wilderness, putting down roots in their communities. Theirs is a different West but a good one, nevertheless. Their semi-urban existence only enhances their love for wild, unspoiled places, and, as a result, they treat the land respectfully.

The Elder's Club

Sometimes it feels like an old timers' gathering to me. There's an informal organization of sorts. We don't have scheduled meetings or collect dues, but we know where we stand. I can tell an Elder's Club member across a room by the look in his or her eyes. A few exchanged words and my confidence level leaps upward. We are an army and may be fighting a losing battle, but there is no giving up. The West is far too grand and beautiful to simply write it off.

Following are a few summary essays from members of the Elder's Club, myself included.

Signs of Hope? John McBride's View

I met Roger Brown in Vail, Colorado in 1963. We had a lot in common.

We were both immigrants to the West—he from Massachusetts, me from Illinois. We were both Ivy Leaguers—Roger, Dartmouth; me, Princeton. We both competed seriously in athletics—Roger, skiing; me, hockey. Both of us made a major break from our homes and family expectations and fled West.

In fact, we both made a commitment to a then very small community: Vail, Colorado. Without really knowing what we were going to do or how, we settled down. We had young wives (and he a small child) but we made contact with a place and a life—whatever the consequences.

Vail back then was tiny. It was a work camp. Although many contractors and subcontractors commuted back and forth weekly from Denver, there were a couple hundred permanent residents like us who had committed totally to the place. Needless to say, life was uncertain and somewhat precarious, but it was exciting.

I have fond memories of those pioneering days and many close friends from that time.

John McBride strolls through the North Forty.

Through the years, all of us have seen a lot of changes to the West. Many of them are discouraging and damaging, which Roger portrays. To me the biggest change from the early resort days is the onslaught of part-time ownership. People who don't live in the West own a lot of it. This manifests itself in second homes, condos, fractional interests and time share units. I fault no one wanting to experience some of what we did, but non-total ownership or part-time residency does not provide the commitment communities need to flourish. And the rules of the game under which such partial ownership is born create a system that is often wrong for the community and Nature in general. Let me give some examples of what I mean.

Columbine.

First, federal tax laws hinder the transfer of family farms within families. The result, especially around resorts where values are higher, is often the sale and subdivision of large, open spaces and the loss of historical ownership. Secondly, there is a slew of realtors, architects, designers, and builders in most resorts ready to accommodate the interested buyer. Since all of them are paid on a commission basis, it is small wonder that so many buyers pay too much, and/or build too much. The result is monster castles or private hotels. This in turn fosters a servant class that comes from everywhere, often living five to twelve people per trailer and ten to forty miles away. And then of course the crowning blow—the need for a regional Wal-Mart to alledgedly serve the needs of the serf class, while country clubs and high end shops arrive to serve the new part-time ruling class. Oddly, the old general store, which used to serve everyone, dies. No one person can be blamed. But we do have a system politically and economically that encourages the demographics changes we are seeing. In Europe this does not occur for several reasons.

One, many mountain European countries do not have punitive death taxes. Instead, they promote preservation of family properties and farms and their transfer from generation to generation. Two, many European mountain towns discourage non-resident ownership of businesses and residences. Thirdly, and most importantly, Europeans tend not to speculate with property. Perhaps it is because land is not as abundant as we think it is in the West, and when Europeans decide to sell, the property is usually offered to family first and friends second.

These attitudes and policies tend to keep the Alps, at least, the way they have been for centuries. Bottom line: there is a stronger commitment to place and to land in Europe than here in the American West.

But all is not dark. I, for one, sense a serious change, or rather reversal, from the speculative trend of the 1990s here in Pitkin County, where I live..

For twenty years I coached ice hockey in the Roaring Fork Valley. During much of that time it seemed that kids who grew up in Aspen, Basalt, or Carbondale would go away and work elsewhere. The claim was that there weren't enough jobs at home and prices for homes were too high. Absentee owners had ruined their chances.

Now I see many kids returning and putting down roots. Some are finding interesting work, others are creating it. And there are now housing projects enabling workers to stay. The North Forty is an example. County rules eliminated speculation. Lots could only be sold to full-time residents, house appreciation was capped, and resales have to be made to similar locally employed residents. In spite of these restrictions the lots all sold in two months. Three years later all but one lot is built upon. Purchasers for the most part do not care abut restrictions because they plan to stay and raise their families right there.

Last year a thirty-eight-year-old builder from Aspen contracted serious cancer. His friends advertised a fundraiser auction in the Jerome Hotel. About 1,000 thirty- to forty-year-old locals showed up and raised $250,000. This is community.

Aspen may be fancy and cater to the "la-de-da," but beneath the surface is a strong, permanent, growing community of youthful people who are making a real commitment to place. They are here. They are coming back. They know and love this valley and her mountains.

In many ways I think these people are just as crazy and committed as Roger and I were some forty years ago. This place we all know is unique, incredibly beautiful, and special. And so I say, I hope there is a new and exciting future for them here in the West.

A real and full-time commitment is what is needed, and it's happening. I'm optimistic. A requiem may be proper for those days Roger and I shared years ago in Vail but perhaps not for the revival of tomorrow.

The Infinite West Reaches Its Limits: Richard Lamm's View

What is the take-home lesson of the West? Some will say truthfully that we have learned a myriad of lessons from exploring and settling the West, but I wonder if there are any great wisdoms that the West has to teach us equivalent to the triumph of democracy and the market that characterizes the American experience. Is there a core message from approximately 200 years of Western experience?

I suggest two conflicting candidates: the triumph of the infinite and living with the finite.

Civilization has triumphed in the West because it has refused to accept limits and has overcome a myriad of obstacles. Our ancestors found a desert and made it into a garden. The culture of the infinite teaches that ingenuity and imagination can prevail over any obstacles and that there are no limits—only lack of creativity.

This is the West of irrigation canals, transmountain diversions, pivot sprinklers and other adaptations that allow us not only to live in a semi-desert, but also to enjoy green lawns and prosperity. The culture of the infinite suggests the future is a logical extension of the past, that all problems have achievable solutions: "Go forth and multiply and subdue the earth" and "Go West, young man."

It is the optimism of "Not to worry: God gave man two hands and only one stomach." It reflects a devout belief in limitless economic development, progress and the perfectibility of the human condition. It is the world of Green Revolution that has given us the potential to eliminate hunger and of technology that some say has repealed the law of supply and demand and discovered endless and unlimited wealth. This is the world built around unlimited people—unsatiated consumers.

The supporters of the infinite are either the modern prophets or the modern alchemists—but to date they say they have been stunningly successful in solving the problem of population and poverty. And in their minds their approach will continue to be successful. Aridity can be solved by desalinating oceans, and wealth (computer chips) can be created out of sand.

The second culture is the culture of the finite. The West also teaches that we must adapt to Nature, and be acutely aware of Nature's fickleness and limitations. It teaches us that there is such a thing as "carrying capacity" and we must respect the fragility of the land and environment. It argues that Nature teaches us that we never can or should rely on the status quo, that climate is harsh and

Arrow-leafed balsam root.

variable, and that the price of survival is to anticipate and prepare. It questions the proposition that growth, population or economic, can go on forever. This is the world of conservation, national parks, wilderness legislation, crop rotation, Planned Parenthood, Malthus, the Exxon *Valdez*. It is the vision of Thomas Berry: "The earth and the human community are bound in a single journey" and it listens to Isaiah: "Woe unto them that lay field upon field and house upon house that there be no place to be left alone in the world."

Only one of these cultures can prevail. They could co-exist when the West was young. We could mourn Glen Canyon while we kayaked the Green and the

Yampa. We could endlessly brag "Watch us grow" and still maintain our quality of life and fragile landscape. But even though the West is no longer young, we are still acting as if it were.

Our industrial civilization is built upon the assumptions that there are no limits, and that we will not reach any sort of carrying capacity. It assumes infinite resources, where scarcity is caused by want of imagination. Civilization in most of the world supports this assumption of the infinite.

The finite culture, with fewer adherents, but equally passionate, contends that the first culture is making "empty earth" assumptions that cannot be sustained. They want to move now to stabilize U.S. population and help the rest of the world do likewise.

Ultimately, finite-culture adherents feel that we cannot and should not have a Colorado of eight million people or an America of 500 million living our consumptive lifestyles. They contend that we live in a hinge of history where society must rewrite the entire script. If they are correct, then our basic assumptions about life, our great religious traditions, our economy are conceptually obsolete. So far, those who sing this song are failed prophets.

But what if—just what if—the culture of the infinite were only a temporary victor? What if Nature bats last? What if the real lesson we should have learned in a place with thirteen inches of rain was the need to appreciate that limits could be pushed and extended but never eliminated? What if the rain forests, the dying coral, the rising temperatures are trying to tell us something?

The lessons I have learned from my love affair with the West support this second culture. I believe we need to transform society from an earth-consuming technological civilization to a sustainable and more benign civilization. I'm impressed with Aldo Leopold's "land ethic" which teaches that human fate depends on our ability to change the basic values, beliefs and aspirations of the total society.

My life's experience confirms Charles Darwin's belief that "It is not the strongest of the species that survive, nor the most intelligent, but the ones most responsive to change."

The Incas of South America saw the sails of the Spanish ships on the horizon, but not comprehending them, took no preparatory action. Ships and sails were inconceivable and thus not real. To modern thinkers, so is a world that must achieve sustainability. But like the Spanish sails, the increasingly burdened environment might be signaling massive, unprecedented change.

I believe that the fate of the world depends on our ability to know when to abandon the infinite culture and shift to the finite culture. Wait too long and we are doomed. Some will say if we shift too soon, we'll give up a lot of fun and exhilaration. I'd rather we shift too soon. For our grandchildren's sake.

Starting at the Beginning

In the beginning of this book we went back in time to the beginning of all life on earth. Now I would like to reflect on what happens soon after the start of a child's life.

My wife, Anne Helene, operates a preschool for fifteen children between the ages of two and five. It's been an educational experience for us as well as for the kids. We also have two sons; Tor Erik is four and Christian is eleven. I was

Learning where we get our food.

traveling a lot when my older boys were that age, but I'm home now and seeing things I missed before.

Basic experiences are important for the kids, such as seeing firsthand where their food and clothing comes from, or standing next to, feeding, and touching a sheep or a llama, or picking an egg out of a chicken's nest, and coming to understand that food does not originate in stores but comes from living creatures that eat and breathe just as we do. Anne Helene spins and weaves the wool from our llama and the sheep, demonstrating the different skills necessary to go from the raw material to finished product. These are simple but necessary connections in understanding how we live, but they are hard stories to get across in a country that once had ninety percent of its population working in agriculture, but now has less than two percent involved in farming. It only takes a generation to lose contact. One mom, a teacher, looked at our vegetables and apples and asked quite amazed, "Do you really make these things?" She was turned on by the whole idea.

Anne Helene and I have both traveled in Third World countries. As we watch the children develop, we are reminded about how the Third World functions and how removed our American society has become from the basic connections to the Earth and natural world.

We are introducing other cultures to the kids at every opportunity. With this comes an understanding that out there in the undeveloped world most people are still farmers and their cultures, their songs, their dances, their art, and the rhythms of their daily life evolve, in part, around growing and consuming food and fiber.

Callawaya weaver near Charasani, Bolivia.

The elders teach morality to the children though traditional myths which have great significance because they are believed by those who tell the stories and those who listen. Scientific analysis is not used to challenge these myths although some urban educated villagers who return home bring doubts with them, not understanding the value of the stories as metaphors if nothing else. When we were in Semikot, in northwestern Nepal, on our way to Mount Kailash in Tibet, a guide came up to us and said, "Why do you film this *Dami* (shaman). He does no good. It is witchcraft." But clearly the shaman was doing a lot of good on a level that the Nepalese guide failed to see. In our society the shaman might be called a psychologist, an herbalist, a healer, or a religious instructor. The rituals he uses: the chants, drums, and fire along with herbs, incense, touching, etc., greatly improves the effectiveness of the treatment because the people believe in the entire process and are optimistic about the result.

The organized religions, of course, still have the ultimate power to direct the course of village life. Religious life permeates most of their lives most of the time. It is not a two-hour Sunday experience.

Shaman dancing above the villge of Sallari in Nepal.

Opposite page— Eagle County Rodeo calf-roping (top) and greased pig contest (bottom).

In the agrarian communities of America's past and the Third World's present rural villages and towns there is an interdependence. The baker knows the seamstress who knows the blacksmith who knows the shoemaker and they all know each other's children. When someone has a problem the whole connected community is there to help solve it. I am always amazed at how quickly the villagers in remote mountain communities find out we are in town and what our purpose is. Crowds always gather to watch us film.

Our American society is very rich in many ways with thousands of options in comparison to a rural Third World country where there are far fewer directions to explore. But are we any happier as a result? We lose something too. We meet few of our friends on the street because we are enclosed in a car. We don't visit our neighbors as often as we might because our televisions and computers absorb so much of our time. We may be able to fashion an interesting independent existence, but we sometimes minimize our social interaction in the process. This gives us a sense of accomplishment, but we have to ask what we have sacrificed during the effort?

Some parents want to foster independence and individualism, letting the children "do their own thing," and they want their kids to get an early start on learning letters and numbers so that they will have an advantage when they enter grade school. While a certain amount of this focused learning is desirable, particularly when it comes naturally to the child, we are careful to keep things in balance. The question we ask ourselves is, do we need to encourage even more

Clouds over the Gypsum Creek Valley.

competition in a world where so many people (at least in the western industrialized countries) seem to be out for just themselves? Do completely egocentric, very competitive people have happier lives? We are not so sure.

Anne Helene tries to foster community values and "getting along" with each other. Selfishness is discouraged, sharing is encouraged. She does not begrudge the silliness, nonsense, and laughter that so often overtakes her attempts at discipline. Aimless play is not wasted time. It is a valuable part of growing up.

Being exposed to Nature and the cycles of life inspires the creative process without the need to be desk bound or room bound in a structured academic setting. We are fortunate to have a spacious rural location where a learning farm is available on the premises and wild nature is only a few steps away. A chipmunk suddenly appearing at the playground, a box turtle lumbering through the grass, or a big hawk flying overhead can capture the child's imagination in a very exciting and positive way.

We are not caught up in theories. We simply believe that a "loving, caring, connected" approach now will result in children who will become responsible, balanced, happy adults in the future.

The Future

I have no crystal ball, nor do I think one is needed. The situation is obvious. We are in a dangerous world. Our present way of life here in America is not only threatened, it is over. Profligate, wasteful consumption on a starving planet is turning everyone against us. We cannot wage war against people so desperate they are willing to die rather than live the way they do. How can we threaten suicide bombers when in their minds they are already dead? If the Israelis cannot control terrorism in their little nation how can we hope to control it around the world? War only exacerbates the situation. Chop off the head of one terrorist and two more will take his or her place.

The welcome mat has been pulled in a lot of places. The last time we were filming in Bolivia our guide told local people we were Canadians in order to protect us from assault. I had to give up on a film project in northern India where we advised it's too dangerous for Americans. The same problems exist in Sarawak, Bali, and Suliwesi where we have made films in the past. Too dangerous. Friends I have in Nepal don't answer their mail anymore.

Americans are seen as the planet's exploiters. As a result, some people want to destroy us, or at least our government. The only solution is to remove their motivation; offer hope, try to end starvation and reduce poverty to a point where life is a better option than death. We cannot do this by ourselves, or overnight, but we can stop flaunting our wealth and power in negative arrogant ways. If the money spent on war can be redirected to help people to help themselves we will find ourselves with friends again. If we can stop wastefully using up the world's finite resources still more people will stop hating us. If we can stop trashing the last beautiful wild places on the planet, we will stop hating ourselves.

In short, life in the future needs to be more about about living wisely and less about spending; more about compassion and less about competition.

In many ways what is taking place in western Colorado is a reflection of what is happening everywhere in the Western World. Our values have been corrupted. We are destroying what really matters in an attempt to find what we have convinced ourselves is "the good life." It's a life based on consumption, not only of goods and land, but of experiences as well. We all want to be winners in the "having it all" game. Unfortunately it is not a scenario based on a sustainable future. We are using everything up.

Can we start over, try to get it right? Here are a few suggestions.

We have already learned a lot from my wife's playschool. The kids love our animals and never tire of feeding and watching them. Finding an egg or planting and later pulling up a carrot delights them. They think it's pretty cool when we tell them the llama poop will help to grow next year's crops.

We should find ways to introduce Nature, natural land, and simple agriculture to more children at a young age. Only people who truly love the land and the creatures that live on it will try to protect it. These children need to understand how the land, the creatures, and the plants nourish them and that these sources of our life must be nourished in return. Let them see how nothing is wasted on a small farm; everything organic is endlessly recycled to nourish new life. In this way, teach them to waste nothing.

It's up to us as parents to teach young people to question an artificial world. Western Colorado is not Disneyland. Human technology is wondrous and amazing but of doubtful value if it disconnects us from the natural world. Nature is not something to be conquered and endlessly manipulated. It is our mother, nourishing not only our bodies but our souls.

Although I'm television filmmaker we aren't hooked up to any of the networks and cables. We don't think we should saddle our kids, or ourselves, with techo junk, and the other often meaningless devices that are being pushed at us. The TVs and computers should not rule us, we should rule them, and shut them off most of the time. They are life-sucking toys that keep us from human interaction. They offer a false view of the world for the most part, giving us incorrect and sometimes dangerous values. We get the kids outside with their friends, in contact with Nature, even in foul weather. They don't have to always be on skis, bikes, boats, and the like. Legs and feet work fine.

We are lucky, of course. Our children live in a place where they can walk to a field, woods, or a stream. We should think about the balance that needs to exist between cities, towns, farms, and wild lands. We need to seriously question losing even one more acre of productive farmland to urban sprawl, and we need to stop letting the Big Boxes wipe out our Main Streets. Smaller homes might encourage us to be more involved members of our communities. Much, if not all, of this can be accomplished with enlightened zoning, a vision beyond the profit motive, and letting go of fear.

Building codes for all new subdivisions and houses could recognize the need for alternative energy sources. Here in Colorado, roofs could be oriented to the south where collectors could be installed to capture solar energy. More passive solar collection could be achieved with properly placed windows and roof overhangs. It would be nice to see these solar collectors on more homes. There are very few now.

Massive transportation systems, energy grids, and information exchanges that create global interdependence are subject to equally massive failures. We cannot urbanize all of America and assume that the rest of the world will provide our food, fuel, wood, other raw materials, and menial labor. Small, self-sufficient units—the family farm, the village, and the town—will always be less vulnerable to catastrophic events than our bigger cities. Optimum size and scale are critical elements in the puzzle. Ideally most of the people in a village or town should know the elected officials that represent them. We need to save, recover, recreate, and support as many of these smaller units as we can, but leave (or create) breathing spaces between them.

In western Colorado, second-home owners could look into retrofitting their trophy subdivisions, remaking them into functional villages (if possible), that are less fossil fuel dependent, more diverse, and more neighborhood friendly. Or these castle owners can continue to hide behind gates that close them in more than keeping others out. It's a matter of attitude and how one sees his or her

place in the scheme of things. Do they, we, hide from the truth, guilt-ridden, knowing half the world lives in sub-human conditions, while we bathe in every conceivable kind of excess?

Lake near summit of Million Dollar Highway near Silverton, Colorado.

Or could these same folks address bigger problems?

If the net worth of the trophy homeowners in Vail and Aspen were added up, I'm sure it would exceed the GNP of several small Third World nations. Yes, many of these folks contribute to charities addressing Third World difficulties, but are we gaining or losing? It seems that the most serious problems are not being solved, only getting worse. I've seen the situations evolve over the years in many places: Africa, Nepal, South and Central America. Each time we go back to these countries some precious part of the culture is gone and more people are destitute. The gap between the rich and poor gets bigger and bigger. Starvation and disease are increasing exponentially as populations in many areas soar beyond sustainable levels.

Gypsum Creek Valley.

Alienation and hate are replacing hope, as America relies increasingly on the military to solve its major problems: problems like keeping cheap oil flowing, stopping drug production in other nations (since we can't stop consuming the drugs here), and labeling desperate suicide bombers in Israel as "terrorists" because they aren't supplied with sophisticated weapons. Instead we prop up an illegal and immoral land grab.

We give lip service to democracy and the idea that all humans are created equal, but we act according to a strange Darwinian economic law based on the "survival of the most wealthy." We talk about "connecting" in this computer age, but it is clear we are becoming more and more disconnected.

Our power has overwhelmed our capacity for understanding and compassion. In spite of our military might, fear rules our lives. As hard as we try, it is difficult to ignore the inequities. So we hide behind righteous indignation. How dare you challenge us? You are either with us or against us, and God help you if you're against us.

On the other hand, it's not easy to understand why we embrace the accumulation of wealth as a final goal when we know we will eventually die just as surely as the poorest soul on the planet. Isn't money accumulation a game after a certain point? Wouldn't it be wiser to depart with a little less personal wealth and the knowledge that we left the world a better place than we found it?

Uh-oh, I see I am digressing again, putting forth arrogant, hard-to-answer questions. Oh, dear. Sorry. Back to the Rocky Mountains.

For the moment it might be a good idea to try to respect the natural world and all of its creatures, of which we are a part. Here on the West Slope, respecting and loving the land may simply mean leaving it alone. We already have done enough damage.

People often say to me, "You're selfish. You've enjoyed this beautiful place for years and now you want to close the door behind you." They have point, of course, but they miss the real intent of my remarks. As big and grand as the Rocky Mountain West is, it is still finite. We can't continue to add more and more people, more subdivisions, more trophy homes, more water diversions, more gas wells, more coal mines, more dirt bikers, more Big Boxes, ad infinitum. As we go from optimum uses of our natural resources to maximum use, we destroy many of our reasons for being here.

I really believe it's more about ignorance than evil. If we think about what's happening and act according to what we know is right, things could improve—or at least not get worse.

Finding Answers in *Small Is Beautiful*

As soon as you own a piece of land your life changes, or should. Of course if you own a potentially productive piece of land or a beautiful piece of land, that is truly a wonderful gift. However, any chunk of the Earth, no matter how small or poor, comes with responsibilities.

We own twenty acres of semi-arid pinyon, juniper, and sagebrush country above the fertile Gypsum Creek Valley on the West Slope of Colorado. The land faces southeast, so it gets lots of sun. Indians camped on it for thousands of years before the European settlers drove them out. They hunted deer and bighorn sheep that grazed on the valley floor and slept on the hillside we now call home.

I have water rights, not as much as I would like but still enough to turn some land close to the house green, grow a vegetable garden and some fruit trees, and have enough grass for a few sheep and a llama. The previous owners put several sheep and cattle on the land and left them there too long. The animals hammered the desert vegetation, but that was twenty-five years ago and it has healed now.

We are at the latitude of Rome but at an altitude of 6,700 feet, which makes for a short growing season in spite of the hot midday sun. The last frost is usually in early June; the first serious fall frost is in September. Some years we lose most of the fruit blossoms to late deep frosts in May, which is a bummer. We have to start tomatoes and peppers inside, but we can get a corn crop from seed. Potatoes are the best producers; but lettuce, spinach, carrots, beets, white kohlrabi, and zucchini also do well. Cucumbers are problematic. All in all, we have a pleasing organic diet, particularly when the fruit and vegetables are complimented with wild game and fish.

I think feeling a responsibility to the land comes naturally. Almost everyone who owns a home has a flower garden of some kind. The more space you have the more you realize you can expand the concept of growing things and self sufficiency. It's satisfying to put seeds into the ground and watch them grow, and there is a whole new level of satisfaction when you are able to eat what you've planted.

These experiences with owning and using land have made me aware of what I have come to see as serious tragedies. First, there is the loss of productive agricultural land to development such as urban sprawl, subdivisions, and shopping centers. This loss is estimated at around one million acres a year in the United States alone. Secondly, there is the misuse of the land by agribusiness: monocropping, artificial fertilizers, loss of topsoil, and the dewatering of ground tables, to mention a few. In looking for a way to articulate my concerns I have turned to economist and philosopher E. F. Schumacher.

In his book, *Small Is Beautiful,* Schumacher states, "It is the dominant belief today that civilization has emancipated itself from dependence upon Nature." He then goes on to debunk this idea. In a long dialectic about how proper land use is really a metaphysical problem, not an economic one he says:

> "There is no escape from the confusion as long as land and the creatures upon it are looked upon as NOTHING BUT factors of production. They are, of course, factors of production, that is to say, means to ends, but this is their secondary, not their primary, nature. Before everything else they are ends in themselves, they are meta economic, and it is therefore rationally justifiable to say, as a statement of fact, they are in a certain sense sacred."

Schumacher then disqualifies metaphysical questions from scientific analysis, and looks to the Bible:

> "But when God saw everything he made, the entire biosphere as we say today, 'behold, it was very good,' Man, the highest of his creatures, was given 'dominion,' not the right to tyrannize, to ruin, and exterminate. It is no use talking about the dignity of man without accepting NOBLESSE OBLIGE, that is for man to put himself into wrongful relationship with animals, particularly those domesticated by him, has always, in all traditions, been considered a horrible and infinitely dangerous thing to do."

The land and what it produces are wonderful gifts, and sacred, for if they fail so will human civilization.

Schumacher has an equally utopic view of labor, or RIGHT LIVELIHOOD as it is referred to in Buddhism. He calls the chapter "Buddhist Economics," but for me that is a little deceiving. It's an ideal that most thoughtful people can embrace.

> "The function of work should be at least threefold: to give man a chance to utilize and develop his facilities, to enable him to overcome his ego-centeredness by joining with other people in a common task, and to bring forth goods and services needed for a becoming existence."

At the core of this approach is the idea that people are more important than goods.

For many of us food comes from the grocery store and that's it. We don't think about the field, the body of a cow, the chicken, or the fish, and we don't think about the farmers and ranchers. Let me stretch a point. In the arts, the producer of the work is usually given credit and applauded if the work is good. Using the land correctly is in some sense an art form as well in that the end product is hard to achieve and beautiful to behold.

Of course that's the kind of farming done by families on a small scale. It's hard but pleasant and rewarding work. There is a close connection between the

Chörten at Thangbboche, Nepal.

farmers and what they grow and a pride in what they produce. Looking closely at factory farming, on the other hand, it's apparent that the work is both impersonal, unnatural, and cruel. Masses of cattle are jammed together in feed lots, standing in their own feces; chickens are raised in giant buildings with wire floors, pumped full of growth hormones for fast turnover; pigs and veal calves are grown in small cubicles with no room to move.

Salsify.

Schumacher quotes the Indian philosopher J. C. Kumarappa:

> "If the nature of the work is properly appreciated and applied, it will stand in the same relation to the higher facilities as food is to the body. It nourishes and enlivens the higher man and urges him to produce the best he is capable of. It directs his free will along the proper course and disciplines the animal in him into progressive channels. It furnishes an excellent background for man to display his scale of values and develop his personality."

Ranching here in the West is a family affair. The kids take on tasks at a young age and seem quite happy helping their folks out. In most cases the "work" is considered fun. The line between work and play becomes blurred.

This is supported by Schumacher when he says, "Work and leisure are complimentary parts of the same living process and cannot be separated without destroying the joy of work and the bliss of leisure". What city kid wouldn't like to ride the range on a horse with his mom or dad leading the way, being taught "the ropes," literally.

When Schumacher addresses mechanization (factory work, assembly lines, etc.) he speaks of two types; one that enhances a man's skill and power and one that turns the work over to a mechanical slave, leaving man in a position of having to serve the slave. A horse and a plow can save a lot of back breaking work, but the farmer is still in charge. On an assembly line the worker gets paid a wage, but there is little other reward.

This view of mechanization, written thirty years ago, still begs the question, not only in regard to having an unrewarding job, but also in regard to our entire lifestyles. Are we slaves to our cars, TVs, computers, ATVs, boats, etc.? Do they allow us to escape our urban prisons, or do they trap us into buying, maintaining, and using an ever-increasing pile of time-consuming junk? What's wrong with just our bodies; our legs, arms, hands, eyes, by themselves, without the constant need for attachments and extensions? Do we need to be slaves to all these things or can a much simpler lifestyle be just as rewarding? Of course tools are big part of what separate us from animals and are necessary to our existence, but it doesn't hurt to occasionally ask, "Can I do without this gadget, toy, or other "convenience?"

Schumacher sums up his interpretation of Buddhist economics this way.

> "While the materialist is mainly interested in goods, the Buddhist is mainly interested in liberation. But Buddhism is 'The Middle Way' and therefore in no way antagonistic to physical well being. It is not wealth that stands in the way of liberation but the attachment to wealth; not the enjoyment of pleasurable things but the craving of them. The keynote of Buddhist economics, therefore, is simplicity. . . . From the economists point of view, the marvel of the Buddhist way of life is the utter rationality of its pattern—amazingly small means leading to extraordinary satisfactory results."

Dawn in the Flat Tops.

A New West?

Yes, the old West is dead and a requiem is appropriate, but there is still an opportunity to shape a new West that is not based on greed but on quality of life. I can say without equivocation, after traveling around much of the world, that there is "no place like home." It doesn't get any better than the Rocky Mountain West, even in its present beaten-up state.

Please be an active member of The Elder's Club. You don't have to be old, just caring and committed. Speak out, behave yourself, be kind to Nature, think in the long term, and listen to your heart. Thanks.